"Veteran reporter John Glionna tells the story of McDermitt, Nevada, population 114, a dying former mining town steeped in poverty where the fielding of an eight-man high school football team is a Sisyphean task that underscores how, even in the face of crushing defeat, sport offers hope by building character. For the McDermitt Bulldogs, winning isn't the goal—simply being able to play the game is."

—**Mike Anton**, former reporter for the
Kansas City Star and *Los Angeles Times*

"Ever a friend of the underdog, John M. Glionna travels the secluded backroads of Nevada to chronicle the travails of a hardscrabble reservation football team. Along the way we encounter all manner of characters, from the young high school athletes and their fans to a supportive if dwindling community clinging to their routines in an abandoned mining town. The McDermitt Bulldogs rarely win, but the players and the town itself remain resilient champions on the field of life."

—**Joe Eckdahl**, assistant managing editor
of the *Los Angeles Times*, retired

"In this terrifically poignant, soulful book about a hollowed-out town and its remaining people, John Glionna makes you feel as though you're walking through lilies in the field, everything blessed and enlivened by his attentiveness, humor, and real affection."

—**Robert Basil**, professor of communications
at Kwantlen Polytechnic University

"While the typical traveler through McDermitt, Nevada, hastens to put this dying, segregated town behind him, John Glionna saw something different, through the lens of the town's eight-man high school football team, coached by a white and a Native American. Having endured persistent adversity in their personal lives, the coaches fielded teams that, though nearly always scoreless, endured failure with grace and dignity. Glionna's plainspoken, inspirational study of these young football failures guides the reader into the rich soul of this community."

—**David H. Wilson Jr.**, author of *Northern
Paiutes of the Malheur: High Desert Reckoning
in Oregon Country*

T0326998

"John Glionna is one of our best narrative journalists. This book shows why—about a piece of our country that's never had it easy, now populated with the Say When casino, mercury mines, Paiutes and whites and their history, and a coach who battles each year to field an eight-man high school football team. Haunting yet peaceful as a ranch at dusk, his story doesn't find endings made in Hollywood but instead in a real and forgotten American small town that no one, not even its own residents, expects to make it."

—Sam Quinones, author of *The Least of Us* and *Dreamland*

"There are few better feelings for a nonfiction bibliophile than to escape life's requirements and return to a cast of literary characters you were reluctant to leave in the first place. *No Friday Night Lights* was that book for me. . . . Small-town football is this story's centerpiece, but those tied to it by seemingly the thinnest of threads are as fascinating as the players and coaches. McDermitt may be a speck on the map, but it looms large in this raconteur's tale."

—Tris Wykes, reporter for the *Valley News* (West Lebanon, NH)

NO FRIDAY NIGHT LIGHTS

Reservation Football on the Edge of America

JOHN M. GLIONNA

Foreword by Glenn Stout / Introduction by Ron Kantowski

UNIVERSITY OF NEBRASKA PRESS / LINCOLN

The University of Nebraska Press is part of a land-grant
institution with campuses and programs on the past,
present, and future homelands of the Pawnee, Ponca,
Otoe-Missouria, Omaha, Dakota, Lakota, Kaw,
Cheyenne, and Arapaho Peoples, as well as those of the
relocated Ho-Chunk, Sac and Fox, and Iowa Peoples.

Library of Congress Cataloging-in-Publication Data
Names: Glionna, John M., author. | Stout, Glenn,
1958– author of foreword. | Kantowski, Ron, author of
introduction.
Title: No Friday Night Lights: reservation football on the
edge of America / John M. Glionna; foreword by Glenn
Stout; introduction by Ron Kantowski.
Description: Lincoln: University of Nebraska Press, [2024] |
Includes bibliographical references.
Identifiers: LCCN 2023035007
ISBN 9781496231499 (paperback: acid-free paper)
ISBN 9781496239679 (epub)
ISBN 9781496239686 (pdf)
Subjects: LCSH: Eight-man football—United States—
Nevada. | Fort McDermitt Indian Reservation (Nev.
and Or.) | BISAC: SPORTS & RECREATION / Football |
HISTORY / United States / State & Local / West (AK, CA,
CO, HI, ID, MT, NV, UT, WY)
Classification: LCC GV953 .G55 2024 |
DDC 796.332/8—dc23/eng/20240309
LC record available at https://lccn.loc.gov/2023035007

Set in Minion Pro by A. Shahan.

Some of the names in this book have been changed.

"DOGS on three! One-two-three DOGS!"

   —Bulldogs huddle break chant

"You can learn a line from a win and a book from defeat."

   —NFL coach Paul Brown

ILLUSTRATIONS

1. Leaving Nevada sign in McDermitt   xvi

2. Bulldogs coach Richard Egan overlooking home field   16

3. Little League coach Ardel Crutcher with daughter Everr   64

4. Todd Murrah outside his house   66

5. Close-up of Todd Murrah   79

6. White Horse Tavern   82

7. Coach Richard Egan before team mural   94

8. QB Lane Barnett   100

9. Lane's father, Kerry   102

10. Assistant coach Jack Smith holding ashes of his father   106

11. Howard "Junior" Huttman   116

12. Lorraine Huttman   121

13. Pastor Dave Lewis   127

14. Martica, Alana, and Alice Crutcher   142

15. Martica Crutcher on reservation   148

16. Dancer Niyla Crutcher   152

17. Young Bulldog with head lowered   157

18. Coach Richard Egan in office   170

19. Coach Egan at rest   183

20. Scholar Thierry Veyrié at Fort McDermit   186

21. Thierry Veyrié around town   196

22. Niyla Crutcher dancing   200

23. Dancer Niyla Crutcher on reservation   208

24. Little League coach Ryan Murrah   222

25. Isabella Murrah on game day   225

26. Everr Crutcher on game day   228

27. Young Bulldog on bleachers   232

28. Niyla Crutcher dancing   238

29. Niyla Crutcher on reservation   249

FOREWORD / Glenn Stout

Once you leave the cities and the surrounding suburban sprawl, much of America can seem disarmingly the same, all farms and fields and forests and scrubland, bypassed by the freeways and connected to one another by narrow ribbons of two-lane roads, where drivers raise a hand and give a small wave to cars heading the opposite direction. Every so often, however, the traffic slows at a crossroads, where a bullet-riddled stop sign or a flashing yellow light that locals mostly ignore announces the presence of a small town. At first, each one seems just like every other small town, marked by a few gas stations, a mini-mart stocked with beer and potato chips, a restaurant or two, a bar, maybe a school or library, and a smattering of mostly ill-kept houses, stray dogs, and barbed wire. Somewhere on the outskirts there is often a football field, and on Friday nights, the glow on the horizon means there's a game, the one time the whole town—what there is of it—comes together in the present to relive the past and dream of the future.

Most of us just keep driving, eager to reach some distant destination that seems more important. But not John Glionna. He has made a career of not just stopping where others keep driving but of getting out of the car and trying to get to know the people and trying to find out who they are, why they live where they do, and what they both love and may hate about the place they call home.

In *No Friday Night Lights* John has done even more than that. Oh sure, when John first came to the unlikely outpost of McDermitt, Nevada, hard on the Oregon border, a million miles from anywhere else, he just stopped and did little more than look around, talking to a few people and hearing their stories, thinking of writing his own about such a remote outpost. But then he did something remarkable. Instead of driving away with his laptop, never to return, soon after John's first stopover in McDermitt, he turned the car around. He didn't just come back for a quick visit to pull another story from a quirky resident like some journalistic vulture. This time he stayed, because among the many stories he found in McDermitt the first time around, one kept tapping at the keyboard in his brain: there was a football field carved out of the hardscrabble ground.

To really know a community and its people, John understood that merely dropping by wasn't enough. He not only moved in, he moved among the people of McDermitt, not just the players and their coaches. With each step away from the highway and each notebook he filled, he discovered that while all small towns might in some ways look the same, their real identity is in the people who are born there and never leave, the families that eke out a modest existence an hour away from everything, and the outsiders who have somehow washed up in an unlikely place and claimed it as their own.

He found a town that had seen better days yet still dreamed that somehow, someway, there might be even better days ahead once more, an eight-man high school football team that had once been the center of a community and that now didn't even know if there would be a next season, a couple of coaches who wanted the next generation of kids to come to understand what it means to be a part of something larger than themselves, a Paiute-Shoshone Indian reservation and its people who rightfully look to outsiders with suspicion, and a cast of characters—minus the cowboys—that Sherwood Anderson would have been pleased to encounter in his mythical Winesburg, Ohio.

Yet that wasn't enough. It's easy to be a bystander and take notes as you just watch the story of a town unfold before you—to be a silent witness. But the real truths emerge once you start to take root. John stayed long enough to earn the trust of some and piss off others, to be both loved and shunned, sharing gossip and a beer at the bar. He experienced both the monotony and the beauty of a place one only comes to appreciate by becoming part of it yourself, a kind of character in his own right, earning his own kind of badge as a local, mostly worthy to be trusted, invited to stop in for a visit, and even welcomed back when he returns.

So welcome to McDermitt, home of the Bulldogs, population 114, a place like every place else yet like no other town in the country, where the stories are true, the lessons hard-earned, and where football still means . . . something. A place where those Friday night lights may have flickered and gone dim, but where the ghosts of season's past still cast long shadows. And if you listen close, as John has done, you may still hear the whispering echoes of the crowd in the wind that whips through the empty bleachers, see the light standing sentry amid the silence, and know that sometime, some way, they might once again light the horizon with a certain kind of hope.

INTRODUCTION / Ron Kantowski

Given that John Glionna has rummaged through more Nevada sage and ponderosa pine than Ben, Adam, Hoss, and Little Joe Cartwright combined, and that I once reported on a record-setting high school football winning streak that had its genesis in a rumble strip town in the central part of the Silver State called Alamo (not to be confused with the one in Texas that Sam Houston insisted his men remember), there's at least a fifty-fifty chance our paths may have crossed long before he asked me to write an introduction for this book.

But let the record show our formal introduction was made via cell phone in Las Vegas. He mentioned the column I had written about the Pahranagat Valley football team defeating another dot on the map for its ninety-fourth consecutive victory, establishing the national standard for the version of the sport played with eight men a side instead of the traditional eleven.

He said he liked that I had arrived early to ask the checkout girl at the Sinclair filling station and general store if she was going to the game.

I had written that the dot on the map called Alamo had a post office and a library and a Mormon church and not one but two filling stations—and a grill inside the Sinclair one called Chester's Chicken; that a little south of town there was a wildlife refuge; and that a few miles to the north was a beguiling extraterrestrial highway, according to a road sign and a beef jerky shop where a frontage road normally would run in towns large enough to have one.

Two years later John Glionna wrote his own piece about eight-man football, for which he virtually traveled the length of Nevada.

If the state were laid out like a football field, the Las Vegas suburb of Henderson (where I live and where John resided at the time) would be the 5-yard line on the southern end, with McDermitt—"an unassuming place where the highway barrels ahead in its rush to get somewhere else," is how Glionna describes it—forming the back boundary of the northern end zone. Wide receivers who fail to get their back foot down in McDermitt wind up in Oregon.

The state line actually runs directly through the recently renovated White Horse Inn—a former hotel and saloon that may or may not have moonlighted as a brothel (smart money is on the may). Food could be ordered and paid for in Oregon to avoid the sales tax in Nevada. This is one of the stones my writing friend John immediately turned over, thereby rendering any encounter with Nicole the checkout girl to the status of irrelevant footnote.

The author's bonafides to tell this story are unimpeachable. After spending four years as the *Los Angeles Times'* foreign correspondent based in Seoul, South Korea, he relocated to Southern Nevada in 2012 to serve as the newspaper's Las Vegas bureau chief. Whenever time and the news cycle allowed, he'd put glitz and glamor in the rearview mirror of his trusty 1998 Mercedes-Benz E320 in the hope of discovering the soul of Nevada and the legacy of its pioneer spirit with frequent forays into its expansive wilderness. The odometer in the Mercedes war horse rolled over like a protected government witness.

No Friday Night Lights: Reservation Football on the Edge of America is John's second book about rural Nevada. He introduced the McDermitt Bulldogs—along with myriad characters bearing colorful names such as Flash, Mr. Cool, Sarge, Smokey, Father Charlie, and Chicken Dave—in *Outback Nevada*, a tapestry of stories woven from travel section features written for the *Las Vegas Review-Journal* in his leisure time.

The McDermitt football team was a significant red, white, and blue swatch in that tapestry. The Bulldogs were winners of five state championships during a halcyon period from 1968 to '84—when the mineral mines indigenous to the remote dusty dot on the border still were pumping out precious mercury, and, ultimately, interior linemen on both sides of the line of scrimmage, owing to the hardy souls who worked the mines and had brought along their families. Or would soon start one.

But when the last of the lode was extracted from the McDermitt crust around 1990, it had the same effect as when the textile mill across the railroad tracks closed in that Bruce Springsteen song: *"Foreman says these jobs are going, boys, and they ain't coming back."*

And neither would the success the sons of the mercury miners once enjoyed on a rudimentary football field whose enduring characteristics consist primarily of a few rows of ramshackle bleachers, horses that graze just beyond the sidelines, and a restroom (of sorts) built by the school's shop class.

Twenty years later there were only a few hundred hardy souls remaining on the combined sides of the border. Most were Shoshone, descendants of the Northern Paiute tribe—Bulldogs coach Richard Egan, a stout Paiute-Shoshone who played quarterback, tight end, running back, and kicker, when needed, on McDermitt's undefeated 1982 state championship team, said the Bulldogs of that era often spoke their native language on the field to confuse opponents.

In 2018—five years after McDermitt was forced to cancel its season due to a shortage of players—Egan cobbled together a nine-man roster consisting of two freshmen, a sophomore, two juniors, and four seniors. Four were Native Americans, two were white, two were Latino, one a Pacific Islander. If diversity were touchdowns, the McDermitt kids would still lead their league. The clashing cultures are a complicated dynamic upon which John Glionna sheds more light than the combined wattage of a typical Friday night in the Dallas-Fort Worth metroplex.

Here, then, is the story of the McDermitt High Bulldogs, a band of brothers in ill-fitting equipment and hand-me-down uniforms, poster children for the time-honored axiom of it not being a matter of winning or losing or even how you played the game—but how much it all meant.

Fig. 1. Leaving Nevada sign in McDermitt, along
Highway 95. Photograph by Randi Lynn Beach.

NO
FRIDAY
NIGHT
LIGHTS

Driving through the northern reaches of rural Nevada is like reconnecting with the past—from a volcano's primordial upheaval to bloody Indian battles and cultural wars fought over God, territory, and a way of life.

You can see blackened rocks hewn during a more chaotic time, and you can almost hear the thunderous fire-and-brimstone church sermons endured by early settlers. When the wind blows, you feel the coarse breath of prospectors, pack horses, and rugged individualists as you traverse a topography of boundless vistas and unbroken space fast disappearing from the American West.

Sixteen million years ago, a long-dormant volcano that is part of the so-called Yellowstone hotspots ranging from modern Wyoming across Idaho and much of Oregon shot fiery boulders toward the stars, steamrolling the land, darkening the skies, and sending untold creatures skittering for cover. It was a very bad time for whatever lived here.

For some it still is.

Native peoples settled in the Great Basin, a series of depressions once covered by prehistoric Lake Lahontan. Paiute and Shoshone tribes took from the land what they needed, nothing more, while raising families and telling stories of great hunts and battles. They were later driven onto reservations by white settlers who felled trees and blocked access to streams and rivers in order to erect fences. One of those tracts, the McDermitt Paiute-Shoshone reservation, lies just south of the Oregon line.

Eons of hydrothermal cooling eventually left a twenty-five-by-fifteen-mile depression known as the McDermitt caldera along the man-made line between Nevada and Oregon. The land retains fantastic caches of buried mineral treasures left over from that big blast: gold, uranium, lithium, and mercury-bearing minerals. In recent years the mineral riches were aggressively mined, bringing jobs and a thriving lifestyle that turned sour when the deposits tapped out and the bosses and earthmovers deserted.

Today this place is still in upheaval.

On a sunny afternoon in May 2021, I arrive in Winnemucca, the seat of sprawling Humboldt County, a busy pit stop along Interstate 80, with

1960s-era casinos, Basque restaurants, and, along a busy drag called Potato Road, a hillside Walmart.

After hours of interstate freeway, I stop for gas, knowing as I head north along U.S. Route 95 that I will punch my ticket into miles of remote, unpeopled isolation. I will leave the last port of call for the mysteries of the open ocean.

From town, the road constricts into two lanes, with straightaways that push on for miles, as I retrace the paths of now fossilized creatures that once ranged here. I continue through Nevada's epochal basin and range, past the Bloody Run Hills and Santa Rosa Range and peaks called Paradise and Minerva.

I'm mesmerized by the ragged music of the road: the percussionist thrum of the big trucks tumbling down on their air gears, the droning hum of automobile engines, the hiss of the wind, the static on the radio.

Ninety minutes from Winnemucca, the straight-arrow highway makes a series of corrections, first right and then left, as though suddenly unsure of itself on its dash to the state line. I pass the reservation and billboards promoting mattress sales in Boise, Idaho, 200 miles distant, as though the people in this intervening space do not exist.

I finally reach McDermitt, my destination, and I am greeted by a tiny sign and a drop in the speed limit. It's an unassuming place without much to keep you, other than a few buildings, as the highway barrels ahead in its rush to get somewhere else.

I pull off U.S. 95 into a way station marked by Chinese elms, Austrian pines, blue spruce, and a clutch of dirt roads that shoot off toward the horizon. McDermitt's anchor—painted orange-red like a shade of woman's lipstick—is the Say When casino, with its long bar and army of slot machines. While its card tables are now a thing of the past, the Say When remains a last-ditch gambling stop for motorists leaving the state and the first spot to lose your money when you enter Nevada from the north. It's flanked by the shells of hotels and a saloon where, generations ago, drunken cowboys rode horses up the stairs to a second-floor brothel.

There are two gas stations, a post office, a public library, and the Quinn River Merc, where a four-pack of toilet paper ambushes the wallet at $13. That's it. A new Subway sandwich franchise, just opened, has town folks giddy.

With a population of 114, according to a recent census, McDermitt is hemorrhaging people, down from 170 in 2010. Students at McDermitt Combined Schools, grades K-12, number just 99, even pulling from the communities of Orovada, Kings River Valley, and the reservation.

More than 90 percent of students come from the poverty of the reservation. Some 84 percent qualify for free or reduced lunch; 30 percent come from single-family homes and 12 percent live with their grandparents. A whopping 36 percent, according to district records, are considered "homeless," meaning that they and perhaps their entire families are living in a transitory situation outside a traditional home. The area's medium income is an abysmal 50 percent of the national average.

Somehow McDermitt stays put. It's among a handful of Nevada towns that closely neighbor a Native American reservation, mixing white society and sovereign land with its own culture and such social ills as joblessness and substance abuse.

It's also a border town, which in Western folklore has always been a romantic concept. The line separating Nevada and Oregon slashes through unincorporated McDermitt like a stalker's knife, in one tavern—the White Horse—demarcated across the ceiling, lending a quirky, schizophrenic feel.

The Nevada side remains a casino-town throwback where little has changed other than the furniture. But steps away in Oregon sits a modern coffee shop called Somewhere Out West, run by a magazine editor and horsewoman. It's a gathering spot for both locals and outsiders, as well as hipsters en route to distant places. The coffee shop sells handiwork by ranchers and Paiute bead workers while boasting Yelp reviews from distant Los Angeles.

I've come to write about high school football off the map. This is a place with the scent of cut hay and alfalfa, where you can hear the creak of wooden front porches and the whinny of wild horses who share this remote landscape. McDermitt features the whiff of rusting tractors and the insult of abandoned houses discarded by those who left.

It's a town without a doctor, dentist, or hospital; a place without a car repair garage, swimming pool, full-time police officer, or movie theater; a place where the nearest mall is an unfathomable 72 miles away.

Teenagers play eight-man football here instead of the traditional eleven because their school is simply too small. They are country boys impatient to become men, white ranch kids and Paiute teens being raised by their grandparents beneath a peak known as Red Mountain, a mythical geographic uprising the tribe considers sacred.

I want to talk to these teenagers about what they expect from playing football in rural America. I want to get to know the two coaches. One is Native American, the descendant of a celebrated chief who shed his blood here 150 years ago during the so-called "Indian Wars." The other is white, a veteran educator who remains in the emotional thrall of his late father, a professional wrestler, boxer, and coach.

For me, these McDermitt High School Bulldogs have a particular story to tell—not one of a championship season but of a long and frustrating epidemic of losing.

And their story is the story of this place.

I take a seat at a picnic table outside the Quinn River Merc and wait for the team to arrive. Pickups and campers ease onto the gravelly lot, drivers pumping their fuel, gazing at the distant brown hills. There's a truck parked next to the table. One window bears an image of Donald Trump—faux-blonde, cartoonish, smirking, as though he knows I hadn't voted for him in the previous year's presidential election.

Yet people here have voted Republican for generations. I'm sitting in rural Nevada's politically red heart, often dismissed as flyover country. As a liberal journalist, I'm a spy behind enemy lines, and I must watch what I say. Breaking the urban-rural divide with these teens and their families will be hard enough without politics intervening.

The previous afternoon, I'd checked into a spartan motel room reeking of fresh paint, and I'd laid sleepless on a narrow bed as big eighteen-wheelers rumbled through town outside my window. Now, as I sit swatting flies, I have the urge to join these gassed-up motorists, to flee this fly-speck place, this metal table outside a gas station. I have rarely spent so much time in places that, at least on the surface, have so little to offer.

The first Bulldog to show is the head coach. Richard Egan is Paiute-Shoshone, a proud man with the athletic build of a one-time ranch cowboy. Three decades ago Egan played on McDermitt's 1982 team that won a state championship in the eight-man division. That was a decade before McDermitt vanished from the ranks of the winners. Now opposing coaches pencil in victories before games are even played.

Egan has witnessed the decline—winning as a player, losing as a coach—yet has never considered bolting to a bigger town with a winning program, perhaps stuck with the notion that he can turn things around. He wears a blue T-shirt with the emblem of a snarling bulldog, and a red Kansas City Chiefs ball cap. His large right hand envelopes mine with a quick crush. He seems like somebody you want on your side.

"How was the drive?" His question is like a rural tic, asked along with queries about the weather and maybe what you had for dinner.

It's 3:00 p.m. and school has finished for the afternoon. Five boys appear—two Paiutes and three white kids—some walking across vacant lots, others driven by their parents. An unemployed Paiute and a white mother look on skeptically: Why would a reporter drive all this way to a town visited by few outsiders of any kind?

The players seem puzzled too. They crowd around the table. Few have ever talked with a journalist.

The spring season had been a disaster, rescheduled from the previous fall by Covid precautions. The Bulldogs finished 0-4, overwhelmed by a total of 300 to 2. In the final game they eked out an improbable safety against the archival Owyhee Braves, a Paiute team from another state-line town a long bus ride away.

At least they *had* a season. In 2008, 2013, and 2017, the Bulldogs forfeited their entire schedule, so merely scrounging up enough players to compete is a victory in itself. For the seniors this will be a last hurrah, a final chance at winning something, to wash away the acrid taste of so much losing.

A few, like Taylor, a Paiute boy who excels in both football and basketball, have plans for the future. He wants to flee the reservation to explore the world. He was born in Alaska, but his family moved to McDermitt so his father, Scoobie, could care for Taylor's ailing grandfather. At seventeen, Taylor is quiet and mercurial, a teen who each evening makes long runs across the rocky reservation landscape. He runs off-road, on the lookout for trouble—the errant gunshots that comprise life among the Paiutes.

For Scoobie, chronic unemployment means focusing his attentions on his son, pointing out this, correcting that. When displeased, he dispatches Taylor out to the yard to pull weeds. The runs are the boy's escape, transporting him to a realm where *he* calls the shots, where there are no weeds to pull. He passes the tribal graveyard, where he can feel the spirits of the players, ranchers, and horse riders who passed here before him. This is where he seeks answers.

Taylor plays high school sports year-round—track in the spring, football in the fall, and basketball during the winter, when the cold wind blows hard and the snowdrifts refuse to diminish. This summer he'll work out with Coach Jack Smith, the football assistant and head basketball coach. With Smith blowing his whistle, the gym fills with sounds of creaking floorboards and squeaking sneakers as the school's best athlete sweats beneath wall banners of opposing teams: Owyhee Braves, Virginia City Muckers, and Carlin Railroaders.

Maverick, the other Paiute at the table, seems an unlikely football player. Tall and gentle, with oversized glasses, he moves at a big man's pace. Maverick lives with doting grandparents who are proud that he rides rodeo, a far-fetched image for a teen seemingly better placed on the couch with a bag of potato chips and his Xbox console. His uncles egged him on to play football, perhaps to relive their own glory days as Bulldogs, when the wins were easier to come by.

Most boys say very little, except two farm boys from Orovada who are friends from the second grade. Elijah is quiet, bodyguard big; Bailey talkative and somehow furtive, balancing traits of uncertainty and bluff, a kid who might need the big kid's protection. The two joke and whisper, but nobody shushes them, neither coaches nor parents, as though after so many years, they're used to such behavior.

Elijah rises early to complete his farm chores before school. The repetitive routine of hefting hay bales has put muscle on his growing body. At 6-foot-1 and 240 pounds, he's the biggest boy on the team, the one who snaps the ball, eviscerating rushers. During basketball season he looms beneath the basket to hoover up rebounds.

Bailey relishes the cowboy lifestyle. Along with playing football he enjoys "mechanizing, welding, and roping" and looks like he was born in scuffed Wrangler jeans, a rodeo belt buckle, a wide-brimmed hat, and handcrafted boots.

Lane arrives last. The New Mexico transplant played quarterback in the Bulldog's forgettable spring campaign. At his last school he mostly rode the bench, but now he competes on every play. As the Bulldog's play-caller, his father assures him he's the team's central nervous system.

Lane's father, Kerry, is a former rodeo rider who's never without his cowboy hat. He moved Lane and his mother here to become the school counselor, the latest in a long line of jobs. By seventeen, Lane is used to an itinerant life that resembles the U.S. military or the circus. He's lived in California, Wyoming, Arizona, and New Mexico but never in a town as remote as this one, where weekends last an eternity and the only respite are the precious hours playing video games and the drive to Winnemucca for groceries.

Lane listens to his father's tales of playing high school football in tiny Marfa, Texas, before winning a scholarship at Oklahoma Panhandle State

University. Lane wears No. 22 like his dad did, the son's way of honoring what the father once achieved. Kerry warns his son about leading a team with a weak offensive line: he's wearing a target and has to think faster and take more hits than he ever dreamed possible.

At the table, heads turn as a woman steps inside the general store. Leslie Muñoz, the school principal, is making a pit stop before her evening commute back to Winnemucca. To the coaches, Muñoz is an enigma. They're not sure whether they have her support or whether she views them as an embarrassment. Muñoz passes without a word and the coaches exchange eye contact: How could she *not* see them? Why didn't she stop, even to just say hello? For the winless Bulldogs, it's another slight heaped upon so many others.

Before we break I explain my plan to return to McDermitt in August, when practices start. I want to witness an entire season, the huddles and the crushing hits, the harrowing defeats and the huzzahs. I want to take the pulse of a team fighting for its survival in a remote town in the middle of somewhere.

The boys line up for a group picture in front of the market's blue wooden wall, within sight of the gas pumps and the highway just beyond. Some smile, or wince, squinting into the afternoon sun.

Maverick shows no expression at all.

I drive out to the reservation to see where Taylor takes his runs and pass the structure Maverick shares with his grandparents. It's a way to begin parsing the puzzle presented by these boys and this place. An hour later, back in town, I see the two coaches still in the parking lot, leaning in conspiratorially, talking about who knows what. In that moment I feel the weight that's upon them, finding a way to win amid the wreckage of losing.

Egan confesses that so much defeat has challenged his style. "I used to bark at those boys," he says. His wife, Lori, a teacher, took him aside several years ago: "You're pretty loud out there." Egan had never once yelled at his own two boys. "What do you mean?" he asked defensively. "I thought that was my job."

Maybe it's not the best way to reach a kid. These days, the veteran coach isn't sure of anything, but he knows that fall is coming and that it's another chance to mentor his boys. Maybe they'll win a game, maybe they won't, but they're sure going to try.

2

As everybody knows, America loves winners.

They relish in those rumbles of joy at center court and the beer showers in the victors' locker rooms. Most sports journalism celebrates winners, teams who overcome drugs, alcohol, and abuse to win games. A reporter captures that championship season and all those hurdles overcome to create a feel-good narrative, as if dissecting a winner's mindset reveals something about the human condition and how we manage to find victory at any cost.

That storyline falls flat with me. I'm more drawn to the misfits of this world, the outcasts and barflies, underdogs who stay under. As a journalist I've sought out the vanquished, those who fail, because that's where I find the most compelling stories: in places without oversized egos or prolonged man hugs.

In the losing locker room, athletes sit on benches with their heads bowed. They punch lockers, speak difficult truths. No true philosopher ever hoisted a winner's trophy, I believe, because the lessons in losing don't occur to winners. Losing says more about our collective experience than winning ever could. We mark our lives by our losses, and we learn from them. Winning is illusory, temporary at best. Losing is what happens to people most of the time.

I know what losing feels like. As a teenager I wasn't good enough to make my high school basketball team and instead played in a church league. I was tall enough at 6-foot-2 to compete but was usually boxed out and outrebounded, finding solace in the camaraderie of teamwork and the victory of just showing up.

My days playing golf in high school and college were marked by snaphooks and missed tournament cuts. In high school I yanked so many critical putts that my coach, an arrogant man named John Pagano, nicknamed me "The Apple," a choker.

Then he cut me from the team.

But I never saw myself as a loser, just as a kid who had tried and failed. My trip to McDermitt is a way to witness how perpetual losses weigh on the spirit of a new generation. Would these rural boys find their own personal enlightenment?

What, if not a trophy, do these lowly Bulldogs achieve on the football field, slamming into blocking sleds and punishing their bodies in the late-summer heat?

What's the end game? How do you carve a sliver of winning out of so much losing?

There are challenges: How can I pry into the fragile mindsets of isolated teenagers usually suspicious of outsiders, who their small-town upbringing teaches them not to trust? And in today's politically correct culture, there's peril in portraying kids who rarely win as losers, even lovable ones. Adults can handle such scrutiny, but maybe kids are too fragile for a journalist to be hounding their innermost doubts.

But what if boys so inured to losing suddenly, inexplicably, win? What's it feel like to bask in the applause from the home bleachers, to have your critical, hardworking father say he's proud of you? Would winning put a coat of shiny varnish on the dullness of continual disappointment?

Considering the odds, will they even get that chance?

The road to McDermitt took me to countless other blips of rural humanity. Between 2012 and 2015, as a national correspondent for the *Los Angeles Times*, I visited countless towns that threatened to vanish from the American West. Most were places where businesses had fled, taking along employees who were integral parts of the community—couples attending church, shopping at the market, sending their kids to school.

My stories took me to Puckerbrush (pop. 28), Mina (pop. 155), Lund (pop. 282), and Duckwater (pop. 368). In Esmeralda County, residents of an outpost called Dyer use fatalistic humor to capture their rural identity. Inside a bar called The Boonies, a sign reads "Where the *hell* is Dyer?" And a faux roadside mileage placard laments, "End of the World: 9 mi. Dyer, Nev: 12 mi."

The trend of diminishing towns has unspooled for decades. As families scatter, school enrollments shrink, leaving too few students to compete in sports. This cultural decay has eroded the rural experience, leaving modern-day ghost towns, boarded-up Main Streets, and too few people.

In Nevada, a state dominated by Las Vegas and Reno, only a fraction of the 3.2 million residents are rural, scattered in eye-blink towns too small for incorporation, some featuring a scant people-to-area ratio that rivals the Australian outback. Yet there's something magical to this Big Empty: Many towns feature the darkest night skies on the planet, where after sunset you can negotiate the road by the wan light of the Milky Way. Really.

After leaving the Times, I continued to report on the threatened species that prefers a small-town life. There was no shortage of stories. In the spring of 2018 I visited the unincorporated town of Gabbs, a former mining town with a one-room high school, an elemental environment that dates back to the pioneer days.

The basketball team, the Gabbs Tarantulas, was a struggling co-ed squad named after the eight-legged arachnids found out here. They travel 300 miles for an away game and barely muster enough players to compete. Nobody knows if the Tarantulas will survive.

Gabbs no longer has a football team. After too many hapless seasons, the school disbanded its program, shipping its uniforms 200 miles south to Beatty High, which uses the same green-and-white colors. In Gabbs the football field now sprouts only weeds and memories.

That image captivated me: a diminished team traveling fantastic distances in old school buses—still feeling lucky to be part of a team, any team. I wanted to find another anemic football program, so I called Dave Jensen, superintendent of schools in mammoth Humboldt County, a district with only a dozen isolated schools. I told him I was looking for a team with so few players that its future was in jeopardy.

"You need to talk to Richard Egan," he said.

That's how I got to know McDermitt's head football coach, the sports mentor at a school many incoming teachers view as a cultural Siberia, light years away from the comforts of the main district office.

For some, the community is Nevada's Chernobyl. When the local mercury mine closed decades ago, operators used quarry waste to backfill pits. Now the groundwater contains unsafe amounts of mercury and arsenic. Despite federal cleanup efforts, many here are afraid to drink the tap water.

In 2021 a state environmental study showed that McDermitt's drinking water was in serious violation of federal standards, significantly raising the risk of cancer. Along with the presence of arsenic, the local tap water contained fifteen times the government's health limits for nitrate and radium—one of mining's ugly legacies.

I call Egan, who stubbornly mentors a football program with barely enough parts to function. For starters, the Bulldogs have no cheerleaders, that staple of the high school rite of passage. Players use hand-me-down equipment, shoulder pads, and tackling sleds donated by better-off schools. Every game, McDermitt kids smell the sweat of a kid who's more privileged than they are.

The football team remains on probation, limited by the league to a schedule of only four games—rather than eight or nine—because nobody is sure whether the Bulldogs will forfeit their season for lack of players like they've done in recent years, leaving holes in league schedules.

Along with his coaching job, Egan is the school's groundskeeper who maintains a playing field in a waterless environment where grass has no right to be. He's also a bus driver who makes the roundtrip to the distant farms and ranches where his players live.

On the phone Egan recites a grim history: when times were good and the Cordero mercury mine was running, McDermitt supported a phalanx of honky-tonks, hotels, cafés, and a population nearing eight hundred. But the mine closed in 1992, and everything collapsed.

That was the last year the Bulldogs made the league playoffs, before mine operators secretly backfilled the pits with waste and laid off its staff, robbing the town of its residents and leaving the high school hungry for athletes and victories.

Three decades ago, the Bulldogs could boast thirty-six players, enough for separate squads on offense, defense, and special teams. Now the team struggles to fill eight starting spots. Kids play both offense and defense while their better-manned opponents send in fresh lineups each time the ball changes hands.

"We lost families when the mine closed, but I thought we could hold on," Egan said. The decline dealt the town its latest flesh wound, this one worse than the others. You could hear the death rattle. McDermitt was bleeding out.

The defections took their toll. Since 2004, the Bulldog's league record has been a woeful 13-61. Some years pass without a single win—if they even have a season.

The league once had a so-called mercy rule to preserve pride among losing coaches and players. When a team led by fifty points, the game was called at halftime. Now whenever one team goes up by forty points, the game clock does not stop between plays. It just keeps running, still a mercy of sorts.

When the Bulldogs play the clock rarely stops.

When Egan saw my call from the Las Vegas area code, he almost didn't pick up. Nobody calls McDermitt from that far away unless they're selling something.

In a way, I was. He listened as I made my pitch to write a newspaper story about his efforts to keep a small-town way of life intact. There was no hesitation.

"Heck," he said. "Just come on up."

In early October of 2018 I arrived in McDermitt for the first time, where I met players who wouldn't make the cut at other high schools. They were too timid, too small, or too overweight, a squad mostly filled out by reservation boys and a few scrawny white kids. They seemed more middle schoolers than teenagers who'd soon be old enough to attend college, work blue-collar jobs, or fight wars.

The two coaches, however, were demonstrated winners. During his playing days, Egan hit so hard he broke bones. He played tight end, running back, even kicker—anything it took to win. Assistant coach Jack Smith played football, basketball, and baseball in rural Idaho. He boxed as both an amateur and a professional. His colorful cigar-chomping father would accept nothing less than excellence from his only son.

Together their coaching task seemed Olympian, rallying boys from continual soul-crushing defeat. That 2018 season, the Bulldogs would eventually finish 0-6, cellar dwellers in Division 1A, Nevada's lowest-level league, comprised twenty-two schools whose enrollments were so small they could only field eight-man teams. Outscored 330-95 the last season, including one 78-0 drubbing, every Bulldog touchdown was celebrated like Christmas. If they couldn't win, the philosophy went, they could score, every once in awhile anyway.

As the team practiced its drills behind Egan, two wild horses grazed a lasso's throw away, out among the dirt and sagebrush. The coach admitted that the previous spring he'd considered quitting altogether. The two recent years when the Bulldogs forfeited their entire season still stung.

Now he was under pressure again. Months before, Principal Muñoz had put Egan on notice: find enough kids or forfeit another campaign. He called players at home, pitched them at the post office and general store. The program's future depended on it. "I approached some a few times, maybe too many times," he said. "They gave me the cold shoulder. So I left them alone. I knew that if they wanted to play, they'd come."

Transportation has always been a problem. Some students live hours from the school, and their parents are too busy to fetch them after practice. So the coaches volunteer to drive them home.

That August, in 2018, Egan bit his fingernails. A 320-pound player who anchored the anemic front line quit after one practice. Finally the coach scored: several farm boys from the Kings River Valley showed up. That's when the real work began. Without a junior varsity program, the incoming freshmen barely knew how to play. The Bulldogs performed drills on a taped-up tackling sled, working with what equipment they had, scrimmaging against themselves, trying to develop skills they didn't have.

The inequities are staggering. One year the Bulldogs played the Eureka Vandals, a high-octane team with wealthy benefactors who paid for a lush new stadium with field lighting and synthetic playing surface. The 2017 game was a scene from a Charles Dickens novel: the worst-of-times Bulldogs stepped off a teetering school bus that barely made the twelve-hour round-trip drive. By late fall, a faulty heater turned the vehicle into a mobile ice box, forcing players to huddle under blankets. For their part, the best-of-times Vandals were ushered around in a sophisticated tour bus, team insignia emblazoned on the side.

Back in McDermitt, the school shop class had cobbled together a humble restroom next to the playing field. In a near-biblical twist, invading insects had turned the grass brown, and Egan worked feverishly to green up the field before the season started. As these McDermitt boys marveled at a far more privileged world in Eureka, Egan would not stand to see his team's heart broken by another kid's birthright. Under *his* watch, he would protect the fragile egos of kids from a poor town few had even heard of. He rallied them like a father. Nothing rah-rah, just humble encouragement.

"These kids are lucky to have everything they have," he said of the Vandals. "But they can only put eight players on that field, just like us. We represent our community, our school, and our families. But mostly we represent ourselves."

They lost 64–12. But to Egan, just by competing, the Bulldogs came out winners, and they celebrated those two touchdowns like it was Christmas morning.

My story ran in the *Las Vegas Review-Journal* on October 14, 2018, under the headline "Rural Nevada Football Team Scores on the Field of Life." After that, I called Egan often to hear his unvarnished take on life that says there's always next season.

I thought there might be a book in McDermitt, but I needed to spend more time there, cover an entire season. It would be a tale of a remote town where many parents are either too poor or unskilled to leave, a fate players worry might infect their own generation. It was a story about rural football, learning how to lose, and either breaking free of small-town bonds or remaining trapped.

The summer following my spring 2021 visit to McDermitt, Egan remained confident. In early August I asked about the chances the Bulldogs would have a season.

"Maybe 70 percent," he said.

That was enough for me.

Moving to a small town like McDermitt is a challenge. A lack of housing forces many to rent crumbling mobile homes. I'd already stayed in the single motel, a place so unwelcoming it was like doing time in the county jail. I considered roughing it, pitching a tent in some field. Then Egan devised a solution. Lorraine Huttman, a school bus driver, rented a bungalow in town. "It's pretty nice," he said, "for McDermitt."

I called Lorraine and her husband, Junior. She explained that a French anthropologist had been renting the bungalow while completing his doctoral work on the McDermitt reservation, but it might just be open that fall. The $600 monthly rent was a bargain.

I'd scored a touchdown before I'd even arrived.

Fig. 2. Bulldogs coach Richard Egan holds ball overlooking
home field. Photograph by Randi Lynn Beach.

3

The skies are raw and smoky from stubborn western wildfires as the Bulldogs begin their first practice. The son of a rancher makes a wobbly throw to a brown-eyed Paiute boy as others stretch tightened calf muscles, moaning as they drop to the grass.

The five seniors are determined. This season they want to score a touchdown and, just maybe, win a game and make their friends, family, and the whole town proud. This is the last-ditch season before heading on to trade schools, blue-collar jobs, or, if they're lucky, junior college. Not a single Bulldog has ever played Division 1 college football. Precious few even attend a four-year university.

Win or lose, these are the glory days. And still, for McDermitt, that means it's mostly losing.

The undermanned Bulldogs are *Friday Night Lights* turned on its head. There are no lights here, no culture of winning, and little more than hope. The last time the team qualified for the playoffs was fifteen years before these boys were born. Nobody at the Say When is laying bets on this team.

When the Bulldogs were winners, supporters even came to watch the team practice on its remote field cleaved in half by the state line. The well-wishers blared car horns and followed the old yellow school bus out of town for big away games. Today the stands sit empty, with just the wild mustangs here to bear witness.

Coaches Egan and Smith make their way to the field, heads down in conversation. Egan looms dark-skinned and muscular, wearing a blue shirt and whistle, along with a camo green ball cap. A thick key ring hangs from his belt. Smith, the one-time boxer, has big hands and a sturdy frame. He wears sunglasses, sneakers, and a red Adidas sports shirt. He carries a clipboard.

A big truck downshifts in the distance, drowning out Egan's whistle. It's 5:30 p.m., time for the inaugural two-hour practice. The boys congregate in a ragged circle. There are five players here, just over half the number needed for a competitive eight-man team.

Egan offers no Knute Rockne speech, no feel-good pep talk. Perhaps he doesn't want to inflate the hopes of these boys only to see them dashed.

Deep down he knows what he's asking—for his players to trust his guidance and run off a cliff without a safety net to protect their egos from the abuse of kids their age, often a clan from another reservation, boys just like them. For years, the seniors have little to show other than losses. Now the coaches are asking for yet another leap of faith.

"Okay, stretches," Smith says. "You remember 'em."

Blonde-haired Bailey leads the others through calf and leg stretches. Jaxon, a tentative freshman who did not play in the disastrous spring campaign, sprawls off to one side as if he isn't yet ready to join this group.

"Get in the circle," Smith barks. "Look like a team."

Smith makes a point to preach by example: his body is compact, without fat or a bulging waistline. He teaches physical education and weightlifting. Come winter he'll head up a boys' basketball team comprised these same players. In a small town like McDermitt, you don't just play one sport, you play them all—that's the tacit understanding. Otherwise there simply won't be enough athletes to field a team.

Smith was born in Carson City but mostly grew up in rural Idaho. Eight years ago he was coaching girls' basketball in Winnemucca when he was replaced by a coach in better political favor. The school principal moved to McDermitt, and Smith went with him. He arrived late on a Sunday, the night before the first day of school.

That's when the first nauseating wave of culture shock set in. What on earth had he just done, moving to this god-awful town? After a few beers Smith found himself walking along the shoulder of U.S. Route 95, with the pickups and semis whooshing past. Eventually he turned around. After his principal mentor left after one year, he advised Smith to do the same. He felt marooned. Rudderless. Yet the veteran coach stayed on, lodging in his rental house on the Oregon side of town with his dog Hazel and a dozen cats.

Over the years Smith had produced instructional videos to inspire young basketball players to adopt the attitude of a champion. He had a reputation as a winner—before he came to McDermitt. The basketball team enjoys more success than the football squad, which isn't saying much. They lose more than they win. "On the basketball court, I'm always pacing, so on the football field I try to relax," Smith says. He turns to Egan: "This is Richard's show."

At this first practice there are no pads or uniforms, no hits, just drills on fluidity and mindset, remembering plays and how to move without the ball. In one routine Smith plays quarterback, stepping back before pausing, as frozen as a Heisman Trophy statue, making pronounced moves from side to side.

As he turns, receivers backpedal, eyes watching his movements. He doesn't throw the ball; the drill is about the connection between thrower and catcher, making sure they're in sync. "You gotta read me, Taylor," Smith shouts. "You're opening up wrong."

Taylor is the strongest and fastest Bulldog who isn't afraid to hit and get hit. "Last year, our guys just would not tackle," Smith sighs. At the end of the games, their opponents' uniforms were muddied and grass stained. "Ours were still white."

The coaches run drills with names like "karaoke," "toy soldiers," "butt kickers," and "bear crawls." Then the boys are dispatched for two laps around the field. Taylor leads the way while most lag far behind.

"C'mon, hustle!" Egan hollers. "You guys had all summer to rest."

"Looks like they rested too much," Smith deadpans.

Egan walks the field like a suburban dad doting on his front lawn. "There's some bad ground here. Yellow spots," he adds apologetically. At midfield there's a small pothole. "It's alkaline. Nothing grows there." God knows he's tried.

At age sixteen, Egan moved to McDermitt from his reservation home in Owyhee, another state-line town 300 miles east. To get there you travel south on U.S. Route 95 to Winnemucca, east to Battle Mountain along Interstate 80, and then north along State Route 225, a two-lane desert road known as the Mountain City Highway.

But there's a more direct way: a crude east-west dirt road that inches between low-slung mountain ranges. The track requires a four-wheel-drive pickup truck with high clearance and plenty of water—in case you break down.

Only a few hardy souls take that route. Like Egan. Driving his trusted brown pickup, a hand-me-down from his late father-in-law, he's taken the direct route many times. He knows both this land and his own limits.

The evening temperatures reach the high eighties, and the fire smoke makes boys stop and grab their knees. One lies down under a goalpost. "Wow, this grass is cool," says Enzo, a Paiute kid with brown eyes and long lashes. "I think I'll just lay here."

Then he rolls over, and his stomach begins to heave.

"Is he puking?" Bailey asks.

"I'm not sure," Egan says. "Wait until he starts wearing those mouthpieces with that funny taste. That'll bring it out."

Egan is nervous. It's the start of another year, time for some revenge against coaches who ran up the score last season. He'd taken a nap after work and tried to eat dinner before practice, but the butterflies wouldn't make room in his stomach.

"It's day one," he says, watching his boys. "You're feeling everybody out."

There are bright spots. Karter, a stout Paiute walk-on, arrived over the summer from Las Vegas, where he played eleven-man football against tough inner-city boys who will likely attend college, get drafted, and perhaps play in the NFL.

Karter is a stocky 5-foot-10 boy who wears a waist-length ponytail. "I'm six-one when I wear my cowboy boots," he says. At just fourteen, he lives on a family ranch that prepares him for football. Earlier that day, he and his cousins moved twenty-two head of cattle out for sale. The following morning, they'll bale six tons of hay due to arrive at 6:00 a.m. The morning after that, another four tons will need work.

"Today I killed one of the meanest snakes I've ever seen," he says. "It was under a bale of hay. I didn't know what it was, but it chased us. We tried to pick it up with a pitchfork, but we ended up killing it."

His father works on the reservation's marijuana farm and isn't always around, so Karter stays with his grandparents. "They warn me there's a lot of substance abuse on the reservation. Even among your own family. Go through a tough time and a cousin will hold out a bottle of whiskey." So far he's avoided all of that.

Nearby, Jaxon stands away from the others, like he isn't sure he belongs. A shy, skinny kid, barely 140 pounds, he arrived here a year ago with his father and younger sister. Pimply and lanky, he speeds down the field with a stride that promises future finesse.

"He needs to put on weight," Bailey observes.

"Nah, he's alright," Egan answers. His mind is playing that coach's chess game, imagining touchdowns to come. "He's good." Egan isn't displeased with this first practice: "This is the most kids we've had in five or six years. Usually it's three."

Most coaches will not tolerate players missing practice. Being soft would set the wrong tone. But Egan is not most coaches. He must wait for boys to trickle in on their own time. Discipline is a fine line. He can't just kick players off the team. He needs them. A few seasons back, one kid begged to be dismissed. One afternoon he threw off his helmet and shouted "Goddamn it, when are you guys going to kick me off this team?"

Egan turned to Smith. "I'm not going to kick him off. I'm building a team here."

Lane, the team's play-caller, is still on vacation. The coaches are eager to see the results of a throwing camp he attended this summer. In the doomed spring campaign, Lane tossed a season total of negative yards, so it couldn't get much worse.

Bailey takes the quarterback position. On the "hut!" signal, he drops back, and one by one, boys lope down the middle of the field, breaking toward the center and then to the sidelines—quick moves designed to throw off a defensive pursuer.

Their eight-man football season will be a track meet on grass, played on a traditional field narrowed to 40 yards wide. It's a high-octane, high-scoring game based on speed and deception rather than power. If a defensive player misses an open-field tackle, there's no one to take up the slack and stop a touchdown.

"If one athlete gets free amid all that empty grass, you'll score a lot of points," Egan explains. "There's no second or third guy to make a tackle. There's just one, and if he doesn't make it, the runner is gone."

As a result many final scores reach triple digits—results that are more like basketball than football. Some believe there's almost too much scoring.

Unless, of course, you're McDermitt.

"Don't throw right at 'em," Smith barks at his young quarterback. "Lead 'em. Make 'em run for it." He shouts out to the receivers, "Don't quit your routes! You gotta sell them!"

On one play, Bailey's throw wobbles. "You getting tired?" Egan asks.

"No," the kid says.

"Then throw that ball. Zip it."

Just then, Jaxon lopes out 30 yards, fluid and unconscious. The ball flies toward him, rising over his head. At the last moment he reaches out and grabs it, taking control, tumbling on the grass.

Both coaches are impressed. "There we go!" Egan cheers.

The next day the team practices with a secondhand blocking sled they acquired from the Carlin team. The coaches sawed the donated equipment in half to fit on the truck for the trip back to McDermitt, where it was reassembled.

Jerseys are also secondhand, faded by the sun and repeat washings. A previous coach had printed "McDermitt" on the back instead of players' last names. "Why would he do that?" Egan scoffs. "The team name goes on the front, the player's name on the back. Just because we're from the reservation doesn't mean we're all related."

Only a few seniors—Bailey, Elijah, and Taylor—show up with the full complement of pads, a helmet, and cleats. Others are missing parts of the ensemble, including mouthpieces necessary for tongue protection during big hits.

"Everybody needs to get their mouthpiece fitted," Smith says. "Take it home and stretch it out. In a game that mouthpiece can be your best friend."

Jaxon, the freshman, complains that his helmet is too big. Bailey tries to tighten the straps so his head doesn't bob inside like a castaway bottle atop the waves. Fighting the heat, other boys remove their helmets between drills, holding up the team as they struggle to snap them back on.

"There's a time to take your helmet off, and it's not after every drill," Smith says. From now on, anyone who removes his helmet does penalty pushups. Jared complains of headaches. His helmet needs its front pads filled with air, and the coaches bring out a small device. The boy watches the quick fix.

"Sometimes, you gotta play through pain," Smith explains. "There's a lot of agony playing football. You'll feel it come game time, and nobody's gonna feel sorry for you. We want to make grown men out of you boys, but you have to work with us."

The next day Enzo shows up wearing a pair of canvas sandals.

"Where are your cleats?" Smith asks.

"There weren't any," the boy says.

"This isn't some casual walk on the beach," the coach snaps. "Did you reach down way inside the box? You gotta dig through there."

Enzo plays in his sandals, complaining that he'll probably break an ankle.

Even out of shape, the boys keep up a banter of teenage humor. In one practice Enzo sprawls on the ground during a water break. He looks up at me as if seeing me for the first time. "Are you writing a book?"

"Yeah," Egan riffs. "It's about you sitting down. He's gonna call it 'Enzo: Sitting Bull.'"

Egan launches a drill where the boys fall on a big circular pad called the big ring.

"Hey, Maverick, this is a big chocolate donut," Egan says. "Have at it."

He then asks Maverick how much he weighs.

"Two-thirty," the boy says.

"Is that before or after the cheeseburger?"

"Biting into it."

Not all the jokes find a receptive audience. During one drill Smith orders the team to take one knee on an imaginary line. "Get down like you're proposing," he commands.

"Yeah," Bailey interjects, "except you guys are all gay. So it'll be to your boyfriends."

Nobody laughs. Questioning a boy's sexual identity out here is like throwing a punch.

"Boyfriends?" Maverick says. "Man, you're like a little kid talking."

On the sidelines, sitting atop gray metal bleachers, Jaxon's family has come to watch. His father, John, is a former oil worker whose job at the Walmart in Winnemucca requires a 144-mile daily commute.

At home the son likes to be called J.P., for his initials. While John was a football lineman, Jaxon has no such intentions. "I was a heavyweight," the father says. "He wants to run."

Next to him is Jaxon's thirteen-year-old sister, Hannah, a coltish tomboy with long legs. There's also his Aunt Roberta and her boyfriend Jimmy. They all share a rental house in town.

As Bulldog receivers drop pass after pass, Jaxon makes three straight catches, trotting back to stand next to his coaches. He hasn't uttered a word the entire practice. All around him, boys are sucking air and grabbing their knees, but not Jaxon.

In another drill, receivers run toward the sidelines, throw a head fake, and then dash downfield. Most sleepwalk through the move, and Egan is confident that Taylor will show them how it's done.

Bailey throws a perfect pass. "Touchdown," Egan says.

But Taylor stumbles, and the ball bounces off his fingertips. He trots back to the group. "I got tripped up on my own shoes," he apologizes.

"Dumb ass," Bailey says.

The boys make eye contact. There's obvious tension, but neither makes a move.

The day's final drill involves six lateral sprints across the width of the field. Boys head out in groups. At the halfway point they turn to run backward before making the final sprint back to their coaches. Taylor worked out all summer, practicing basketball with Smith, and he lost fifteen pounds. Bailey's determination to best his nemesis drives him on. But Jaxon's speed surprises everyone. On the evening's last drill, three laps around the field's perimeter, Bailey and Jaxon make a determined dash for the end line. Bailey is confident, but Jaxon keeps pace, his father and sister shouting from the bleachers, until the older boy edges ahead in the final yards.

Bailey fist pumps the young receiver whose speed, he knows, may pay dividends for the Bulldogs. It's a gesture to show this oddly quiet freshman, the only boy without a cell phone, that he's really a part of this team.

Then the Bulldogs rally in a tight circle, holding their helmets over their heads. Bailey leads the traditional chant. "Dogs on three! One-two-three Dogs!"

As the team walks off the field, Jaxon lags behind with his family. As they near the locker room, Hannah unconsciously keeps walking. In a few more steps, she'll be inside. That's when Jaxon goes from quiet freshman to taunting older brother.

"Go ahead," he says, grinning. "They're changing clothes, but go on in if you want."

The girl blushes. But Egan knows that the locker room dynamic could soon take a dramatic turn. All summer he has tried to win over an incoming freshman named Nicolette, who could make history as the first girl to play eight-man football in Nevada.

Mixing the sexes in such a physical game is an obvious risk, even for a team without enough players, but Egan has little choice. Nicolette is an athletic Paiute teen from the reservation, where most girls ride horses and perform in the rodeo. Most refuse to take any lip from a boy. They're ready to fight.

One day Nicolette told Egan she might want to skip women's volleyball and try football. She didn't have to say it twice. Nothing, he knows, would prove these teenage boys' mettle than defending a female teammate singled out by opposing teams. Most have gotten wind that Nicolette might play. "I'm sure she'll be able to take care of herself," Lane will later say. "But if kids came after her, tried to intimidate her because she's a girl, we'd stand up for her."

Just weeks before the Bulldog's first game, Egan cracks a reserved smile.

Maybe they'll win a game after all.

4

During the 1950s the barflies who squandered their paychecks in McDermitt's saloons got bad news about one of their own: well-respected rancher Chet Wilkinson had died. The boys all tipped their hats and asked what they could do to help.

Among them was Herman Hereford, a schoolteacher and imbiber who decades later wrote down what happened next. In the days before the backhoe, Hereford and fellow drinkers Dora and Satur volunteered to dig the six-foot grave by hand in the town cemetery. Chet's nephew, a fellow rancher named Dave Bankofier, made the funeral arrangements.

An hour into the backbreaking work, Dave arrived with a six-pack of beer. "It was a warm day," Hereford writes, "so Dave's thoughtfulness was greatly appreciated." Dave finished his bottle, wiped his mouth, and said, "This is going to be a full-case job."

The others agreed.

Four feet down, the diggers hit a huge, immovable boulder. That's when Dave returned with more beer. The men took a break, and after more alcohol, they turned philosophical. "Sometime later with still half a case left, Dave took a new look at our problem and said, 'Chet wants to be the first one out anyway so four feet is deep enough.'"

The men concurred and finished off the rest of the beer.

This kind of story often gets lost in a town's recorded history, or it never gets written at all. But it wasn't the first to involve McDermitt's impassioned affair with alcohol, a relationship that began sometime after the volcanoes erupted and European interlopers pushed the Native Americans off the land; in other words, way back. Hard liquor runs through McDermitt's story like coolant through the radiator of an old ranch pickup.

In 1865, the year after Nevada became a state, President Lincoln dispatched U.S. soldiers to protect a growing white population during a series of wars involving the resident Paiute, Shoshone, and Bannock tribes.

The army established Quinn River Camp No. 33, a rudimentary fort overseen by Lieutenant Colonel Charles McDermit, who spelled his last name with one *t*. Based at nearby Fort Churchill, the young colonel was also tasked with protecting the Carson City stage lines that passed through northern Nevada en route to the Idaho territory.

On August 7, 1865, McDermit was mortally wounded during an ambush by two Paiute warriors not far from the Quinn River Camp. He died within hours, and his dejected men transported their leader's body 220 miles back to Fort Churchill for burial. Yet the tribe's victory was short-lived. U.S. officials sent even more soldiers, reinforcing Camp 33 to create a larger fort named after McDermit.

For twenty-five years the outpost—consisting of adobe and stone barracks, a three-room hospital, a storehouse, and a stable surrounding a central square— played a central role in the conflict between invading white settlers and the area's original peoples. In the 1880s the U.S. military sought to decommission Fort McDermit, which by then was Nevada's only army post still in service.

Pushback came from post trader, Charles Bowling, who wanted the fort to remain a part of his nefarious business interests. For years Bowling had been illicitly selling liquor to Native Americans who had settled around the camp, breaking U.S. laws against alcohol sales to tribal members.

And, according to Thierry Veyrié, there was more. The French-born anthropologist has spent years in McDermitt. In his doctorate thesis on the history of the fort and subsequent Native American reservation, he infers that Bowling's nefarious behavior not only involved alcohol sales but also Native women.

In fact, on May 9th, 1889, the camp's commander, U.S. Army Captain R.J. Armstrong, wrote to request that the U.S. postmaster general in San Francisco revoke Bowling's standing as the fort's postmaster. "The Indians are encouraged to congregate about Mr. Bowling's place," he wrote, "and in many instances it has been reported to me that men employed by Mr. Bowling— his nephews and others—have given liquor to Indian men for the purpose of gaining access to the Indian women."

An irate Armstrong banished Bowling, who immediately opened a new settlement known as Dugout, located just outside the military reserve, presumably to continue his alcohol sales to local tribes through the saloons that quickly sprouted there.

On September 16, 1889, Fort McDermit was abandoned and later converted into a Native American school. Dugout was relocated several miles west, where the new settlement was rechristened McDermitt to honor the Army officer slain decades before. The name was spelled with an extra *t*, reportedly due to a military clerical error.

In the ensuing decades, not much was written about McDermitt as one of the many thriving communities across the American West. Too small to support its own newspaper, the rhythm of daily life in such a remote frontier town just didn't resonate in bigger communities such as Winnemucca, Reno, or Carson City.

Few outsider accounts captured what it was like to call McDermitt home. No one chronicled how the local bank failed during the Great Depression or, as rumor has it, the bank president called his secretary one night and advised her to withdraw all of her savings because the institution would be shuttered in the morning.

Real small-town stories about miners, cowboys, Paiutes, farmers, and ranch hands, written by the people who actually lived there, were not recorded.

Then came Herman Hereford.

In 1948 Hereford and his wife, Ruth, arrived from Missouri to teach at the reservation school. They checked into the White Horse Inn before taking a tour of the town. Days later they moved into their reservation quarters, a house that offered a commanding view of the old fort's parade grounds.

A half century later, in 1995, Hereford self-published "McDermitt in Retrospect," an irreverent collection of his frontier adventures that's alternatively sexist and even racist by modern standards. Nonetheless the book serves as a living document of its time. Hereford painted the area as he saw it, with scenes of teaching Paiute children and even washing his own clothes. Like the rest of McDermitt, the reservation lacked electricity and running water, so the Herefords made do and washed their dusty garments without detergent in the mineral-rich hot springs located just north of town.

The book's first twenty-five pages show a certain disrespect for Native culture, with reservation residents used as foils for humorous pokes. Hereford writes, for example, how he strictly enforced a rule that Paiute children only speak English while on school grounds, and he seems bemused over the lengths many children went to bypass the restriction. "Never were we able to catch them unawares for they early learned to keep a sharp lookout for our approach and we often overheard the loudly whispered warning, 'Talk English, talk English, come teacher.'"

Neither do adults escape his digs. Hereford notes that teachers played movies on a reel-to-reel projector inside a Quonset hut each weekend "to keep as many of the adults as possible from enjoying the entertainment provided by the peyote priests."

He also describes waking up many mornings to several Paiute elders sitting in his kitchen. Rather than see this as proof that he was accepted into Native culture, Hereford complains. "We became reconciled to the fact that here, so far from towns and cities, we were to enjoy no personal privacy whatsoever. All day long our visitors visited and even far into the night."

A year after he arrived, Hereford received his reprieve when he was hired to teach in town, where he rejoined his own kind. That ended any attention he paid to reservation residents, who remained punchlines for inebriated townsfolk, as though Hereford viewed them as wooden dime-store statues: inanimate and part of the scenery.

Hereford's experiences are indicative of the frayed relationship that still exists today between the town and its adjacent reservation. Paiute children comprise a vast majority of students at the McDermitt Combined Schools. They're necessary to maintain current levels of state and federal funding and to populate the various sports teams, including the football squad. They pick up their mail from local post office boxes like everyone else. But a not-so-subtle divide continues to exist.

Eighth grade teacher Penny Lancaster arrived in McDermitt a few years ago to find a reading list dominated by historical accounts written by whites, championing the nineteenth-century drive to colonize the American West. "I couldn't imagine being a kid having to sit through the death of my people being taught in school year after year," she says. "There were details of the Donner party and settlers attacked by so-called savages. And you're like 'What the heck, is this still a thing?' It was even worse when these kids' grandparents and parents were in school, but even today it's still happening."

While Paiutes aren't banned from the Say When casino like they were from local bars in Hereford's day, they're not exactly welcome. "Endured" might be a better word. One evening I sat at a table near a line of squawking slot machines. I was with Thierry Veyrié, the French anthropologist, and his friend Harley, a local Native artist.

We'd already had a few beers. When I ordered another round, the owner motioned at Harley. "This one's had enough." I pretended I hadn't heard her.

"Make it three, please," I insisted.

Veyrié believes that the owner was merely protecting her establishment from some reservation troublemakers. I asked him if she would have treated a white rancher in the same manner.

"I don't know," Veyrié said. "It's a good question."

The anthropologist has witnessed the cultural divide firsthand. "In the old days there used to be fistfights in town between whites and Natives on every holiday," he said. Even today no Pauites are buried in the town cemetery, a regimented place where the graves of whites are separated from those of Basque settlers. But the chasm is slowly being closed through intermarriage.

Mixed children play the equalizers. Still, while Hereford's book is available at the local library, few Paiutes check it out.

In the 1960s, the town and reservation began bonding through Bulldogs football. Players and their parents were able to put differences aside to better compete as a team. And there was another reason: as the mines closed and McDermitt's white population fled, Pauites came to comprise a majority of the players.

The town and its football team needed the reservation for its very survival.

In his book Hereford is most entertaining when he writes about the foibles of his fellow townsfolk, families with such surnames as Reeves, Mentaberry, Albisu, and Wilkinson, whose descendants still live here today.

"McDermitt in Retrospect," is a celebration of the madcap, alcohol-lit events of his adopted hometown. Elderly residents still shake their heads at the high jinks captured within its ninety-eight pages. The author had an eye for telling details and an ear for dialogue; he was a man-about-town who made it his business to get to know just about everyone.

Hereford was also a consummate drinker, a consumer of "liquid necessities," who felt at home in a settlement with six rollicking bars to serve a community that in 1948 numbered just sixty-five residents—an average of one saloon for every ten and a half people. Mining and ranch work made men thirsty. Long before the Bulldogs arrived, drinking was the only game in town.

As the town's unofficial biographer, Hereford interprets a long history of boom times followed by failure and rebuilding, and then more failure. He outlines how the decisive Indian wars played out generations before the Paiutes moved on the reservation, and white homesteaders planted endless fields of hay to feed their cattle and horses.

A succession of harsh winters devastated the ranching industry, and many cattlemen turned to raising sheep, Hereford writes. They brought in Basque settlers to manage their flocks, establishing McDermitt as a prosperous center for wool exports.

When that industry failed and banks foreclosed on many operations, McDermitt turned to its surrounding mercury deposits. A Basque herder named Tomas Alcorta was looking to clean his backside after defecating among his sheep, Hereford writes, when he picked up an odd red-colored rock. It turned out to be cinnabar, a mineral formed during volcanic activity, prized as a high-grade form of mercury.

The finding attracted the Sun Oil Company, which bought up area claims and opened the Cordero Mine, which soon employed 150 men. Most were single drifters who labored underground and preferred to slake their thirst from atop a barstool, veterans returning from World War II seeking safer adventures and good times.

In 1948 McDermitt was home to such thriving enterprises as the Highway Bar, Rancho Bar, and Orveda Dance Hall. Locals traditionally imbibed in turn at each establishment before calling it a night. Or not. There were ranch owners, farmers, gas station and motel owners, schoolteachers, buckaroos, and random passersby who populated the rowdy drinking establishments that served as McDermitt's town square.

Hereford recalls one out-of-town motorist who handed his keys to Vic at the Shell station to quickly service his car while he moseyed across the street to the Highway Bar. When Vic dropped by to say his car was ready, the traveler insisted on buying him a round. Well, Vic never let anyone buy him a drink without reciprocating. "After two days," Hereford writes, "the man in such a hurry to be on his way" finally got back on the road.

He also chronicles the high-spirited carousing of ranch characters like Basco Joe and Coyote Sam; businessmen nicknamed Donuts, Patch, and Dynamite; bar owners Concha and Sundown Sam; Tim Payne the snake man; Wilma the wild waitress; and legendary drinkers named Sap, Dora, Pinky, Blackie, and Boat.

Hereford's favorite haunt was the old Commercial Hotel, built in 1915 and later rechristened the White Horse Inn—the place where he and his wife spent their very first night in town. The owners ran a saloon on the main floor and, during prohibition, carved out a thriving business peddling bootleg hooch from the basement. Upstairs were twenty-one cell-like rooms, each with a narrow bed and a small sink, with a shared bathroom down the hallway, rented nightly by cowboys who'd had too much drink. Rumors said working women also plied a trade there.

The state line ran through the building, and its demarcation on the dance hall ceiling allowed boozy patrons to order drinks and gamble in Nevada but pay on the Oregon side to avoid the sales tax. A stone jailhouse outside was reserved for troublemakers who couldn't hold their drink, which included just about everybody in McDermitt.

Hereford writes about boys who drowned in nearby reservoirs, observing that most Natives "have never learned to swim as there are no swimming pools or water in the local streams for them to learn." He tells how several locals owned airplanes and carved out a small strip on the Oregon side of town. Then wealthy rancher Locke Jacobs decided he needed a larger airfield for his jet. He twisted the arms of politicians for funding, and by the 1950s tiny McDermitt wound up with a modern airstrip large enough for commercial planes. Not many came.

Hereford's journal includes a collection of personal photographs that include shots of all six saloons, framed with as much reverence as if they were taken at Mount Rushmore. There's a picture of Dora Lasa cutting Chuck Johnson's hair on the sidewalk; Sam Albisu holding up two lines of just-caught trout; and Charley Lows's little shack, built in 1904, that became an unlikely dance hall. There's even a shot of Hereford himself, taken in 1948. He wears a fedora and holds a Paiute boy in his arms as he stands in the back of a dump truck that served as the announcer's stand at his first reservation cattle sale. An American flag unfurls in the background.

Once Herman Hereford arrived, McDermitt was never quite the same. It now had a story and a storyteller to relate the tales that allow us to come to know a place and its people.

Hereford was still new in town when he got his first taste of McDermitt hospitality. As he was about to leave for an extended Christmastime trip, the paycheck from his government teaching job failed to arrive on time.

Everybody soon knew of Hereford's misfortune, because he told them all about it. Hilda Reeves at the post office offered him $100. Next door, the Chevron Service Station's owner Batista "Boat" Albisu stuck two $100 bills in his jacket pocket. At the Quinn River Merc general store, proprietor Chuck Ford offered him another $200 and a bottle of whiskey.

Hereford turned down all of it, except for the whiskey, which he considered a holiday present. He knew then that these townsfolk were *his* people. "They worked hard and they played hard," he writes. "The best compliment paid to anyone regardless of his station in life is 'He's a hard worker.'"

Hereford established himself as the town's de facto events planner and social secretary. One morning he and his cronies were drinking coffee at the State Line Cafe when somebody mentioned they ought to plan an event for the upcoming Fourth of July holiday.

The teacher suggested they reprise the rodeo, an annual party comprising downtown horse races and bucking contests. Dating back to 1913, the rodeo was the oldest in Nevada, a major social event for remote ranchers who saw one another once a year. The rodeo was discontinued during the war, and now Hereford wanted to bring it back.

Dave Bankofier, Chet Wilkinson's nephew, offered to hold the event at his Ten Mile Ranch. Dave was a so-called rodeo "pick-up man" who rescued fallen riders before they were trampled by angry bulls and broncos. When there was no rodeo, Dave could still be found atop his horse, guiding his mount into local bars, quaffing beers while still in the saddle—until the day the horse lifted its tail and defecated on the barroom floor in front of mixed company. After that, Dave's horse had to do his business outside, and Dave was only allowed in on foot.

The town took Dave up on his offer, and business owners pledged to build a rodeo arena, but they needed grandstands. So the hardworking locals bought some used event seating in the nearby town of Paradise. They sawed the grandstands in half for easier transport, headed back to McDermitt, and put them back together.

The shindig, first known as the Twin States Stampede, soon became one of the wildest rodeos in the West, with hard drinking, fistfights between winners and losers, and horse races through the middle of town, with many big bets placed on the results.

As Hereford recalls, Dave rounded up a few scruffy-looking mustangs, which caused quite a stir among competitors. The feisty wild horses, unaccustomed to even the sight of a rope or halter, threw more riders than anyone could count.

Each night after the rodeo, saloon fights spilled out onto the streets, many between whites and reservation residents. Hereford mentions that he opened up the Pioneer Bar as rodeo headquarters "and as a gathering place for youngsters and Indians who were not allowed in the bars."

Early one morning he wandered down a deserted street "where [he] observed an Indian sitting on a bench outside the Rancho Bar." Just as the Paiute slowly raised his head, Hereford heard laughter. The head dropped and rose to more guffaws until Hereford spotted a clothesline looped around the man's neck, extending to the roof above, held by a man named Santa Blackie.

"What are you doing, Blackie?" he inquired.

"Havin' fun," Blackie answered. "I've always wanted to hang an Indian, and now I'm about to do it."

The teacher who had once instructed the Paiute man's children wasn't outraged but bemused. "Of course," Hereford writes, "Blackie was still a bit under the influence of his favorite brandy but I think for the Indian's sake it was just as well I had gotten up early."

Today the Twin States Stampede is known as the "McDermitt Fourth of July Rodeo," which is supported by the reservation residents.

Without them the event might cease to exist.

Over the decades Hereford witnessed under-the-influence acts performed by townsfolk that could easily take their place in a Mark Twain novel.

One cowboy named Donuts, after a bit of revelry, roped passing cars from atop his horse. Buckaroo Dave Castro came to town to ask a wealthy widow for her hand in marriage but had so many drinks to build up his courage he eventually forgot why he'd shown up in the first place. Hereford never tells us what happened to either Dave or the widow, but considering the pickings around McDermitt, both probably stayed single.

At one time the Orveda Bar hosted high-stakes poker games, where ranch titles were sometimes won and lost. In one epic showdown, rancher Coyote Sam stared down a woman named Blanche who was widely known as a sore loser. Once, after a losing hand, Blanche reached out to retrieve her coins. That's when Sam belted her in the face, knocking her from her chair as he pocketed his winnings and walked out the door. "Of course," Hereford concludes, "Sam did not know the meaning of chivalry and in a poker game of high stakes it didn't exist anyway."

Still, McDermitt women usually called the shots. One day, rancher Leo Turner and the wife of his cook, Pinky, hit the town for supplies. After a few drinks at the Highway Bar, they began to argue over who was the better buckaroo and decided to settle their differences in a contest Hereford refers to as "squaw wrestling." "Mrs. Pinky," as Hereford calls her, borrowed the pants off a fellow drinker, placed them over her skirt, and whipped her husband's bewildered boss in a tussle right there on the barroom floor.

Hereford and a crony named Dora once drove five McDermitt youngsters to Winnemucca for a fishing derby. The men loaded the boys—the youngest, a three-year-old toddler named Skeeter, and the oldest, Jimmy Naveran, at eleven—into Dora's 1949 two-door Chevy. But the day turned too cold and blustery to fish. The pair sent their wards into a movie theater and retired to the Farris Bar and Hotel for a few rounds, where a bartender named Alabama did the pouring. It wasn't long before Hereford saw five noses outside, pressed against the glass, so he gave the boys more money and told them to go see the movie again.

Hours later the two drinkers ran out of money. "All I could find in my pockets," Hereford writes, "is a jar of salmon eggs which Alabama took as a pawn for one last round." When it was time to head back to McDermitt, both men were staggering drunk.

Since it was *his* car, Dora drove first but finally relinquished the wheel to Hereford who, equally sloshed, didn't do much better. The road ran through undulating landscape, presenting a challenge for two men who'd been drinking all day.

A few miles out, they pulled over, eyed the boys in the back seat, and made a decision. Hereford notes, "Dora and I always considered this to be the first driver education lesson in the state of Nevada as Jimmy Naveran became an excellent driver."

McDermitt's good times eventually ran their course. In the early 1970s, the Sun Oil Company abandoned the mercury mine, selling off buildings and equipment for scrap. A Canadian company called Placer Dome then launched an open-pit operation within view of the old shaft, which they renamed the McDermitt Mine.

The new owners preferred family men, workers who could move into houses built near the mine and, after five years, claim the properties as their own. Overnight, the tenor of downtown McDermitt felt a shudder of change that would continue for decades. "This meant the end of the old-time transient miner with his free-and-easy life of turning his paycheck over to the bartender," Hereford writes. "The arrangement spelled disaster for the local bars."

The advent of television also kept most folks at home and out of the saloons. Then the McDermitt Mine closed in 1992, further sounding the town's death knell. By 1995, when Hereford published his book, only two bars remained: the Say When casino, built at the site of the old bank, and the Orevada Bar just across U.S. Route 95.

At its end, Hereford's book ponders the future of his adopted town. He outlines how McDermitt could make a comeback, with ample minerals to attract new mining enterprises and a highway that's becoming a major artery for all kinds of tourism.

"McDermitt is ready," reads the book's boosterish last line.

The town still waits for more good times and a chronicler like Herman Hereford.

Maybe that's me.

Today this diminished town is graveyard quiet. As I pass the ruins of the White Horse and Orovada Bar, I want to hear Herman Hereford's voice and the laughter of those drinkers past, the ghosts of McDermitt revelers now dead and gone. But all I hear are passing semis along the highway, in a hurry to reach somewhere else.

5

On my very first day in McDermitt, I head out for a country walk. As I move down the gravel driveway of my rented bungalow, I hear a voice.

There's a man in the next backyard. He's dressed in a farmer's cap, purple "wild rag" around his neck, work pants, and a denim shirt. He reminds me of Mr. Green Jeans from the old children's TV show *Captain Kangaroo*.

The man has raked the thin dirt on his lot into straight, parallel lines, as if preparing the land for planting, leaving walking paths in between each row like a gardener might do, or perhaps like the pathways between graves in a cemetery. Along his back porch railing, stones of different colors and styles are arranged like a religious offering.

The scene reeks of mystery: Midwestern crop circles or the grounds of an abandoned mental hospital, a glimpse into an obsessive-compulsive mind. At the fence line sits a rock grave topped by a crude wooden cross, something makeshift that a wagonload of pioneers might have left behind along the Oregon Trail.

Who, or what, is buried there? Do I even want to know? I notice that the man is talking to someone with a tinge of urgency, but there is no one there.

I don't interrupt. I walk on.

Days later I visit my landlords, Lorraine and her husband, Howard, whom everyone calls Junior.

"What's up with my neighbor?" I ask.

"You mean Cowboy Bob?" Lorraine says. "He once worked as a buckaroo on isolated cattle spreads." He's a simple man, a lost soul. "I'll tell you one thing," she says. "When he was young, Bob was one good-looking man."

"What's that?" Junior calls out from the couch.

Lorraine repeats herself. "*Man*, he was good-looking."

Junior has issues with Bob. "I call him SpongeBob," he says. "He's got sticky fingers."

"Oh, Junior," Lorraine says. "That's just the way he is. He doesn't understand."

"I don't care," Junior continues. "You've got to watch him." Weeks before, Bob made off with some plastic piping that Junior kept in his yard. Now the man can't be trusted.

Lorraine shakes her head. "Junior, you hadn't touched those pipes in years. He probably thought you'd just abandoned them. That's how he is."

"No, he took them. Now I've got to keep my eye on him."

"Oh, Junior."

Cowboy Bob, I realize, is a Herman Hereford story come to life, a slice of old McDermitt still present in the new. Still, I give Bob a wide berth, which is difficult in a small town. Every time I leave my house, he's there in his yard, pulling weeds real and imagined. I pretend not to see him. One day, as I sit in the town's tiny public library, Bob hurries inside, as though looking for something that's gotten away, like a horse that's fled the barn.

Then I realize that thing is me. He makes eye contact for several long, uncomfortable moments and then suddenly turns on his heels and walks out.

I ask the front desk librarian about the visitor. "That's just Bob," she says.

Bob's visits soon hit closer to home, to my one-bedroom rental house with its period details: ornate cabinets, doorways, and crown molding. One day he walks onto the wraparound porch. I hear his footsteps and peer out the window like a suspicious old spinster as he raps at the door, hiding in the bedroom until he finally gives up.

It's like living next door to a rural boogeyman.

People joke that Bob waits inside his house with a pair of binoculars, ready to ambush unsuspecting passersby. One evening as I walk past, he appears in his yard, raking dirt. There's no way to avoid him.

After weeks of playing the timid mouse, biased by gossip, I finally ask myself: Why am I so afraid of this harmless old man?

"Hi, Bob," I say. "You sure keep a nice yard."

He jumps back in theatrical surprise. But there's also a kind of joy in his eyes, maybe from just being acknowledged.

"Do you know how old I am?" he squeaks.

"Forty-nine?"

"Nope."

He hands me his driver's license. "I'm eighty-one! Says so right there."

His posture is ramrod straight, a buckaroo from those Old West paintings. He really is *Cowboy Bob*. He seems less menacing. One day I look out my window to see his face right there below. Is he peeping? I once might have thought so. Now I walk outside.

"Am I in trouble?" he asks.

"Why?"

"Because I've been bringing your trash barrel in from the road."

On Monday nights I roll the container in front of my gate. The next morning it's magically back in place.

"No, you're not in trouble," I say. "Go ahead if it makes you feel better."

Bob has manic energy that needs an outlet. One day he pulled up a neighbor's flower bulbs. He thought they were weeds, and out they came. He even manicures the public alley, raking straight lines in the dirt, creating patterns that make no sense to anyone but him.

It's crazy, but "Cowboy Bob" crazy.

Around McDermitt, opinions on Cowboy Bob are divided. Many cringe when they spot his brown Dodge Ram truck with the muddy Nevada license plate, rakes and shovels stored in the back.

He accosts strangers who stop along U.S. 95, at the two welcome signs for Oregon and Nevada, depending on which way you're headed. Within minutes after someone stops for snapshots, Bob rolls up in his truck, offering to take their pictures.

Junior calls him the Town Greeter, a nickname that conjures Forrest Gump, someone without an agenda. Not a menace but a mild irritation, a fly that won't buzz off. "He's eccentric and, frankly, quite lonely," says Vickie Easterday, who has lived here for decades. "He doesn't know his limits."

She offers a truth about small towns. "People judge. And once you're judged, your reputation stays with you. People don't know Bob; they know the rumors. I often worry what people say about me."

Joe White Buffalo, who runs a rock-and-gem lot, suffers from PTSD and doesn't trust many people. But he lets Bob inside the wall of his disease. "He'll knock on my door at 6:00 a.m. I have to be stiff with him," the old rockhound explains. "I tell him he can't come around until after noon. He'll pop up and invite my customers to his house to look at *his* rocks."

Every afternoon White Buffalo offers Bob the same goodbye: "I love ya, but not that much. What you need is a wife."

White Buffalo suffers Bob like a coyote skulking his property at night. "He essentially has nothing to talk about. He repeats what I call mindless drivel. It's the same thing day after day. I'll say to him, 'Bob, do you know how many times you've told me that story? I'm tired of hearing it.' He's not a worldly man. He can't talk about a lot of stuff. Cowboying is a lonely life. You live in a cowboy camp. You work, and that's about it."

Bob, he says, is a creature of habit. For breakfast he eats two Little Debbie donuts and a banana with a cup of coffee. Lunch is a peanut butter and jelly sandwich, and dinner is a bowl of Cheerios and bacon salad. He talks about himself in the third person. He'll slap his knee and say, "Well, ole Cowboy Bob is gonna make me a sandwich."

One day I have a professional reckoning: Cowboy Bob is more than just the strange man across the fence. In a way he's McDermitt, or part of it.

To understand this small town, I have to learn more about Bob. I've already asked questions out of perverse curiosity. Now I have to do some reporting.

That evening I spot Bob, rake in hand, and head over to the fence at our property line. I say I want him to be a character in my book. He says nothing but points up at a passing jet.

Something changes after that encounter. Suddenly Bob no longer knocks at my door. I realize the cowboy boot is on the other foot. Now Bob is ghosting me.

Another day I spot him at the gas station. As a motorist cleans his windshield, Bob is there like a sidekick. He flexes his right bicep and makes the muscle twerk. He produces his driver's license to show his age.

And I realize this: I actually miss Bob and the days he turned up just about everywhere.

"Hello," I say after the motorist drives off.

But Bob doesn't feel like talking. "I've got things to do," he says.

He drives off, and I realize that, apart from the stories locals like Lorraine and Junior have told, I know little more about Bob than the day I arrived.

One day Bob showed up outside Lorraine's front door.

"I need a haircut," he said.

"Well, it's gonna cost you," she answered.

"How much?"

"A hundred dollars."

"Okay."

"Bob, you know I won't charge you," she said. "I'm no professional, so you're going to be my guinea pig." Days later Bob told Lorraine he'd pinned up community notices advertising free haircuts. Each gave Lorraine's number.

"Bob, you march back over there and take those down!"

As it turns out, Cowboy Bob does have a support network. Bruce Easterday, Vickie's husband, keeps Bob's shovels sharpened. Lorraine helps him decipher his bills. Another woman does Bob's laundry but doesn't want much else more to do with him. He leaves his clothes on her stoop and picks them up the next day.

But the woman's mother shakes her fist when Bob comes over. She tells him to leave her daughter alone. Not everyone chooses to endure Bob.

One day Lorraine tells Junior that Bob needs help with his television. Junior once went a year without even talking to Bob. "I got a hammer," he says. "I'll fix his TV, alright."

But Junior's antipathy is mostly bluff. "He doesn't have a vicious bone in his body," he says. "I've irritated the hell out of him, just to see if I can get a rise. Nothing bothers the man."

"That's because he's afraid of you half the time," snorts Lorraine.

"Well, he should be," Junior shoots back.

He knows Bob's repertoire. "He puts one hand up, and when he's got your attention, he grabs something of yours, like a wrench," Junior explains. "He thinks it's fun until I say I'm going to stab him with my screwdriver, then he puts it back."

Once, entering the Merc, Bob playfully stepped in front of a woman walking out. When she tried to let him pass, he moved with her, like in a dance. "It was harmless," Junior says, "Bob's idea of a joke."

Still, the woman's husband wanted to beat Bob up. "There's no harm to what he did," Junior told him. "Your wife just took offense, is all."

Lorraine scolded Bob for that escapade. "You're irritating people," she says. "Never joke with anyone you don't know."

She remains his biggest defender. The two can talk about anything, until Lorraine has had enough small talk.

"I'm going into the house now," she says.

"I'm not done talking," Bob replies.

"Well," Lorraine says, "I'm done listening."

When Lorraine was postmistress, Bob stopped in daily to collect his mail. Rather than use his key, he reached around inside the public window to feel if his box was empty.

Lorraine told him to behave himself, but he tried the stunt again the following morning, so she swatted him with a handful of magazines.

"You hit me," he protested.

"That's right, and I'm gonna hit you again if you do that." Then her soft spot returned. "Did it hurt?"

"No," Bob said.

"Okay then. You learned your lesson. You're just an irritating little boy."

Word spreads quickly around town: Cowboy Bob has been robbed.

Everybody knows he carries $100 bills in his wallet. People have seen him hand $20 bills to children. "He does it to buy friends," Lorraine says. "But it gets him into trouble."

Bob doesn't have many demands on his monthly social security check. His house and truck are paid for, so all he buys are gas and Little Debbies. But he's got bad habits. He picks up hitchhikers and invites them to his house. People figure he gives them wads of cash before sending them on their way.

When Bob once met a derelict named Debbie, everyone feared the worst. She took up residence in the Diamond A Motel, and Bob gave her the keys to his truck. As it turned out, Debbie had a gambling problem, and Bob gave her all of his social security checks, too, so he was left walking around without a single dollar bill in his wallet.

Then Bob's crazy generosity went too far. He gave money to two drifters who broke into his house with a gun and demanded all his cash. The robbery is the final misadventure.

For awhile now, Bob's sister, Charlotte, and her niece, Michelle, who own a ranch outside town, have been his absentee caretakers. Now Charlotte files for power of attorney, so the social security checks are delivered to her, and she dispenses Bob an allowance. No longer flush with cash, he drops by Lorraine's house asking for a loan.

"Don't loan him any money," Charlotte urges.

Before the holdup she gave him $70, which he handed over to the drifters.

As Lorraine tells the story, Junior shoots her a glare. "So, now it's all coming out," he says. "You told me it was a lot less than that."

"Oh, Junior," Lorraine says. "You're only told what you need to know."

I decide I need to speak to Bob's family. But will they talk to a stranger poking into family business? Junior picks up the phone and calls Charlotte. "Can the writer come visit?"

Charlotte gives her hesitant consent. Lorraine tags along as my emissary.

Charlotte sits inside her ranch kitchen, tucked into the foothills of the craggy canyon range. Michelle, a capable woman who handles most of the ranching chores, sits by her side, and they start to tell me about Bob, whose full name is Robert Donald Grubaugh.

He was born in Arock, Oregon, a town even smaller than McDermitt. His parents, Don and Lois, ran a ranch, and Don made extra money driving a school bus. Bob was the second youngest of five kids.

Bob had a pet pig, says Charlotte.

"He loved that little pig," she tells me. "It grew into a nice big sow, and he'd rub her belly, and she'd lay right down. He had a horse he called Blue. Bob broke her all by himself. Anybody could ride her. He had her for years."

When Bob's oldest brother, Chuck, moved to California, Bob followed. He didn't even finish high school. "He was shy," Charlotte says. "He didn't like school."

Bob got a job as a mechanic at a San Mateo wrecking yard and married the boss's daughter, Pam. They had five children before they separated a decade later. Charlotte says there was no question about who would take custody of the children. Bob quickly fell out of touch with his kids, a situation that persists today.

He then launched a life as an itinerant cowboy. He worked with his hands, drank beer, and womanized whenever he got the chance. He moved between Idaho, Utah, and Nevada—including a gig near Area 51, which, both women joke, is how Bob became so damned weird.

Charlotte could only guess what her brother was doing. "There weren't many holiday calls, mainly because Bob never had a phone," she says. "He did his thing. He liked his beer. He'd go home after work and drink a few six packs."

She surmises there were a few more kids, including a now-grown boy who popped up not long ago. "Bob got around." Michelle laughs. "Bob had a bunch of little Bobs."

"You go to the bar and drink," Charlotte says. "That's what happens."

He eventually picked up the moniker Cowboy Bob. He got a puppy, a blue healer he named Whisper, and the two became inseparable. Charlotte believes Whisper represents the single meaningful relationship in Bob's life.

After eighteen years Bob clashed with a new boss, a woman. "Bob does not like a woman telling him what to do," Michelle says. "Not me, not her, not anybody."

In 2004 he showed up in McDermitt. He bought a house in town and worked at the Lucky Seven Ranch watering cattle, cleaning the barn, and building fences. When he turned eighty, the ranch let him go. By then he'd quit drinking and found the Bible.

Suddenly Bob didn't have anything else to do but drive around in his pickup and scarf down Little Debbie donuts. When Whisper died at age sixteen, Bob buried the dog in his yard, under that stone pile. He keeps Whisper's photo in his wallet—right beneath his license—and still talks to his old friend like he was the day I first met him.

Michelle understands her eccentric uncle. "Bob is a very smart man," she says. "He's just peculiar. He was a cowboy, and that's all he had to worry about. He never paid any bills. The ranch owner did all that. And then came all that isolation."

He loves animals. "He just isn't comfortable around people," Michelle says. "He was around them horses and them dogs. And that's what he loves more than anything in this world. He relates more to animals than his own kids."

Now he clings to his warped sense of humor. It's all that's left of who he once was. "He spent his life way in the middle of nowhere, 40, 50, 60 miles from town. That's why he doesn't understand the way the world works, because he was always isolated," Michelle says. "McDermitt's a small place. Can you imagine Bob in a big city? They'd put him in a nuthouse."

When Bob gets into trouble, the police come visit Michelle. "The first thing they ask: 'Is Bob ready for a nursing home?'"

No, she always answers, he is *not*.

In what is nothing less than a small-town tragedy, Bob is now convinced that his sister and niece are embezzling his money. He distrusts the women who are his last defense, the ones who protect the independent life he's always known: the freedom to start his pickup each morning and cruise McDermitt's backstreets, to play his pranks and get on people's nerves and rake his yard and talk to his long-dead dog, to just continue being Bob for Bob's sake.

I accompany Lorraine to check on Bob. As we knock on the door, huddling close in the hard morning rain, we eye the back porch lineup of oddities. There's an antique child's spoon he found in the dirt, once dull but now polished. Like a fish or a field crow, Bob likes shiny things.

We carry two plastic jars of peanut butter to bribe our way inside, if necessary. Lorraine opens the screen door and calls for Bob.

Suddenly he's there, appearing like an apparition. His blue eyes widen until we hand him the peanut butter, and he quickly morphs into an engaging social host, leading us into the living room.

As Lorraine asks Bob about his favorite religious shows and old TV westerns, my eyes drink in every detail. Here I am, finally inside Bob's coveted personal space, as if I'd entered King Tut's tomb, notebook at the ready.

On the cable box Charlotte has taped a letter warning Bob not to start giving away his possessions like he's done before. "Bob, do *not* send this back or give it away," it reads. "It belongs to your sister Charlotte, not Direct TV or your friends."

There are stuffed animals, bears and birds, a poster of Marilyn Monroe wearing a Los Angeles Lakers basketball jersey, and several calendars, each with the dates marked off with a large *X* like Bob is a convict marking time.

He leads us into his bedroom. On one wall, above a picture of Whisper, hangs a list of a dozen people, their birthdays penciled in. In the second bedroom he points toward the bed where a woman hitchhiker he'd recently picked up spent the night.

"Bob, that's dangerous," Lorraine clucks. "These days, people will hit you over the head for less than a dime."

As a gag, Bob reaches out suddenly to tweak her nose. She grabs his arm to show that he's written his age, eighty-one, on the side of his hand, as if he couldn't let himself, or anyone else, forget.

We turn to leave, back out into the steady rain. On the back of one door I spot another handwritten sign, no doubt from his two women protectors.

"We love you!" it says.

I buy a painting one day depicting a herd of wild mustangs from the coffeehouse near my house. As I walk home, I run into Bob raking leaves. I show him the painting. He's silent for a few moments.

"There used to be a lot of wild mustangs out there in those mountains," he says, motioning toward Oregon. "Cowboys used to catch 'em, take 'em home, and break 'em. But they put a stop to that."

He talks about Whisper. "I got that dog when it was just an itty-bitty thing," he says, cradling the air in his arms.

"Why don't you get another dog?"

He shakes his head.

"It doesn't have to be a puppy. You could go to the pound and pick out an old dog nobody wants. That way, it'll be old, just like you are."

Bob likes that idea. Then he lies again, saying he's seventy-one.

As I walk away he yells, "See ya later, alligator!" and "After awhile, crocodile!" Then he goes back to sweeping outside somebody else's house.

Every Sunday Bob visits the local cemetery and keeps his parents' gravesite as manicured as his own yard. He doesn't know this, but Charlotte and Michelle have already purchased his gravestone for when it's Bob's time to join his mother and father.

The epitaph will read "Robert Donald Grubaugh: Cowboy Bob" and will include a likeness of Whisper there so they'll be together, the eccentric old buckaroo and his beloved canine companion.

For now Bob stays in tentative touch with the outside world. He keeps a letter from one of his daughters who wants to reconnect. Bob tells people she's coming to visit next summer, but it never comes to pass.

Charlotte and Michelle hope it never does—that she doesn't take Bob away. They want him to live out his years here in McDermitt, a town that mostly accepts him for who he is and the only place where he'll be remembered once he's gone.

6

The Bulldogs are sprawled on the ground, doing their stretches. It's the first week of practice, late-August hot and humid, the smoke from far-off wildfires looming like a storm cloud that threatens the entire season.

"Where's Mav?" Smith suddenly asks.

"He'll screw around in the locker room and join us at quitting time," Egan says.

"Probably," Smith says.

Maverick is the team enigma, doughy and quiet, a dark-skinned kid with middle-of-the-night black hair, the last straggler at any event other than the cafeteria line.

Over the summer he joined Taylor, the team's pumping heart, for a private gym workout with Smith. The session kicked Mav's ass. He never came back.

Days before the start of classes, Egan is arranging his chess pieces. Other than Lane, who's still on vacation, Maverick is the biggest question mark, once again holding his coaches hostage with his lethargy and indecision.

He's made only one practice, and everyone figures he's quit the team. Then, as the boys run end-outs, dropping most balls thrown their way, a minor miracle happens.

It's Maverick.

The others watch him inch his way toward the field, barely moving.

"Mav!" Egan calls out. "You're here!"

"I'm tired," the boy says. "I had to work all day long."

With the other boys looking on, Egan can't be seen to play favorites, but he doesn't have the luxury of kicking anyone off this team. Even Maverick.

"I work all day long too," he says. "And I'm here."

Maverick moves sluggishly through the evening's drills. On breaks, the boys guzzle from water bottles. A big truck blasts its air brakes out on the highway. When there's no traffic, the field is quiet, isolated, as though these Bulldogs have been left on their own at the edge of this dying town, with the outback slowly creeping in.

A hawk lingers above the field, wavering in the weakening wind. The boys watch, perhaps curious about a creature that can leave this town at will, fly away from a high school with just twenty-seven students, but chooses to stay.

Maverick lingers the longest. Only Egan's whistle breaks the silence.

The following night, Maverick is late again. The coaches see him coming.

"Is he running or walking?" Smith asks a player.

"Walking."

"He can't pull this shit," Egan says. "He says he can't get a ride. Well, he lives with his grandmother. All he has to do is ask."

Maverick still hasn't reached the field.

"He's got one gear," Jack says. "And that's first."

As Maverick reaches the group, he turns to big Elijah. "Don't get near me," he says.

"Why? You got Covid?"

"Nah," Maverick says. "I'm just sick."

Elijah is himself recovering from Covid but still attends practice, wheezing and grabbing his knees. Egan warns him to sit out a few practices, but the big kid waves him off. Elijah is a farm boy. It's a dangerous life, and the last thing Egan needs is a season-ending injury that would doom the team. So no messing around, he says. Be careful around those horses, tractors, and motorcycles.

Egan ends most practices before the sun weakens so his boys don't drive home at night, especially those who live far outside town. They could hit an antelope or collide with some speeding tourist.

During a break on this day, boys amble over to a water spigot. Maverick drops to his knees to slurp his fill. "You gonna drink that?" Bailey asks. "That shit is full of arsenic."

It's McDermitt's legacy: water fouled by mining waste. Yet despite studies showing that the water is unhealthy, many here deny the science. "I've drank worse," Egan says. "Growing up on the reservation, you'd kneel down at some water hole and swat the flies away, animals doing their business all around."

Still, Egan is never without his big bottle of iced tea, the ice inside rattling as he tips it to his lips. He calls out to the boys at the spigot. "Don't drink too much. Swirl it around in your mouth and spit it out. That water's not gonna do ya any favors."

Maverick doesn't listen. Soon he's on the ground, trying to retch.

"Let it out, Mav!" Taylor yells.

He spits out a heavy fluid. He gets up but falls again. "Man!" he says. "I just fell in my own spit!"

"That won't hurt ya," Egan says.

On the final laps around the track, Taylor finishes first, rejoining the coaches, sweaty and breathless. "Did you beat Bailey?" Egan asks, stoking the rivalry.

"Yeah, here he comes."

Taylor sees Mav moving zombie-like. "I'm gonna go do a few laps with Mav," he says.

The two friends finish together, mostly walking. But at least Mav is here.

The Bulldogs know their practice drills as well as their computer passwords. "Playboy" is sitting up on the grass, one leg stretched over the other like a posing model. "Hurdler stretch" is extending one leg, the other tucked behind like you're leaping over a hurdle, reaching out to grab your outstretched toe.

"Toy soldiers" is running, thrusting out your legs like fascist soldiers. "Karaoke" is running sideways, swinging your arms side-to-side in rhythm. "Foot fire" is running rapidly in place. "Defensive back," or DB, is running backward 5 yards before turning to sprint downfield. "Drop steps" are dropping in your tracks for pushups.

The most tortuous drill of all, the Grand Poobah of pain, obviously dreamed up by the crazed ghost of Vince Lombardi himself, is the "bear crawl," which involves scrambling on your hands and feet without your knees touching the ground.

The boys call out weakly during their calisthenics. In Egan's day, Coach John Moddrell had his boys slapping their helmets and pads as they bounced up and down, calling out so vociferously that their voices echoed off the school buildings.

Moddrell's name falls softly from Egan's lips. "John made us do bear crawls up and down the 100-yard field. There was a fireman's drill where you had to carry your partner 100 yards and then switch, with him carrying you back."

He sighs like a disappointed parent. "These boys aren't ready."

Smith has heard enough. "If you call like that and I'm your opponent, I just want to hug ya," he taunts. "I'm certainly not afraid of ya."

Inspired by talk of his own playing days, Egan calls for a series of bear crawls—not for 100 yards, only 15. Maverick grunts and almost immediately falls onto his stomach.

"I'm tired," he says.

The original Claude Reeves field is located directly behind the school. But in 1988 the town outgrew its original playing space, like a young boy sprouting through a pair of pants. The mercury mine was thrumming, and times were good—or so everyone believed. No one knew the enterprise would pull up its stakes just five years later, dealing McDermitt its latest blow.

Moddrell received a grant to create something bigger. After all, there was so much space. Maybe it was time to push back the ghosts of those early pioneers. An Oregon rancher donated land for a field where the state line crosses the 50-yard marker. Now the walk from the locker room is longer, each step a lesson to a town that became too full of itself.

The next night during practice, Egan spots Maverick trudging toward the field. The boys gauge his progress. "You can tell it's Mav," Bailey says, imitating his gait. "He's like a snail."

Maverick wears a T-shirt showing Bart Simpson on a skateboard.

Egan sighs. "Get with it, Bart."

Coaching these Bulldogs is more like corralling baby pandas. Elijah announces that he needs to take a toilet break, and his heavy frame ambles toward the field-side public restroom. He milks every second.

He tries one door, but it won't open. "Try the other!" Egan yells. Both doors are locked. Other players follow his progress. Finally Taylor calls out. "Looks like you're going to have to go in the bushes!"

Smith hustles over to give him a key. When Elijah gets back, it's Mav's turn to go.

When Egan announces a handoff drill, Bailey asks, "We're gonna do that without shoulder pads?" The pads add a bit of gut protection.

Egan leans in low, whomping the ball into the receiver's stomach with such force you can feel the impact. "Crouch low when you get the ball," he shouts. "Remember, people are trying to take your head off!"

Smith grimaces. "This is important! If we fumble the ball, we'll look like the Three Stooges out there! Guys will be out there, trying to strip it!"

Each time he receives the handoff, Bailey extends his hands, unwilling to take a gut punch. Finally Taylor smirks. "Bailey doesn't want anyone to hit his baby skin."

The Football Team That Barely Exists practices with the full complement of shoulder pads, helmets, and cleats. But nothing comes easy to these Bulldogs.

Maverick grabs the wrong pads, and Egan helps him loosen the smaller set on his pudgy frame.

"Hey, you've been working out," he tells the boy.

"No, and it shows," Maverick says.

"I meant at the dinner table," the coach quips.

Under their bulky equipment, the players move sluggishly in the ninety-degree heat. Their cuts are lazy, more arcs than ninety-degree angles.

"Square-ins, not flares!" Smith barks.

They drop wobbly passes that hit them squarely in the chest. Or Bailey's hapless throws sail over their heads, uncatchable. "Throw at the numbers!" Egan says.

"My bad," Bailey says. "That one got away."

Egan counts two dozen misses. "This thing is a hot potato. Has *anyone* caught one?"

Just then Taylor reaches high, looking like he's going to reel one in.

"Right there!" Egan says. But the ball once again bounces off his hands.

"Somebody *please* catch a ball!" Egan shouts.

Egan's newfound coaching philosophy means less barking. The practices take on a forgiving feel. No Marine Corps basic training here. This is more like a sixth-grade summer camp for violinists.

Taylor has a close relationship with both coaches. He calls them *Dad* to their faces. But he's particularly close to Smith, who supervises his summer training. Their familiarity breaks down the usual coach-player boundaries.

Taylor runs by Smith as he blows his whistle. "Hey, you blew that thing right in my ear," he says. On the next pass Smith does it again. The boy smiles.

On a break Taylor stands on the 30-yard line and motions toward the goalposts. "Ten bucks says I can make this kick from here."

"You're on," Egan says. The boy hesitates as though called out on a poker bluff.

"C'mon, I'm waiting," the coach prods.

Taylor flips the ball in front of him for the punt, his eyebrows furrowed. He shanks it. "I'm gonna pay you," he says, embarrassed.

"No, we weren't really betting. Buy me some chips," Egan says, a reference to the boy's Hot Cheetos habit.

Bailey sees his chance to one-up Taylor. "I made the most punt yards last year."

"Yeah," Egan says, "if you count all the rolls."

The next evening, Taylor sticks a $10 bill in Egan's hand. "No," the coach protests. But the boy will not have it. Egan shoves the money into his back pocket.

Then Maverick speaks up. "A dollar says I can kick this through the goalposts."

"I'll give a bag of chips," Egan says, having learned his lesson about cash bets.

The boy splits the uprights. A lightning bolt of pride flashes across his face. It doesn't last. Egan barks a command for bear crawls. "Fuck, I hope I don't shit my pants," Maverick says.

Egan turns to Smith. "They should be glad we're not hitting tonight."

Then Maverick farts. "Woah," Egan says, "easy on the shorts."

"Maverick can clear out a room," Taylor says.

On this night, a dozen cars pack the parking lot, but they're not there to watch the Bulldogs. They're parents watching their kids practice in the town's newly revived football Little League, which is using the far end of the field.

The seniors look on with longing. They never got the chance to play Little League, which Todd Murrah formed in 1977. It gave McDermitt kids something to do, and freshmen started as Bulldogs ready to play. Then, like McDermitt itself, the league went dormant for thirty years.

Egan and Taylor watch the cars pull up. Neither says the obvious: nobody comes to watch the Bulldogs practice. In tiny McDermitt they know which car belongs to which local. "That's Frankie in the Dodge," Taylor says.

"No," Egan corrects him. "Frankie is in the suburban with the dented fender."

The two watch a husky eighth grader make a tackle. They can see the boy's plumber's crack from across the field. Egan knows the Little League means a renewed feeder system for his hapless Bulldogs. "He'll be playing for me next year," he says.

Just then a toddler playing flag football starts to cry. "It's like a lamb calling out for its mother," Egan says. Then he turns to his own lambs.

Then Egan gets the bad news about Nicolette, the freshman he'd hoped would forego girls' volleyball for football, giving him another much-needed body.

Nicolette's mother called just before practice: the girl had decided to stick to volleyball. For Egan, the desertion provides another hole he'd hoped he'd filled.

Still, quarterback Lane has returned from vacation. If everybody shows, including Jaxon, the timid young freshman, the Bulldogs will number exactly eight players, enough for another season.

Will the boys show up? Now it's a numbers game, a fool's gambit of three-card monte the hustlers play on urban street corners—one Egan can't afford to lose.

As if on cue, Taylor sidles over to the head coach. "Where's Jaxon?"

It's an hour into practice, and so far nobody has seen the freshman, which is unusual because he's usually the first player on the field, standing under one goalpost, throwing a football into the air while the rest of the boys are barely on time or mostly late.

Just then Egan spots two figures approaching: a boy and a woman.

"Here comes Jaxon," he says flatly, as though expecting the worst.

Jaxon keeps his head down, walking next to his aunt, Roberta, a blonde, buxom woman in a T-shirt and jeans. Along with Jaxon's younger sister, Hannah, Roberta has watched every practice from the small set of home bleachers.

She's like a strict teacher marching a student toward the principal's office. Everybody knows who's in charge. Egan walks over to greet them.

"He's restricted," the aunt says without greeting.

She hands Egan paperwork describing injuries to the boy's left hip and ankle. His father is taking him to Winnemucca on Friday for a CT scan. "Meanwhile the doctor says no running or hitting," she explains, "but he can do stretches."

Jaxon keeps his head on his chest. "Did the injuries happen at practice?" Egan asks.

"I did it a few weeks ago," the boy says, pointing toward his hip, "but I thought I could play through it."

"His ankle is giving him trouble too," Roberta interrupts.

"We can tape that up," Egan offers. He tries some public relations. "I was wondering where Jaxon was." He smiles. "He's never late."

He turns to the boy. "In the future please let us know if you can't make practice so we'll know where you're at."

"We didn't have your number," Roberta says. Egan gives her his cell number, then turns to Jaxon. "We're glad you're here. You can shag footballs."

The freshman runs down a few balls and retreats to the sidelines to play catch with his sister. Egan shakes his head. The boy doesn't *look* hurt, but who knows?

Egan's mind races. So *this* is what it has come to, the water-drip challenges of coaching eight-man football in a town without bodies.

Without Jaxon he's down to six players. Karter has been in street clothes after injuring his knee a week ago. Now he may be ineligible to play because he lives with his grandparents while his father travels out of town.

The rule seeks to stop Nevada's football powers from moving prospects into relatives' homes in their district—a ploy to add talent and stack the deck. Now the regulation is hurting a runt of a team, perhaps the feeblest squad in the tiniest league of rural wannabes: boys who almost never win, hailing from a town that barely exists.

Egan knows he can't blame these boys. It's not just the disinterest of a softer generation. Being outscored 300-2 this spring was no anomaly, but the status quo. No wonder kids hide behind their lockers when they see Egan coming.

He fears more defections. "They show at first, but once you show 'em the pads, they vanish," he says. "Once we start hitting we'll know real quick who's going to play."

After his visit with Jaxon's aunt, Egan shows a rare flash of bitterness.

"You guys need water?" he asks. "You need to powder your nose?"

He turns to Karter, who sits on the ground rubbing his sore knee. "You got a girlfriend to massage that for you?" he asks.

The boy blushes. "It looks like you're in trouble then," the coach snaps.

Both coaches seem on edge. "These drills are for running, not walking," Smith says. "No 7-Eleven ambles, unless you're preparing to get life-flighted out of here."

Bailey wants to do the drill called "tackling the wheel," where players hit a padded, movable blocking barrier. "We gotta go over our form first," Egan says. "Right now that wheel might hurt you guys."

Then the storm passes. Egan backs off. Elijah lines up for a tackling drill. "Okay, Dick Butkus," the coach says. The boy smiles, absorbing the compliment.

At the end of practice he summons his players. "Once you get into shape, everything is a breeze. I'm glad we're going to have the chance to build a team together. Now we've got to learn to mesh as a group. We're thinking we've got time, but we don't. Time waits for no one. These next three weeks of practice will pass before we know it."

He wants to let them head off for the locker room, but more needs to be said. "We want to be better than we were last year. I don't want to be standing out here on the field after another loss, saying 'We are who we are.' We're better than that."

Elijah leads the final session. The team gathers in a circle, helmets held high as they wish for things to go their way for once. Elijah says what is on everyone's mind. "We need people, guys," he implores.

They break the huddle. "Dogs on three! One-two-three, Dogs!"

Later, as Egan sits at a table, Jaxon emerges from the locker room. The coach has a mind to tell this timid kid that he has to man up like he once did, like a lot of kids who came through this football program learned to do.

Instead he plays the gentle father figure. "I hope everything checks out good tomorrow on those medical tests." He pauses, letting his words settle.

The boy is still quiet, his head still hung low.

"I need ya for this year," Egan whispers.

Finally he's said it. The comment is almost a plead.

The boy nods his head and joins his sister for the short walk to his house in town. Egan watches them go. Then he gets up and slowly heads toward his red pickup, knowing he's already late for dinner.

7

The first hint of trouble comes via a Messenger text.

How dare you write such terrible things about our town, dragging these kids through the mud like that! it reads. *Keep away from my nephew.*

Where on earth did *that* come from?

I have only been in McDermitt for a few weeks, but slowly a story is emerging: how a struggling high school football team reflects the fate of a dying town where scholastic sports are the last bit of social fabric that still binds them together. It's a riches-to-rags saga about the decline of small-town America. The Bulldogs once won championships; the town once thrived. Now there's little left but the memories.

I sit down each night to write vignettes about that day's practice that I publish the next morning on my public blog, *Persona Non Grata*, to hopefully develop a following.

With each installment I try and capture the team's unique character, noting how coaches interact with players, observing the give and take among boys, and the talents and liabilities each brings to the team as a whole.

Using a journalistic precaution, I offer only the players' first names. Otherwise I don't hold back. Some boys are skinny, shiftless, late to practice, slackers. They're also dedicated, fleet-footed, and sometimes sure-handed. I call it as I see it.

Many urban newspapers omit last names in stories like this, providing a cloak of anonymity for any character, good or bad. But McDermitt is decidedly *un*-metropolitan. Everybody here knows everyone else, from remote ranches to the reservation. Whether I use last names or not, they *know*, something I didn't recognize when I first arrived.

My posts are analyzed like a farmer studying the weather report. And many do not like what they read, including the online heckler.

Tempers boil over during Labor Day. Suddenly *I* am the town's *persona non grata*, the subject of their unvarnished scrutiny. A powder keg has been lit.

My McDermitt days are about to ignite.

This is not my first small-town reporting rodeo.

In 2016 I took a six-week gig in the tiny southeastern village of Haines, Alaska, at the weekly Chilkat Valley News. Haines residents don't just read their weekly newspaper, they *consume* it. Offending reporters must face their critics at the grocery store and joints like the Fogcutter Bar, where the blue-collar fishermen sharpen their hooks.

If I wrote something critical of some politician or busybody in Haines, I'd soon run into them at the local market. So I devised a defense against this particularly rural torture: I saw people but *didn't* see them. I waltzed past them in the frozen food aisle, pretending to be lost in a price comparison of tater tots and Hungry Man frozen dinners.

To beat back the darkness of the encroaching winter, I began posting about my experiences in Haines, missives that appeared under a heading I often saw in local police reports: "Alcohol Was a Factor." I thought it was harmless.

One night at the Haines Brewing Company, while nursing my second pint of Black Fang imperial stout, I spotted a carpenter I'll call Sam and bought him a drink. He was a *real* Alaskan. Bearded, burly, and quiet. Maybe I'd found a new friend.

The next day in the newsroom I mentioned Sam to the newspaper's gregarious owner, who leaned over to impart some juicy gossip. "Don't tell him *that!*" his wife said. "You know he's writing about the town!"

Sam had dated a woman who fell and hit her head on the ice while skating, resulting in some chronic sensory deprivation. No longer able to *smell* Sam, she lost her attraction to him. The pair eventually broke up.

Without mentioning Sam's name, I posted the tale. I thought I was safe. But the shit soon hit the snowblower. Someone in Haines showed my post to Sam. After that, he wouldn't even look at me. I'm lucky he didn't deck me.

Hoards of locals were whispering about this nosey outsider throwing shade at their beloved Haines. I crept out of town a few weeks later, never to return.

I had obviously not learned my lesson.

In McDermitt, this newest backlash is again my own fault: one of my posts includes two reservation brothers who had been disruptive as Bulldogs the previous year. I foolishly throw in a loaded descriptor I'd heard: "developmentally disabled."

Dawn, the boys' mother, is irate. I don't blame her. After all, I hadn't checked out whether this was even true. I've always needed a good editor to backstop my work, and this time I wrote without considering the ramifications.

This is very bothersome to me, Dawn writes on social media. *[My younger son] is underage and I never gave anybody any permission to use his age!!!*

I need to apologize to this mother *and* her sons. I remove the offensive descriptor and develop pseudonyms for all the boys. It's like stopping a deluge with your bare hands.

The next day the entire town knows about my blunder, like someone has stood on Main Street with a blowhorn. At practice the boys are standoffish. I'm now marked in town with my own uncomfortable descriptor: slimeball journalist.

I have a meeting scheduled that day with Principal Muñoz. She's an aloof woman with an advanced degree who prefers to be called Dr. Muñoz. The coaches recall how the office staff once printed T-shirts that read "Muñoz's Minions."

One staffer meets me at the sign-in window. She's hyperventilating. "I don't like what you've written," she fumes, "how it reflects on this town." Moments later, Muñoz strides past me as though I'm a ghost. I'm told I'll have to come back tomorrow.

Things are spinning out of control. I worry Muñoz might ban me from the school, ending my time here before it even starts. I call Superintendent Dave Jensen. We have a cordial relationship. Dave was the first person I called when researching the project.

"Hey, Dave," I begin, "it looks like I've messed up here in McDermitt."

"I heard," he says.

Clearly the word has spread.

Principal Muñoz claims that I've broken district rules by identifying an underaged student. Jensen doesn't agree. Since I have used only first names, he explains, I have not actually identified either boy. While most people in McDermitt know who they are, people in, say, Winnemucca, where most of the district lives, will not.

So I have broken no rules, at least technically. But I have broken something else. A sense of community trust.

"Look, John," he warns, "you're living in a remote place where people are very defensive." I get it: tread lightly.

The next morning I walk into Muñoz's office chagrined but no longer fearing banishment. We sit at a large meeting table, and she levels me in her gaze. This isn't just about the brothers, she says. I have committed other crimes.

She produces a post that mentions Jaxon, the freshman, and reads it aloud. *At age 15, he's funeral-home quiet, barely saying a word, even to the other players, his voice a whisper when the older boys call out their drills. At a mere 137 pounds, with bird-like legs, shoulders hunched, his head swimming inside his helmet, he isn't one of those strapping kids you see playing varsity sports in many towns across America.*

She pauses theatrically. To her, this is a put-down. "He's fifteen! He's just a boy!"

I've also written about an eighth grader who plans to play for the varsity Bulldogs next season. He'd walked up to me at practice and asked, "Are you a writer?"

I said that I was.

"Can you give me some writing tips?"

He's an earnest boy, a Paiute, just thirteen. After dinner he types short stories on his laptop. Writing about other places and inventing make-believe characters, he says, gives him focus. He likes being alone with words.

He sends me a piece about a small-town quarterback named Jamal who falls into trouble and becomes hounded by a street gang. He's also being pursued by a girl at school. The boy watches TV, and even in McDermitt he knows something about gangs and girls.

The eighth grader is big for his age. *Really* big. That day on the field, I asked how much he weighs.

"Two seventy-five," he said.

Before I published the post, I sent him a copy to show his mother. The boy said he liked the piece, with one caveat.

"Do we have to put my weight in there?" he asked.

Of course not. "We'll just say two hundred and change. Would that be okay?"

The post read in part: *He's shy and stocky, a Paiute-Shoshone boy who lives in town with his mother, just a few steps from the high school football field. . . . He knows he's big for his age. Weighing 200 pounds-plus is a lot for a boy.*

He goes only by his initials. *He likes their brevity,* I write. *They're not too much, not overweight, like him. They're skinny.*

Muñoz glares. "You celebrate a boy who wants to be a writer. Why do you make such a big deal about his weight? Did you ever think he might have self-esteem issues?"

She's right, of course.

I was once that self-conscious boy who, at this same age, sprouted nearly a foot. But instead of taking pride in my newfound height, I began to slouch just to fit in, no matter how many times my mother harangued me to stand up straight.

Today that fault remains. A sin of the boy that still haunts the man.

I telephone Dawn. She listens as I offer to apologize to both of her boys. She says she will speak with them, but the damage has been done.

Days later I am attending a presentation in the high school cafeteria. Students go table to table, refilling glasses of water. A Paiute girl I've seen around school silently replenishes my glass.

I make sure to thank her.

"I'm not your waitress," she huffs and walks off.

The next weekend I am standing along the sidelines of a Little League football game. The stands are packed with parents there to watch the next generation of Bulldog football players. Paiute women sell drinks and corn bread at the concession stand.

Suddenly I hear a voice behind me, close, almost in my ear, and it startles me.

"Keep my kids out of your *bullshit* stories!"

I turn to see a Paiute woman, her face twisted in anger. Is this Dawn, here for my public reckoning?

"Dawn?" I say.

"No!" the woman shouts. "Just keep my kids out of your *bullshit* stories!"

She moves off, still glowering. People look at me like a jury reproaches a courtroom defendant, ready to pronounce the verdict: Guilty as charged. No chance of parole.

Later I see the woman standing alone. She's not Dawn, and I will never know her name or whether I have even spoken to her children. I consider walking over to apologize, but I don't. I know that such a conversation will not end well.

My misery continues as I watch a young player with a black braid take down a runner with fluidity and force. "Wow," I say to the man standing next to me. "That girl can hit."

"That's not a girl. That's my son," he says. "Here on the rez, just because you got a ponytail doesn't make you a girl." After that, I keep my thoughts to myself.

Days later I spot the owner of the Quinn River Merc, sitting atop an ATV in the parking lot, chatting with a friend. When I approach, he eyes me warily. "I'm not talking to you," he says. "I don't like what you're writing about this town."

His anger takes me by surprise. "Well, then," I hear myself saying, "I guess I won't be patronizing your store in the future."

"That's just fine," the owner says. "You're not welcome here."

The brush fire of public scorn, it seems, has engulfed the entire town.

I have my sympathizers. "You didn't write anything that wasn't true," Lorraine says.

She's mystified by a call from a Paiute friend who knows I rent her bungalow. "You better watch out," the woman said. "Somebody's going to burn that house down."

Now *that* startles me. So I call Thierry Veyrié, the French anthropologist who wrote his doctoral thesis about the McDermitt Paiute Shoshone Reservation. One Sunday we sit in my tiny living room, and he offers a cultural translation of sorts.

Our experiences here could not be more different. Veyrié spent years on the reservation, cultivating mentors, learning the language, earning trust. He wrote nothing until he was sure it was true. I shot from the hip.

When I wrote for daily newspapers, I stayed in a town just long enough to get the information I needed. This is different. I *live* in McDermitt and have unlimited time to check my facts. And just as I observe and pass judgment on others, people in McDermitt are doing the same with me. It doesn't feel good.

Veyrié says the threat to burn down my house may not be an idle one. Historically fires on the reservation have been used as a message. Tribes once burned the winter hay supplies to vex U.S. soldiers, leaving them little to feed their horses. Even today there are unexplained fires here that many believe are arson.

The anthropologist and I do have *this* in common: we're both outliers in a place with a complicated history with the white world. The town has watched mining companies pollute the land. Over generations the reservation has developed an even deeper mistrust for white outsiders, with their false promises and broken treaties.

I must be patient as I repair the damage, Veyrié says. Rather than quit, I have to do a bear crawl through McDermitt. And not for just a few yards, but all the way down the field, no matter how painful.

Days later Muñoz tells me that one of the brothers is in school that day. "Do you want to talk to him?" Soon I am standing in the linoleum hallway before a shy fifteen-year-old boy who studies me like I am some sort of space alien.

"Adults make mistakes," I begin, "just like kids do."

I realize that it's an awkward apology, but I let the matter rest.

He says little, and we shake hands before he turns and walks back down the hallway.

Later he tells his friends that he wants to beat me up.

Slowly I make breakthroughs.

One night I meet Ardel Crutcher, a former Bulldog who now coaches his daughter, Everr, on the Little League football team. I want to interview him about how football has helped him cope with reservation life and his battle with substance abuse.

The elders warn him against talking to me. But days later he invites me to his house. As we sit at his kitchen table, he explains why he changed his mind: "People make mistakes," he says. "I know I have. So I'm going to give you a second chance."

Over the coming weeks I visit Ardel often. We drink coffee and wander around his spread with the view of sacred Red Mountain. He talks about personal loss and addiction, and sometimes tears well in his eyes.

Gradually he exposes emotional wounds. Sometimes he goes silent, and I let the lull linger, allowing him space to express himself. Then he reveals something personal he has yet to confide to anyone else, a fear no father would ever want to contemplate.

This time I don't write about it in my blog; I just listen. In that moment we approach something that feels like friendship.

I also seek to interview three generations of one family, all strong Paiute women, about reservation culture. Veyrié has told me about them. He's friends with Alice, the matriarch. The two take regular road trips together. She treats Veyrié like a son.

Alice is a private woman, suspicious of a reporter with a reputation around town. Veyrié tells me I must wait. One Saturday he takes me to visit a Paiute family for dinner. In Veyrié's company, I am welcomed like a relative. We sit at the kitchen table as women cook over a hot stove and toddlers run in the living room.

Fig. 3. Little League coach Ardel Crutcher and his
daughter, Everr. Photograph by Randi Lynn Beach.

I try the fried flatbread, a reservation staple, drawing laughs with my
comment that it tastes hot and wonderfully greasy, like french fries on a
toasted bun. Then I notice a woman across the kitchen table. She has been
watching me closely.

Veyrié introduces us. "This is Alice Crutcher," he says.

"*The* Alice Crutcher?" I say.

She nods and smiles, and we leave it at that.

Days later Alice agrees to be interviewed. Apparently I have passed the test, or at least a quiz. Slowly other tribal members open up to share their culture. I begin to better understand this place and realize how badly I screwed up.

Yet I never make amends with the angry woman from the football game. When I see her at the Say When, I give her a wide berth. What more is there to say?

Much later, during my last week in town, I approach her at a slot machine. I don't know precisely what I am looking for.

"I'm leaving town this week, for good," I say.

She looks up. "Why are you telling me this? Do you think I care?"

"I just want to apologize."

"Well, apology not accepted," she says. "Now get out of my face."

And then she turns back to the spinning wheel. For a reporter who writes before he listens, some doors will forever remain closed.

Fig. 4. Todd Murrah, star of 1973 championship team,
outside his house. Photograph by Randi Lynn Beach.

8

The line is ringing.

The old high school running back places the phone on speaker mode so with his diminished hearing he can better track the conversation. He sits on his living room couch in a tiny home just behind the Say When, babysitting his two-year-old grandson.

Todd Murrah spent his glory years here on the Nevada-Oregon line, playing eight-man football for the hometown Bulldogs. By age seventeen, he dipped Skoal, drove cars fast, and wrecked more than one. But his family owned half the town, so there was always another vehicle, another chance. He chased girls, and they chased him back. He was voted biggest flirt in his senior year along with Dixie Swisher.

One year the kid broke multiple bones in both hands. Yet prior to each game the coaches removed his casts, taped him up with padding and gauze, and he hustled out onto the field. He was young and indestructible; nothing could stop him.

But a lot has changed in the forty-seven years since Murrah made all-state and smashed the face guards of would-be tacklers with those big bruising mitts. He's sixty-four now, retired, his hair receding. He's diabetic. He doesn't take good care of himself.

He still uses Skoal. Some habits die hard.

Even though Murrah quit drinking three decades ago, his body has lost the physical skills of that tough-minded boy with the watch-me attitude. After all that physical abuse, he's just happy he's still here.

Malcolm, his grandson, sleeps on the couch beside him. Earlier the boy had pulled apart both of the old man's Bluetooth hearing aids, so the old athlete struggles to hear. The phone is set at high volume as the line buzzes.

Then a voice. "Hello?"

Other than a father, there are few men more important in a boy's life than his high school coach. For one season, in the fall of 1973, when the running back was a senior, a new field leader showed up on the McDermitt football scene.

Dan Armstrong was barely out of college, an arrogant, hard-drinking disciplinarian, commanding a clutch of boys who seemed more like his younger brothers. The Bulldogs won the state championship that year.

What followed were both scores and fumbles: marriage, kids, grandkids, divorce, remarriage, and the car wrecks that killed so many of their teammates.

Now both men are on the line. The retired running back sees daylight. He gulps.

"Coach Armstrong, this is Todd Murrah."

"Call me Dan," the old coach says. He's been expecting the call.

It's one of the few times the two have spoken in nearly half a century.

"Can you hear me?" Armstrong asks.

"Yeah, I can hear you," Murrah lies. "Can you hear me?"

The coach isn't listening.

"How you doing?" he begins.

Murrah can barely make out the words.

"What's that?"

"I was just asking how you've been."

If Murrah concentrates, he can hear. Well enough, anyway.

"Ahhh, I've been doing pretty good," the former player says. "Just getting older. And you're really old now. So we're just getting older together."

They talk about grandkids and past players. "I've been sober for thirty-five years now," the coach says.

"Dang," Murrah says. "I've got twenty-eight." He glances at his sleeping grandson.

The handoff has been a success. A touchdown scored. Time, for now, defeated.

For nearly an hour the two old teammates bridge the decades, reliving a time when Bulldog football was a force to be reckoned with.

But there's one major difference: one would escape McDermitt; the other would not.

Todd Murrah was born McDermitt royalty, groomed from the start to take over the family real estate empire.

His grandparents, Claude and Hilda Reeves, owned most of the land here. Claude was the town constable, and Hilda was as sharp as a set of cat's claws. Todd's father, Clifford, was a prolific drinker and ex-boxer who got his nickname when someone remarked, "That guy's a Tuffy." Together with his mother, Claudia, they owned a gas station and a motel in town, and in 1973 they opened the Say When. For years Claudia served as the town's postmistress, following in her mother's footsteps.

Hilda knew how to do business in McDermitt. "Mines come and go," she told her grandson. Then she pointed at U.S. Route 95, the highway that runs through town. "That road is the thing you've got to keep open."

Like a lot of country kids, Todd started driving—and drinking—early. He was always behind the wheel, a bored teenager with unlimited gas from his family's service station. You drove everywhere when you lived in McDermitt. The nearest swimming pool was all the way down in Winnemucca, for God's sake.

The wrecks came quickly. First Todd totaled the 1963 International Scout Tuffy had bought him. Years later, on homecoming night, he crashed his father's cherished Ford pickup. After Tuffy got it fixed, the boy smashed it up again. He didn't come home for a week after that, but even then Tuffy slapped the boy around good.

When Todd was in middle school, an English teacher wrote: "For all your bluster and bluff, you are a kind, generous and quite sensitive guy. Your crazy sense of humor will make life enjoyable and that's a gift a lot of people don't have."

Before Todd's freshman year, Tuffy hauled him into the White Horse for a youth boxing smoker. The chubby boy couldn't pack a crate of oranges, much less a punch. But Tuffy still wanted bragging rights at the bar.

He told his son, "You're gonna play high school football."

Organized prep football arrived in McDermitt in 1964, when Todd Murrah was still in elementary school. All those farm boys and miners' sons needed something to keep their minds off all that isolation.

They needed a playing field, not just for football but also for the school's nascent track-and-field program. Junior Huttman, who is my landlord, along with his wife Lorraine, was a McDermitt high school hurdler back then and recalls being teased by competitors.

"You don't even have a track? What do you do, run out among the sagebrush?"

Well, yeah, that's precisely what they did.

Not for long. The year after the town's sports field was finished, the Bull-dogs won the state track and field championship in Las Vegas. Underdog McDermitt swept the afternoon events, dominating in races like the 440 and 880 sprints.

But all that would come later.

Claude Reeves, Todd's grandfather, donated land for a field right outside the brick schoolhouse on the Nevada side of town, and the school sent boys out during gym class with rakes and shovels. The property had previously served as a dumping ground of sorts, and Mike Mentaberry recalls finding an old coffin before the mine workers arrived with their bulldozers. Even when it was done, the rancher's son says this was no field of dreams. "It was stickers and stubbles and gopher holes."

Decades later when Coach Richard Egan played, athletes surrounded the field in their vehicles after dark. When a teacher gave the word, they'd all turn on their headlights and chase the burrow-digging rabbits with baseball bats. "We never killed any rabbits," Egan says. The football field was raw and rural and imperfect, like McDermitt itself.

Football game days became a big event. Local boosters turned referees played on-field Houdinis who manhandled the yardage chains to give the home boys the advantage. During halftime Mentaberry played baritone saxophone in the band, not even changing out of his cleats. "We got a government grant to buy uniforms," recalls Mentaberry, now seventy-two. "They came blank, so our mothers cut the numbers from patterns. I wore No. 34 with those huge two-foot numerals on my blue-and-white jersey."

For two years McDermitt played six-man football before being able to switch to eight-man.

There was a succession of colorful coaches, such as Denny Britt, a drawling English teacher who once played at Ole Miss. Many times he grabbed a helmet to show the boys how it was done.

Six years after the field was completed, McDermitt won its first championship in 1970 and finished as co-champions the following season.

During his senior year Todd Murrah got the chance to honor his grandfather when the school named its football grounds Claude Reeves Field—and it wasn't just because he'd donated the land.

Claude had handled tragedy with particular McDermitt grit. Herman Hereford chronicled how Reeves was hauling gasoline in his pickup when he was clipped by an oncoming cattle truck along a narrow gravel road: "Claude felt a spray of moisture and he was sure the impact had ruptured one of the metal barrels," Hereford writes. This wasn't gasoline, but his own blood. "His arm, severed just below the elbow by the impact, was lying in his lap. He picked up the arm and threw it from the window."

A doctor sent somebody to look for the arm, but it was too late.

Claude still worked as well as any man with two good arms. He could hammer a nail and tie his shoes with one hand. At the dedication ceremony Todd Murrah gave his grandfather his football letter jacket. Because this was Claude Reeves, the old man didn't need any help; he put it on just fine with only one arm.

As the two men talk, they admit they were immature when they first met. The running back was seventeen, the coach twenty-three. Now they're both just old.

The coach lives in Carson City, 275 miles and an entire universe away from McDermitt. People tend to go their own ways, even players and coaches. They keep their memories to themselves. But not today.

Just days before, the running back was thinking about The Play.

It took place in a game against Gabbs, another school in the middle of nowhere, during that memorable 1973 season. In Todd's mind the running back is still there. He's been there for nearly fifty years. The Bulldogs are once again in command, driving for yet another score. Todd's on the 5-yard line, wide open, poised to score a 2-point conversion. He has one man to beat, a hulking 240-pound lineman.

The two make contact, and Todd freezes. He doesn't dodge or dive. It's as though his feet are suddenly grabbed by something lurking deep below the surface.

He doesn't move. He can't.

In a split second, Todd tumbles face forward. Tackled. He doesn't score, not this time. He runs back toward the sidelines. His coach is shouting at him in that red-faced way that coaches do. The boy who can do it all has failed.

"What the hell happened?"

The boy can't answer. He walks to the bench and throws off his helmet, lost in private misery. All these years later he wants to set the matter straight with his coach and with himself. There's a ghost to dispel.

So one afternoon a week before, on a whim, Todd dialed the coach's number. As the voicemail recorder beeped, the running back wished he hadn't called. But he left a message anyway.

The words he spoke were abrupt, stumbling slowly out of his mouth. There on the couch, his young grandson by his side, he leaned forward as though in pain.

Then he began talking.

He didn't score on that day, he told the machine, because that big god-damned lineman had been laying across his toes, pinning him to the ground. He'd tried to dig his cleats into the dirt to keep moving. But he was helpless. And then he fell.

Back then it was a failure he could not accept, much less talk about, especially to his coach. It would have been making excuses. But old men are more willing to make up for the sins of the boy.

The coach got the phone message. And whether or not he even remembered the play, the call opened up a galaxy of memories long forgotten.

The coach wanted to talk to his old high school running back who's now a man, who has experienced so many more letdowns than failing to score on a high-school playing field.

A busted marriage. Too many wrecked cars. Bad financial decisions.

The coach has had his own losses too. He knows what it's like to fail, to carry regrets like a football held close by your side.

As a freshman, Todd Murrah disliked everything about football, especially the muscled seniors who were more like men. He was a flabby kid getting punished by monsters twice his size.

Still, girls liked him. In eighth grade one wrote in his yearbook: "I hope you have a lot of fun in MHS because you'll be popular and have all the girls wrapped around your finger. Darn it. Well, stay a good kid and don't forget me. You probably will anyway. PS. Hey, whenever you're lonely I'll be around. Just kidding."

Some swooned over Todd, but not football coach Burt Polkinghorne. He was an algebra teacher and heavy drinker who'd one day cause a minor scandal when he married one of his former students.

He's eighty years old now, living in Jackson, Wyoming. In 1966, while working on a ranch after college, he was approached by the McDermitt principal, who'd just lost his football coach and science teacher, who both quit. Polkinghorne didn't have a teaching certificate, but that didn't matter. The principal put him on the books as a custodian. He never mopped a single floor. Instead he coached football and, even without a degree, was made head of the science department.

As Polkinghorne recalls, the team scrimmaged in a hayfield south of town rather than tear up their home field. "We had more players injured slipping in cow shit than from taking hits," he says. Then one day Todd, in the eighth grade at the time, showed up at a Bulldogs practice on a new motorcycle.

The kid let quarterback Arnie Zimmerman ride the bike, which he quickly wrecked after hitting a gopher hole. Zimmerman badly sprained his ankle. "I was so goddamned mad I couldn't see straight," Polkinghorne remembers. At school he warned Todd to avoid his algebra class. "Take general math," he said, "so I won't have to fail you."

Todd played end his freshman season—"As in, end of the bench." But when the regular kicker got injured, Polkinghorne threw him onto the field. He was the team's only kicker from then on.

Back then the field was just south of the state line, and fans murmured when Todd booted a perfect spiral that seemed to travel into space. Referee Jim Salme said Todd was the only kid he knew who could kick a football from one state to the next.

As a sophomore, Todd got a chance to run the ball, and he made sure nobody took it away. One day Polkinghorne said, "I guess Murrah's gonna be my fullback."

At 5-foot-9 and 185 pounds, with his center of gravity low to the ground, Todd was a bowling pin that would spin and wobble but never fall. "I just went straight ahead," Todd recalls. "I'd hit a kid in the face mask. Doink! And he usually went down. A lot of times I could have side-stepped guys, but I never thought of that. I just went through them."

When he broke carpal bones in both wrists, Polkinghorne told Todd not to go to the doctor. "I said, 'He'll just say you can't play.' We were reckless in those days."

Todd *wanted* to play. Still, it was tough getting up from a tackle when his wrists throbbed. That year he went to the homecoming dance with Eddie Ann Ugalde. The girl kept forgetting and grabbed his broken hands, sending jolts of electricity up and down his spine. That hurt as much as the tackles.

At the start of Todd's junior year, the Bulldogs scrimmaged against Lowry High School in Winnemucca, coached by one of Polkinghorne's drinking cronies.

"What kind of team does McDermitt got this year?" he asked.

"We got a good little running back," Polkinghorne said. "Name's Todd Murrah."

The coach smiled. "We'll take care of him."

"We'll see," Polkinghorne said.

Nobody took care of Todd Murrah. The running back dominated that day. He was named all-state running back that season, running for 1,060 yards in only six games for a career total of 2,400 yards and 26 touchdowns.

Todd had gotten stronger from those hits from bigger kids. His arms were sledgehammers. Under his grandmother's guidance, he lost fifteen pounds, replacing fat with muscle. Then Polkinghorne left the team. Just when the running back was ready to rumble into his senior season, a new mentor arrived on the scene.

Danny Armstrong's father had run a drilling firm in the Kings River Valley and wanted his son to follow in his footsteps. "One night I was working a twenty-four-hour shift," he says. "It was the middle of the night, and it was cold, and those drills were going, and I said, 'I'm not gonna do this. I want a career in sports.'"

Coaching in McDermitt was Armstrong's first job out of college in Reno, though he'd spent three years coaching church sports while in school. He already knew the town. He'd played football in Winnemucca and faced off against the "rough and tumble" Bulldogs.

Years later when Armstrong took the job in McDermitt, he walked into a thriving football culture in full bloom. There were parades and pep rallies that required him to make speeches. Everybody wanted to know the new coach's philosophy.

Before away games, townsfolk cheered and blew car horns as the bus drove out of town. "It was like a Gene Hackman movie," Armstrong recalls.

Football was a bridge between the town and the reservation. Students from both races began dating, something that had rarely happened in McDermitt. "When you played sports, you weren't whites or Paiute," said rancher John Hill. "Everybody was a team. Nobody better offend anyone, or we were all offended."

By then McDermitt was a legitimate football powerhouse, stacked with the sons of miners. Whenever Cordero bosses hired a new man, everybody wanted to know whether his boy played football. "If you were a Bulldog back then, you needed to win," said Hill. "There were expectations."

Luckily Armstrong also knew Polkinghorne, who invited him for a few beers at a Reno bar called the Little Waldorf Saloon to hand over the coaching baton. He made one thing clear: Todd Murrah should be team leader.

Polkinghorne was now assistant coach for Lowry High in Winnemucca, where he would oppose the feisty Bulldog who'd once performed so ferociously for him. He counseled one Lowry defenseman on how to tackle Todd. "I said you had to hit him low or he wouldn't go down," Polkinghorne recalls.

On a sweep from scrimmage, the boy hit Todd on the thigh and injured him. He had to come out of the game. "I tried to tell you," Polkinghorne told the player. "But you tried to take on Todd Murrah, and now you've paid for it."

Todd became known as "the teenage Walt Garrison" after the bullish Dallas Cowboys fullback. "Todd was the toughest high school player I ever knew," Armstrong says. "He was just not afraid to get tackled. I had to teach him to avoid the hits, not relish them. The kid had no finesse; he just didn't like to go down."

Todd also had that sense of entitlement, a kid used to getting his way. That year, he quit the basketball team—also coached by Armstrong—and took several players with him as though the team was just another car to be crashed, one Tuffy would replace. There were also head knocks between player and coach on the football field.

Armstrong played a delicate game with his star running back, whose powerful family took care of the coach. Anything he needed, they were there with a checkbook.

He also knew McDermitt's drinking culture, with Tuffy as its ringleader. Many nights young Todd had pulled his father off his barstool at the Say When. Now the teenager himself had unlimited access to alcohol.

And that was a problem.

Early on, Armstrong told Todd he was a special player, but one infraction could end his season. He proposed a deal to the team: if no one got caught drinking, he'd buy everyone a keg of beer at season's end.

But the tensions did not end there. The Bulldogs went undefeated in their conference. The headlines used such verbs as "romps," "belts," "drubs," and "nails." Moments before the final game, Armstrong approached Todd in the locker room and slapped the boy's shoulder pads.

"You ready to go?"

"I don't give a shit," the kid responded.

A fight with his girlfriend? Who knew why?

"Well then," Armstrong told him, "you can sit on the bench."

At the start of the second half, with the Bulldogs leading 30–0, Armstrong shouted over to his sulking superstar, "You ready to play football?"

"Yeah," the boy said, now chastised. He ran for 180 yards that day.

After the final whistle blew, Tuffy jumped in the coach's face. Why hadn't he played his boy the entire game? He'd ruined his career, robbed him of vital statistics.

"Shut up, Dad," Todd intervened. "This was my fault."

Armstrong blames himself and his ego. He'd met Bobby Knight, listened to John Wooden speak, and hung out with Hall of Fame coach Bear Bryant who drank him under the table. He thought he knew it all.

"After five drinks there wasn't a man I didn't want to fight or a woman I didn't want to screw, and they were usually together." In McDermitt there was little else to do but drink. On the field Armstrong was equally bullheaded. "I was going to do it my way regardless."

Former Bulldog Cash Miner recalls Armstrong's tactics. "I'm still sorry I never got the opportunity to put pads on and take him on one-on-one," he says. "I wanted to thump his ass. He was young, arrogant, and smart-mouthed. I was a big kid, and I wanted to strap on those pads and go after that coach."

Armstrong laughs. "I used to infuriate Cash," he says. "He was a gentle giant. He was almost 6-foot-3 and weighed 225. I stayed all over him. I called him our immovable object on defense. I said, 'When the season is over, if you want to do that, I'll put the pads on, and we can do it.'" They never did.

Finally it all came to an end. The Bulldogs beat Smith Valley 66–42 to win the state championship. They had their trophy. Armstrong stayed on another year, but the final whistle had blown on Todd Murrah's Bulldog career.

On the telephone the coach confides that he, too, struggles to hear.

"I got an ear cut off in a car wreck a few years back," Armstrong explains. "I have hearing aids in both ears. It's tough sometimes. Especially on the phone. You can hear the sounds, but you can't make out the words."

"That's right," the running back says.

They throw out names of players past, old girlfriends, people they both knew.

"Who'd you marry?" the coach asks.

"LaRae McClintock."

"Not Cindy Albisu?"

Cindy was the head cheerleader. But she married someone else.

"You and LaRae had how many kids?"

"We didn't have any."

"I saw LaRae at the stock car races years back. She said she was living in Boise."

"She's still living there."

The men move on to the subject neither can forget: those players who won the eight-man state championship in the 1973 season.

They talk about where everyone is, where they last saw them. One works as an accountant in Elko, another runs a bar in Lamoille. Some are dead now. Taken too soon. Todd flips through his old yearbooks and points to boys wearing their game faces, men who are now gone.

Armstrong ran into one at a rodeo a few years back. "He'd been in a car wreck, had a huge scar across his face."

Todd says his second wife, the mother of his kids, also died in a wreck. She was on her way to Boise and flipped her car.

Why so many car wrecks?

"Around McDermitt there was nothing to do but go out and party," the coach says. "There was a lot of distance between places. A lot of open road. I count my blessings now, how many times I drove drunk."

Talk returns to football and the running back who was as tough as raw shank steak. "You scored touchdowns," Armstrong says. "You didn't care how you got them. You were the leader of that team. I'd blow the whistle, and you'd run and score a touchdown and then come running back."

The running back mentions the game theory the coach drilled into his head.

"Primary responsibility," Todd says.

The coach picks up on the theme as if they were still at practice.

"Know your job. Each and every play," Armstrong says. "If everybody does it, we form a cohesive unit. Nobody can beat us."

Yet the Bulldogs didn't always win back then.

In the first nonconference game of that championship year, they played Crane, a private school full of big Oregon farm boys.

They led Crane 18–0 with eight minutes to go. Then Dave Holloway, No. 43, fumbled, and Crane picked it up and ran for a touchdown. The coach gave Holloway a second chance, and he fumbled again. Crane rallied to win 20–18.

"I'd like to play that Crane game again," the coach says.

"Me too."

Todd talks about showing off his talents to the coaches at the University of Nevada in Reno. His mother knew a booster at Stanford University who also wanted to take a look. The kid hated Reno and didn't even know where Stanford was. Anyway, neither worked out.

"I didn't do too well," Todd says. *"I couldn't kick leather. But I could kick a rubber ball."*

"You could kick both," the old coach says.

After high school Todd married LaRae. For two years the couple lived in Boise, and he changed tires and painted signs before they got divorced.

Then Todd came home and never left.

He worked at the Cordero Mine, drilling holes for dynamite blasts. Then he took over the Say When, named after a bartender's words to gauge the size of your shot pour. He ran the place until 2009 when his sister, Chloe, bought him out.

For years Todd staged the biggest show in town when he drank more shots than he poured. He remodeled the place four times and brought in blackjack tables and twenty-four-hour gaming. Party boys from Boise would show up after 1:00 a.m.—closing time in Idaho—and wager all-night gambling sessions, with Todd pouring drinks.

It was tough to find help in McDermitt, so Todd hired his drinking buddies from Boise. That's where he met his second wife. They had two kids, a girl, Chelsea, and a boy, Ryan. The marriage didn't last. Ryan was thirteen when his mother died in a car wreck.

The workers didn't last either. Todd put them to work before they'd earned their police ID cards. When outstanding warrants surfaced, the sheriff's deputies arrested them right there at the casino.

Tuffy's death was another excuse for Todd to keep drinking. He bought a few motorcycles and a four-wheeler that he wrecked right away, breaking his hip and slowing him down for eighteen months. He got into trouble and lost friends when he extended too much credit to gambling cronies.

He saw gaming's uglier side. One father lost all his money en route to Disneyland with his kids. Todd fronted him the cash to get home. A long-haul trucker lost his company's money at the tables and then shot himself in the head inside the cab of his truck. He survived, and Todd forgave the debt so the trucker could keep his job.

In 1977 Todd began coaching Little League football. He liked the kids and the winning, but the volunteer job took too much time away from the bar. The league folded a decade later.

Armstrong had left McDermitt long before. He took various teams in northern Nevada to the playoffs and won few titles. People called him "Phelps,"

Fig. 5. Close-up of Todd Murrah. Photograph by Randi Lynn Beach.

the character from *Mission Impossible*. Along the way he got a divorce and quit drinking.

He coached at the Northern Nevada Correctional Center, something out of the movie *The Longest Yard*, where his football players left the prison for away games in buses with armed guards and bars on the windows.

Those convicts taught Armstrong something about coaching. "I found out real quick you don't yell at grown men. You can't treat them like high school kids. It was more about reasoning. You didn't punish them when they made a mistake."

The coach worked at a prison; the running back feels like he'd always lived in one.

The phone call is coming to a close.

The two men talk about throwing a fiftieth-anniversary party in 2023 to celebrate their long-ago championship. Both promise to round up those players who are still alive.

For the running back, the call has stirred up memories.

Todd wishes he would have left this town when he had the chance. "I could have gone out and done something. Done better with money management, watched the money I did have," he says, spitting another stream of brown tobacco juice. "Hell, I've been a diabetic for fifteen years and still can't even spell the word." He pauses. "I didn't think I was good enough or big enough to play college ball. I could have been a good kicker though."

Todd paces his living room, yelling at the family mutt, Fido. He sees a bull-dozer rumble pass and shouts, "Buy my house. Buy me out!"

Then Fido barks, waking the grandson.

The Man Left Behind takes the child in his arms. Maybe it will be different for this boy. Maybe he'll be the one to get out of McDermitt.

9

Most evenings, both in summer's heat and winter's chill, Bulldogs coach Jack Smith walks McDermitt's deserted streets. With his small dog, Hazel, pulling on the leash, he often pauses outside the long-shuttered White Horse tavern, a sagging sun-bleached hulk located a block off U.S. Highway 95.

The walks are an escape from football and the frustrations of herding high school boys. They're a time to revisit ghosts from the past, with one in particular: his late father.

Donald "Moe" Smith was like a Sunday morning cartoon character. Sparkplug sturdy, his mouth working a fat unlit cigar, he was a compact man with oversized hands who worked as a bartender, tavern owner, bouncer, carpenter, and car salesman. All of them were sideshows to his real passions: professional wrestling and later, boxing, first as a fighter, then as a promoter, manager, trainer, and cutman.

In the 1950s, before Jack was born, a young Moe was forever on the road, uninhibited and undomesticated, hooting out of car windows, those big mitts clutching the steering wheel as he toured the Northwest with wrestling cronies like Mr. Fugi, Haru Sasaki, Gorgeous George, Lonnie "Moondog" Mayne, and the Claw.

The White Horse was a favorite stop, back when McDermitt boasted a half dozen taprooms and drunken cowboys rode their horses into buildings. Moe and the boys minded their own business but brooked no bullshit. Hell, they'd even buy you a beer before they crammed back into the station wagon, moving on to the next outlandish wrestling match before screaming secretaries, loggers, and teenagers.

Each night Jack pauses outside the White Horse and wonders: Is this tavern the reason he stays in McDermitt? A decade ago he immediately regretted taking a job in a lifeless town of crumbling buildings surrounded by vast open space.

Then he stumbled upon the White Horse and it suddenly made sense. Here he could summon the spirit of his father at a bar where the exuberant

Fig. 6. Shot of shuttered White Horse Tavern. Photograph by Randi Lynn Beach.

Moe once sewed his wild oats. The White Horse helps him remember. But some reveries hurt.

As a boy, Jack wondered if he really ever had a first name among his father's roughneck cronies. He was always Moe's kid, the chip off the old man's unvarnished block. He lived in Moe's shadow; no matter what he accomplished, his father had done him one better. For his part, Moe wanted his son to work hard in the boxing ring and take the big hits with poise just like he had.

"You're a Smith," he'd say, "and my kid doesn't quit."

Moe was 5-foot-7 and weighed 240 pounds, a man whose hardened hands could slap and crush things like beer cans and the dignity of opponents. He was a retired light heavyweight wrestling champion turned boxing manager, and his wards respected him. He was tough and wise, with a plan to make the big time. He taught them how to become better fighters, and they loved him for that.

And those cigars. Moe couldn't afford the Cubans, so he smoked the cheap ones, rolling them on his lips as he barked instructions. Today whenever a cigar smoker asks Jack, "Is this bothering you?" he'll wave his hand. "No, it's good," he'll say, because when he smells that sweet aroma, Moe is there.

A life with Moe meant a life on the road. After his parents divorced, eight-year-old Jack jumped into the back seat of his father's station wagon, which served as his first-class seat to wrestling and boxing tours, allowing him to bunk next to fighters who counted on Moe to turn them into contenders. None made it, but some came close.

When Jack was young he assumed that every kid was dropped off at baseball practice by a carload of miscreant professional wrestlers. Early on, Moe taught him to box, to throw combinations and straight right-hand jabs. He later competed as a collegiate, amateur, and professional fighter.

But he wasn't Moe. Jack finally gave up boxing to become a high school basketball coach with a gritty mentoring spirit inherited from his father. Still, even at sixty, he's pained by the thought of failing to live up to his father's standards. Moe was the priceless original while he was merely a photocopied imitation.

Few in McDermitt know about Jack's past—those days when he laced up his gloves and headed into the breach, knowing his father was there, ringside, cigar in his mouth, rooting him on. "I always had one eye on my dad," he says. "When I threw a punch or hit a jump shot or ran the football, my radar went right to him, to see his expression. He always had this little grin. I cherished that smile. It meant the world to me."

Now he misses that formidable shadow. Most summers he returns to Spirit Lake, Idaho, where he and Moe lived for years, to see the people who still know him as Moe's boy. "I'm Jack Smith," he said at his father's funeral. "Most of you probably know me as Moe Smith's kid."

Inside his pickup, on the long drive to away games, the past pummels his brain—the father's success, the son's failure. And sometimes he cries.

But almighty Moe remains on a pedestal. Jack preserves his memory through those walks past the White Horse. And on a shelf next to his bed, in a pair of vintage boxing gloves, he keeps his father's ashes where he knows they'll never be far away.

Jack was born in Carson City in 1960, the first boy after three girls. Imagine Moe chomping on his cigar the day his son was born. Finally here was a boy to mold into his own image.

Moe's real first name was Donald, and he grew up in Weiser, Idaho, a kid who loved history and pored over details of the battleship Missouri, known as the great "Mighty Mo." As a teen, Donald learned to fight and adopted the moniker "Moe." He also used "Jack," the name he gave to his only son.

Moe taught boys to box at the Police Athletic League gym, known as Mighty Mite's. By the time Jack was six, he'd already gone undefeated in four fights, the gloves on his hands almost bigger than his head.

Moe also owned a joint called The Cave, a popular steak house and bar that featured lit tiki torches, where drinking regulars slapped each other's back amid talk of boxing, knockouts, and spilled blood. The place was Moe's stage. With his wrestling photos on the wall, the old, apron-clad man poured shots at a polished wooden bar where he kept bowls of single cigarettes. He'd even slide you a free beer if you could make him laugh or one-up his stories.

Sometimes a barfly would spot Jack inside the place and call out, "Moe, do your routine with the kid." Then it was Show Time, a routine where Jack struck Moe's big hands and shouted sound effects. Bam! Slam! Pow! Moe would switch off the jukebox as the boozers turned on their barstools. He'd get down on one knee and hold out his large hands as the boy's punches landed with unusual fury. Jack's feet were always moving as he performed a pugilistic dance across the barroom floor: Straight jab. Uppercut. Duck. Spin. Repeat.

When the punches stopped, the place erupted. The kid was Mini Moe, the barflies insisted. "When he's gonna turn pro?" they'd ask.

Moe waved a paw, secretly pleased. "He's not gonna do that. He's going to school."

"Bullshit, Moe! I've never seen a six-year-old do something like that."

Moe didn't want the kid to repeat his life: get his daylights punched out in hundreds of amateur and pro matches. Still, he couldn't help himself. Moe's *life* was *boxing*. There was a Smith legacy to uphold.

When his son entered the ring, Moe enforced rules. "He kept it simple: if a guy snaps your head back, make sure you snap his head back," Jack recalls. "Always snap his head back more than he does yours."

Jack's mother accused Moe of railroading her son toward boxing at the expense of other sports. So Moe bought a basketball hoop and tossed Jack baseballs, schooling him on the fundamentals of stepping into a catch. Jack soon excelled in football, baseball, and motocross, and he was later offered a college scholarship for pole vault.

"See?" Jack's mother said. "I told you so."

The couple separated in 1968. Moe sold The Cave and emptied out the family's sprawling Carson City house. He loaded up his station wagon along with his son and the family dog, the pit bull Cummings—named after a wrestler the old man had idolized.

Then Moe and the boy hit the road.

They headed to Sin City—Las Vegas. The so-called "Boxing Capital of the World" had always understood misfits, offering fighters the bright lights they craved.

Riding in the front seat was Larry "Irish Pat" Duncan, an emerging heavyweight boxer Moe had managed in Carson City. Over his career, Duncan won 44 of his 58 pro fights—half by knockouts—against boxers like Duane Bobick and Earnie Shavers. In 1974 he was ranked No. 7 in the world and came one fight away from facing Muhammad Ali.

For Jack, the good-natured Duncan was the older brother he never had. He was also the boy's babysitter and taskmaster, throwing jabs at his inflating ego.

Once they arrived in Las Vegas, Moe frequented a gym run by promoter Bill Miller that drew mostly Latino and African American boxers. Moe asked a Black veteran trainer to work with his fighter. He wanted a smoother rhythm to Duncan's punches, and this was the place to learn it.

Jack recalls the sweaty basement gym and restaurant upstairs. Sometimes his was the only white face there. It reminds him of the scene in one *Rocky* film when Apollo Creed takes Sylvester Stallone's character to the Los Angeles gym where he trained.

"That scene in Rocky," Jack says. "I lived it."

The place had a Mafia feel, crawling with tough guys, not all of whom fought in the ring. One day, in an encounter that made Jack gasp, Moe ran into Sonny Liston.

Charles L. "Sonny" Liston was the era's dominant contender who became world heavyweight champion in 1962 after knocking out Floyd Patterson in the first round. The next year Liston lost to a young underdog named Cassius Clay.

When Moe introduced the legendary fighter to his son, Liston got down on one knee. "To me he was like Godzilla," Jack recalls. "At first I was afraid. I flinched. But his words just calmed me down. He asked me about boxing and life and was looking me right in the eye. It was man to man, as much as it could be with an eight-year-old."

Jack later dismissed the rumors about Liston's organized crime connections. "To me Sonny Liston is the most gentle soul I've ever met," he says.

"After that talk he had with me, I could care less about what he did. As I got older, no matter what I read about him, he was my guy."

Along with his father, Moe, of course.

Jack and his dad moved into a three-bedroom bachelor pad with a stable of flashy boxers who treated Moe's kid with respect.

Along with Duncan, there was "Cowboy" Don Moore, a former wrestler who dealt cards at a local casino, and Manny Gillette, one of Moe's old boxing chums. Moe enforced strict rules: no drinking, no carousing, and no women. He didn't want that atmosphere for his boy, whom he enrolled in a local school.

Their stage was the Silver Slipper, a saloon that opened in 1950 before being bought by the reclusive billionaire Howard Hughes. Unlike other casinos, the Slipper lacked a hotel but advertised a chuckwagon buffet—the first ever in Vegas—and the town's best-known showgirls.

And boxing, lots of boxing. It became Jack's home away from home.

On Thursday nights Bill Miller staged the "Strip Fight of the Week," featuring boxers, booze, smoke, and lightweight gamblers. Moe piled his boxers into the station wagon and drove to the Slipper to fill out the card, or lineup of fights.

One night Manny Gillette faced a Native American puncher nicknamed Squirrel. The bout was a vicious affair that had patrons throwing money into the ring, hoarse from shouting. Moe liked Squirrel's moxie and invited him home.

At the apartment Jack loved the ring talk and living room wrestling matches. His sidekick was his dog, Cummings. The pit bull was actually the second Cummings. The first was an English bulldog whose death provided Jack with a compassion for animals that he carries to this day.

Two years before, on a hot day in Carson City, Jack ignored his father's order and took the original Cummings along to the store, where the dog succumbed to the hundred-degree heat. Moe was livid as he dug the dog's grave. "He made me look at the corpse. 'See what happens?' he told me. Never do this to one of your dogs again!'"

Now inseparable, Jack and the second Cummings were a handful, even for a crew of rowdy boxers. Jack caught reptiles and horned toads and brought them into the apartment. One morning a boxer awakened to a lizard staring at him.

"Moe! What the hell!"

Then he realized the culprit.

"Jack!"

Even Moe's kid couldn't bring reptiles inside the apartment after that.

Jack recalls the night Moe's whole crew won their Silver Slipper matches and broke out some booze to celebrate. Duncan sprawled on the grass outside the apartment, swigging from a jug of wine, rolling on the ground as Cummings licked his face.

"Pat was howling, and I was jumping on his back, and Manny and Squirrel were wrestling," Jack says. "My dad was like, 'Somebody's gonna call the cops on us!' Nobody cared. We were all so happy."

Nothing good lasts forever though, and eventually most boxers drifted away. Only Duncan remained, and he soon set out to break Jack of his boyish bad habits.

Without any other kids at the gym, Moe allowed his son to spar with a national amateur nicknamed Bird Legs, the lightest fighter there. The boy held his own, or so he thought. Bird Legs handled Jack with kid gloves because he was Moe's son. His dad played it up: "You're doing good. You're doing good."

But the kid was getting on Duncan's nerves. "If I didn't get my way, I'd say things like 'I hate you,'" Jack says. "Most of the time, Pat was pissed at me."

One day Duncan poked the boy's fragile ego. "Jack, you know that guy's carrying you, right?" he said. "So don't think you're that good."

He said it in front of Moe.

Jack didn't know what the phrase "carrying" meant. He asked his father, "Is Bird Legs carrying me?" Moe was flummoxed.

"Duncan!" he yelled.

"Yeah, Moe?"

"Knock it off!"

That's when Jack learned he wasn't a contender. He was Moe Smith's kid, whom everybody was afraid to hurt. "I remember crying," Jack says.

It was a lesson in humility he quickly forgot.

With Jack in the station wagon's back seat, Moe drove Duncan to fights in distant western cities like Seattle and Salt Lake City. The boy listened as the men reminisced about boxing matches and bar brawls.

Both were heroes in Jack's eyes, and whenever conversation lulled, he'd ask a question to get things moving again. One day Moe called his mother, Elizabeth, and got an earful about how he was raising his son.

"Why are you dragging Jack all over the countryside?"

"Ah, he's having fun," Moe defended himself.

"Come back to Carson," she pleaded.

"No, Ma."

One Seattle gym was home to the famous trainer Jack Hurley, who always wore suits, even to the dankest ring. After his death in 1972, his *New York Times* obituary cited the fact that Damon Runyon once said that he'd known only two honest prize-fight managers: "One is Jack Hurley, and I forget the name of the other."

Moe would watch Hurley's training sessions as his eyes scanned the gym for other legends. One was Eddie Cotton, a retired light heavyweight contender who lost close decisions in his two championship fights.

"This guy's good, Jack," Moe would say.

Whenever Jack saw Moe talking with Cotton, he'd rush to the nearest bag to jab, pivot, and punch, longing for encouragement from a boxer with Moe's stamp of approval. "The whole time they talked I'd just keep going."

Then Jack would interrogate his father. "What did Eddie Cotton say?"

"He said you could really move."

"How'd he say it?" The kid wanted every detail. "Then what?"

He couldn't get enough attention. Despite Duncan's intervention, Jack's head was swelling again. He believed that this fraternity of men accepted him, not because he was Moe's son but because he *belonged* there.

In Seattle Jack began sparring against other kids his age. He dominated most contests. He had swagger, a fact that wasn't lost on Pat Duncan, who wanted to teach the boy a lesson that would stick.

One night, following a professional fight card at the Everette Firefighters Club, Duncan asked the promoter to arrange a sparring session for Jack. The following afternoon, Jack swaggered into the Everette gym, Duncan beside him.

"You got your best boy?" Duncan called out.

Duncan was big, over 6-foot-5, and he was grinning. He looked over to gauge Moe's reaction. "Knock it off, Duncan," Moe spit. It was all part of the two men's repartee.

Jack eyed the kid who was summoned to teach him a lesson. "He looked like a spark plug, but I could move with anybody," he says. Jack flashed his pre-fight punching repertoire, figuring the affair would be over quickly.

Then the bell rang. "He was like a Tasmanian devil," Jack recalls. After the first round, he sat on his corner stool, the roar of those punches in his ears, and he felt the tears come as Moe and Duncan hovered with water, a towel, and words of advice.

Then Duncan turned to Jack's father. "Moe, are those tears?" He paused theatrically. "Hang on, Moe. Wait, are those *tears*? No, that's gotta be sweat, right Moe?"

Moe shook his head. "Duncan . . ."

Jack lasted three rounds, each worse than the one before it. On the drive back to their motel in a pouring rain, the kid heard the clack of the windshield wipers as he slumped in his seat. He'd just taken his first real beatdown, and it hurt.

Duncan was still grinning. Moe glanced over at his fighter like he wanted to swat his head. "Don't Duncan," the look said. "What are you gonna do, Duncan?"

It was time to deliver the lesson, the knockout punch. "Moe, it all just came to me," Duncan began. "I've got the perfect fight name for Jack. It's perfect."

"Duncan," Moe warned.

"No, Moe, I got it." He launched into a riff like a ring announcer from the old days. "From Carson City, Nevada, fighting out of the blue corner, the pride of the capital, Crying Jack Smith!"

The boy lost it. "Dad," he yelled. "I'm not Crying Jack Smith!"

"Ladies and gentlemen, we're all here tonight to see Crying Jack Smith!"

"Duncan, knock it off," Moe said.

But his father was grinning too. Jack could see from the back seat. Duncan was laughing so hard that tears welled in his eyes.

"Dad, tell him!"

"You're not Crying Jack Smith, son."

"Tell him! Tell him!"

The moment scarred Jack's boxing psyche; his ego got KO'd in the back seat of a car on a rainy night in Seattle. Today he replays the scene on every long drive in his pickup truck. Sometimes he laughs. Sometimes he's Crying Jack Smith.

Duncan soon got his own comeuppance during a fight in Salt Lake City. Jack assured the fighter's domineering mother who'd driven up from Carson City that "Irish" Pat was going to knock the guy out.

The bout turned into a free-for-all with both fighters wrestling one another to the mat. A brawl erupted ringside, and Moe pummeled the other guy's trainer. Duncan's mother had seen enough and quickly took her son back to Carson City.

Suddenly Moe was without his contender, and Jack had lost the minder who kept his ego in check.

Without Duncan around, Moe accepted an offer from an old wrestling chum to become night manager at a motel in Eugene, Oregon. Jack ate his meals in the adjoining restaurant. He felt like a rock star, but his father kept him in line.

One night he insulted a waitress, and Moe gave him a thump. "You don't talk to working-class people like that. When she comes back, you're going to apologize." And Jack did. That was probably the last blue-collar worker he ever maligned.

Moe worked the graveyard shift and woke up about the time Jack got home from school. At 3:30 p.m., they'd watch *Star Trek* together. Moe loved the show as much as Jack.

Then in 1970 Moe reconnected with some aging wrestling mates for one last tour. There was Anthony Wayne Osborne, a.k.a. "Tough" Tony Borne, and Lonnie "Moondog" Mayne, who wore a cloak and a Viking helmet. They were joined by Harry Masayoshi Fujiwara, "Mr. Fugi," and Beauregarde, whose signature move was "The Thumb." The big Oregonian held his thumb behind his back for the jeering audience to see, and then he jabbed it into the other wrestler's Adam's apple, finishing him off. The crowd hated him, and they loved him.

Finally there was James Donald Raschke, a part-time substitute teacher who wrestled as Baron von Raschke from Germany. The bald, diabolical-looking Raschke goose-stepped into the ring wearing a mask, repeating his mantra "I am *ordered* to win! I *must* win! And I *will* win!" Raschke had a move called the "brain claw" that was always booed, and he was often billed as "The Claw."

The ensemble hit the road for a northwest tour they called "The Loop," with Jack along for the ride. But the old man kept a secret from his impressionable son: he never let on that the matches were staged.

In one politically charged tag team event, Moe fought as the villainous "heel" alongside the Japanese fighters, Mr. Fuji and Haru Sasaki, who specialized in taboo hair-pulling, eye jabs, and sand-throwing. Jack knew the pair as the Fujis.

The pranks played off World War II prejudices, and most bad guys who climbed into the ring were cast as either German or Japanese. "People hated the Japanese," Sasaki told the Portland *Oregonian* in 1997. "I got booed all the time. I got death threats, and in some small towns I had to leave hidden in a trunk."

Over his career, "Tough" Tony Borne relished his bad-guy role. "I was not in there to make friends," he told the *Oregonian*. "I was in there to make money. Some guys got a flat guarantee, but most wrestlers fought for a cut of the gate. You had to have ring color. You had to be liked or disliked."

But on Moe's tour, Borne was a good guy—or "face"—usually alongside Lonnie Mayne. With Moe as their teammate, the Fujis would use cheap-shot sleeper holds, raising the crowd's ire. Moe would soon lose his match before the angry Fujis turned on him, kicking him and beating him with chairs.

Eventually the good guys rescued Moe from the foreign onslaught. Rallying from his stupor, Moe would leave arm in arm with his new mates, the Fujis now a twisted pile of human rubble. The crowd ate it up. Every night it was the same fight with the same result. Jack recalls, "I sat there thinking, 'Oh my god, why is this happening again?'"

After each match, the crew stopped at a roadside diner where they were less likely to be recognized. Jack would sit wide-eyed as the Fujis walked in and took their seats. "Moe, did you order me a cheeseburger?" one would say.

Then a baldheaded man would join them. Years later Moe told his son, "You know you had dinner with The Claw about five times?"

"I did?" The Claw never took off his mask in the ring, so how was Jack to know?

"One night he even gave you 'The Claw' handshake, and you still didn't figure it out."

The wrestlers became a colorful backdrop to Jack's life in Eugene, where he played shortstop on a Little League baseball team called State's Veneer. Moe would drive him to practice, always arriving late, with a coterie of professional wrestlers in tow.

"You never get here on time," one player remarked. "We always wait for you because you're good. And when you *do* get here, you arrive with all these giant people. Who *are* you?"

Jack never revealed the real story; he just blushed.

A half century later, around McDermitt, Jack keeps his memories to himself as though they would lose their emotional power. But Moe is never far away, his ashes inside those boxing gloves Jack keeps on the shelf near his bed.

Standing outside the old White Horse, recalling his father's crazy life, Jack no longer feels marooned in a dying town. He's back with his mentor, lovable Moe, the man who made him the man—and the coach—he is today.

Now if he could only rally enough kids onto that football field.

10

The coaches arrive on schedule, unlike their players. Jack Smith rolls up in his brown pickup, Richard Egan atop a four-wheeler, and we sit in my living room on a hot afternoon. I keep the door open for airflow, a necessary move that also lets the flies in.

The two men are an odd rural pair. One white, the other Paiute-Shoshone; one divorced, the other married with grandchildren; one a relative newcomer, the other homegrown. Both are one-time athletes whose love of sports led them into coaching.

They've forged a brotherly bond through continual losing and dealing with the whims of an unpredictable principal neither is sure has their back. And now they're sitting on my old couch looking a bit uncomfortable as though on a first date. Both sink so far into the sagging furniture that it might be difficult for them to get up again.

I fetch them water and face them in a kitchen chair as their interrogator. Our subject matter is as comfortable as that old couch: the spring season's four lopsided losses that mark an all-time low for McDermitt Bulldogs football.

Football, after all, has no business being played in March when the northern Nevada cold still braces each breath. The game is meant for the fall, starting when the weather is hot and the leaves are green, ending only when many trees have no leaves at all.

But Covid-19 made for some strange bedfellows.

The Bulldogs numbered six players to start: Dawn's two disruptive boys, along with Enzo, Maverick, Elijah, and Lane. Taylor didn't show up until the season was half over. Too late, as it turned out.

"Our plan was to win at least one game," Egan begins, "but not knowing what we had, and what little experience we had, it was a challenge just to win a ballgame."

A challenge, for that matter, to score a single point.

Being walloped 298 to 2 can make any coach reach for his antacid tablets. The scoreboard becomes an insult, a heckler, some drunk who just won't shut up.

The game results: 100–0; 58–0; 68–0 and 72–2.

Fig. 7. Coach Richard Egan holds ball before team mural. Photograph by Randi Lynn Beach.

In the eyes of some, however, the Bulldogs were winners. They kept their cool as boys their age imposed on-field carnage. They made time to be boys, finding things to laugh about. In one play, Maverick hit the opposing quarterback, who fumbled. Mav searched for the ball in panic, and there it was all along, between his legs.

On those long bus rides home, the boys discussed how close they'd come to scoring a touchdown or busting out for a big run. Then they would get tired and drift off to sleep, slumped against the bus windows, the highway passing beneath their feet.

The season brought disappointment even before the first snap of the ball.

Peyton Smart, an athletic 170-pounder, was slated to start as the team's quarterback, following his older brother, Duane Horse, who'd been both a standout play-caller and running back. Peyton was a sort of second coming, a kid who could bring change, impose daylight over darkness, produce wins instead of losses.

Then his father, Tilden Smart, an ex-tribal chairman who had served as both a football and basketball assistant, moved to Battle Mountain for a gold mining job, taking Peyton along with him.

It was just McDermitt's luck. Peyton was like a lottery draft pick, with a young arm to build a team around. And then he was gone, snatched away like a crop that withered before harvest.

So the coaches go with the untested Lane as quarterback, and he ends the four-game season with negative offensive yards—the yards lost to sacks far outpacing his completed passes. But nobody is keeping track. The Bulldogs no longer keep statistics on individual and team performances. "We don't record game film either," Egan says. "None of the kids want to do it."

Maybe it's just too painful.

Egan holds both himself and his players accountable. "Coaches can only do so much. We can call in a play, but the guys have to figure it out inside the huddle, how they're gonna run it, who they're going to block. You can't just leave it up to the coaches."

The first game was played on a blustery Friday in early March. The Bulldogs got up at 5:00 a.m. and loaded into two SUVs for the 265-mile one-way trip to Eureka, which fields one of the state's best teams, one that has embarrassed them in seasons past.

This one would be the worst yet.

Game day came windy and cold, following an overnight storm. Standing on the sidelines of Eureka's pristine field, the nervous visiting coaches joked about the weather. "You normally start football during August and you're worried about heat protocol," Smith says. "But on that day, it was just the opposite."

The game was played as a scrimmage because, amid the last-minute pandemic scheduling, not enough Bulldogs had completed the requisite ten days of practice to compete in a sanctioned league contest.

Still, for the twenty Eureka Vandal players, this was the real deal. "I got upset because our kids didn't have their games faces on," Smith says, sinking deeper into that couch. "They were in joke mode. They didn't realize we were going into battle."

At halftime the scoreboard read 50–0. So officials reset it to zero for the second half, offering a morale boost to the hapless, outplayed visitors. The Vandals scored on the very first play of most possessions.

The coaches winced at one missed tackle after another, with Dawn's boys even jumping out of the way to avoid contact. McDermitt's offensive front line was repeatedly pushed back. They went the wrong way on every play.

The defense wasn't much better. "We had shown rushers techniques to slice through the line—the swat and swim move—but once they got into the game, they just threw everything out," Egan explains. "I think it was something like stage fright. They just forgot what we'd asked them to do."

In the tiny bungalow the two coaches are two movie critics, a small town Gene Siskel and Roger Ebert, parsing memories that are like a horror flick.

"That first game was not good," Smith says.

"Not very good at all," Egan adds. "We ended up with a total negative yardage."

"Meanwhile," Smith says, laughing, "they amassed a world-record amount."

"Even in the backfield, they were good-sized kids, pretty athletic too."

"Real swift quarterback."

After the game a ray of kindness graced the McDermitt sidelines, blue skies after a steady rain. The Vandal's quarterback, wearing No. 24, ran across the field to shake hands with every Bulldog player, looking each in the eye, offering encouraging words.

"He came over all by himself," Egan says. "Not many kids would do that alone, so it showed some real maturity. He told our boys, 'Keep your heads up, keep playing, you did a good job.' Other than that, they kicked our ass."

Yet the Bulldog players seemed unmoved. "They were okay with the defeat," Smith recalls. "If it had been me, I would have been upset. They jumped into the trucks and got on their phones. They were more worried about where we were going to eat."

Even with five times as many people, the town of Wells, Nevada, is about as luckless as McDermitt. Once known as Humboldt Wells, it burned to the ground in the late 1800s. A century later, in 2008, the town center was damaged by a magnitude 6.0 earthquake.

One saving grace is Wells' proximity to Interstate 80. The town sits in the middle of the highway's 410-mile run through Nevada, from the Bonneville Salt Flats in the Sierra foothills to the town of West Wendover at the Utah border.

That's the road that the yellow McDermitt Combined Schools bus took to reach town for a game against the Wells Leopards, a team that fielded sixteen players that day, twice as many as the undermanned Bulldogs.

The ride was quiet, with the boys eyeballing their smartphones, a far cry from the days Burt Polkinghorne was coach, when the entire football team wrestled the two big linemen, John Hill and his brother Gene, in the back of the bus as a way to kill the boredom of those long rides.

Egan worries the internet distraction might cost his team its focus, but he's never considered an iPhone ban on the bus. "If we did that," he says, referring to the principal, Muñoz, "we'd probably get called to the office. I don't know."

It was a Friday evening game, the closest thing the McDermitt Bulldogs would get to those vaunted Friday night lights. The team left early for the near four-hour drive. A few parents followed, but not many.

The Leopards began with their starters but soon resorted to the second string. The Bulldogs had no second string and struggled in the late August heat.

Wells led 48–0 at halftime.

But just like it did in Eureka, a tiny bit of moonlight shone upon those McDermitt boys. The girls' volleyball team had also made the trip. After their game they sat in the stands to support the boys' team.

It was like a light had been switched on. Suddenly the Bulldogs had something to play for, and that something was pride. Now nobody jumped out of the way of oncoming runners. They made tackles. The offensive line dug in against the Wells pass rush, allowing the Bulldogs to keep possession of the ball for longer periods, even though the clock continued to run, with the mercy rule in effect.

Each time they made a block or tackle, the McDermitt boys glanced toward the sidelines. "I don't think we should have waited for the girls to play better," Egan says. "We should have played better from the beginning. Whether we have a crowd or no crowd, that should be up to our kids to decide."

Wells totaled only seven points in the second half, although McDermitt was once again held scoreless. "When we were heading home, they were proud of themselves, boasting, 'We made a tackle!'" Smith says. "They were learning on the job, so by the time the second half came around, they started to get it."

The volleyball players rode on the same bus, making the mood even lighter. Still, the coaches brooded. While the Bulldogs had made a few tackles that evening, they still had not completed a pass in two games, settling for a total negative yardage.

If the Eureka game scored an *F*, Wells was a *C-*. It was certainly no way to win any games. Regardless the optimistic Egan was proud of his boys. "We played better than we did the week before," he says. "And we held them in the second half."

Then came the Carlin game, when everything went to hell. If you ask Egan, it never should have happened. The Bulldogs were playing in front of hometown fans, with entire families sitting in lawn chairs on a warm evening. They'd been rooted on from the first whistle blow.

The Carlin Railroaders fielded only eight boys as well. For the Bulldogs this was a real chance for victory. But that didn't happen. The Railroaders dominated 68–0. "Carlin overpowered us," Egan says. "They were better than Wells."

Here's where his anger rises. Coaches seem to forget that these games are played among young boys with fragile egos. The purpose is to win, of course, but not dominate, not to step on the throat of your opponent until you see the lights go out in his eyes. But that's what Carlin did.

Egan saw a visiting coach who had lost control of his team. Rather than reel in the aggression after the Railroaders went up big, he left his starters on the field. The Carlin kids didn't offer to help up a downed Bulldog as Eureka had done. Instead they stepped over them like they weren't even there.

"They were kids," Smith says. "They didn't know."

"And the coach was young," Egan adds.

Years before, when another generation of Bulldog players beat Eureka by the unlikely score of 98–18, Egan told his kids to take a knee whenever they pierced deep into Vandals territory. He didn't want to embarrass anyone. He knew that one day the football cleat might be on the other foot.

Now that day had come to pass. After the game, during the lineup of player handshakes, Egan didn't complain to the Wells coach. "I don't remember if I said anything to him," he says.

"You kind of let him off the hook, didn't ya?" Jack says.

Three games, three monumental losses.

Next up were the Owyhee Braves, a team dominated by Paiute kids from the border near Idaho. McDermitt always marked the game on its calendar, tribal pride at stake. The Bulldogs took a deep breath and then exhaled.

There's something about reservation football that brings out bad blood among a bunch of Nevada teenagers. When two high school teams dominated by reservation players take to the field, the crowds come and they are loud from the start. Mothers shake their fists; grandfathers storm off on missed opportunities.

The intensity is heart-stopping when you're a Paiute kid playing against your father's extended clan. What happens that day will be discussed, analyzed, and broken down moment by moment for months to come.

"Many reservation kids are related, so there are bragging rights, even among the parents," Egan says. "When you hear that Owyhee is coming to town, you'll see people who normally don't show up at ballgames. They'll be the first ones there. There's more attendance in both places."

The rivalry dates to the 1970s when Egan was growing up in Owyhee. He moved to McDermitt and lived with his uncle so he could enroll in school and play football. He morphed from a Brave to a Bulldog—as player and then coach—but there are demons to slay every time he takes on that team.

As a coach, those Owyhee losses visit his dreams long after the final whistle is blown. But Egan knows that revenge is sweet. That spring, the Bulldogs were at home against their mortal foes. "I knew Owyhee was gonna have a good team," he says. "They had fourteen kids, four of them seniors. They were bigger across the line, seasoned athletes. Our kids from the reservation know those kids. They know their names."

The Bulldogs were down 34–0 at the break. Then sometime during the fog of the fourth quarter, something redemptive took place. With the team well on its way to its fourth straight defeat, the Bulldogs scored.

It wasn't a touchdown, but nobody cared. The Braves were deep inside their own territory, and Enzo—the baby-faced freshman—hit the quarterback, who went down in the end zone for a safety.

"I didn't know it was Enzo," Egan says. "Well, he was the hero of that game then."

Enzo had recalled hitting the quarterback so hard he heard the air leaving his lungs.

"He could have," Egan says.

Nobody was going to take such a precious moment away from that boy.

Perhaps no one feels the brunt of a football ass-whupping more than the losing quarterback. He feels the hits when unblocked defensive linemen stampede him like untethered horses; he knows when his passes flutter like butterflies rather than bullets.

Fig. 8. QB Lane Barnett outside town rodeo field. Photograph by Randi Lynn Beach.

Months after the Owyhee defeat, Lane sits in his father's office before a computer screen, watching a video of a game that produced only failure. His father, Kerry, looms just over his shoulder.

Kerry is a school guidance counselor, a Billy the Kid lookalike who dresses in blue jeans, a denim shirt, and a cowboy hat, a scarf pulled over his face to protect him from skies laden with woodsmoke, even though the wildfires are hundreds of miles distant.

He played high school and college football, then rode professional rodeo. He looks pained as his son relives the torture of a 72–2 defeat, stopping the footage to try and articulate what went wrong. In the video, the mountains east of town are snowcapped and wind howls into the microphone. Conversations resound with a tinny static, like transmissions from space.

Watching the game tape, it's easy to see what happened. The Bulldogs get the ball first that day, and what takes place next is a bitter taste of what's to come. On the initial play Taylor scrambles to the right for a 10-yard gain, but the play is called back because of an offsides penalty.

Then a lost Bulldog fumbles at the snap. On the very next play, the opponents run 50 yards for a touchdown when a McDermitt player misses an open-field tackle and the Braves runner is home free. They add a 2-point conversion.

After only four plays, McDermitt is down 8–0. Lane stops the video. "Our front line was too scared to move in on defense," he says glumly. "Those kids could basically do anything they wanted."

On McDermitt's second possession, the first play is whistled for an illegal formation, then Lane is tackled in the backfield. On third down he lofts an anemic pass that's picked off for an interception and run back for a touchdown. After another 2-point conversation, the Bulldogs are down 16–0.

The Braves romp for more than 400 yards. They score on every possession, usually on the first play from scrimmage. With the Braves up 24–0, Lane stops the video again. "They're not going to let up," he says. "It's a Paiute versus Paiute thing."

The only bright spot comes when Taylor recovers a fumbled punt. Otherwise the video unspools a harsh reality. The snaps come high, making Lane leap to corral them. His passes are flails of desperation. Play after play the Braves are quickly in his face, untouched on the line. "This was our last game," Lane says. "We should have been getting first downs by then."

In the video, the coaches remain mostly silent as Bailey is summoned toward the huddle with one of an arsenal of ten plays: eight runs and two passes. There are no timeouts, no pep talks. The video picks up groans from the McDermitt crowd.

"The thing is, they weren't that good," Lane says. "We just made them look good."

Lane knows he didn't live up to the standards of his heroes that day—missile throwers like Peyton Manning and especially Seattle Seahawk quarterback Drew Lock, whom he calls the most mobile man on the football field.

He also likes college football's Alabama Crimson Tide. But on this day, the only thing reddened are the shamed faces of the McDermitt players. "They're probably up to 70 by now," Lane says of the Braves. "They never had to punt. Scored on every drive."

This wasn't in Kerry's playbook when he moved his son to McDermitt to get more playing time. After the game he offered some encouragement. "I told him I was proud that they had finished the season," Kerry says.

Then Lane turns off the video, and nobody says anything.

Fig. 9. Lane's father, Kerry, poses on fence. Photograph by Randi Lynn Beach.

Kerry wasn't the only one who closely watched McDermitt's last game.

Alden Donston called it a thing of unpolished beauty. In the Bulldogs' game against Owyhee, he saw things others did not see.

As a referee working high school games across central Nevada, Donston hears the chatter along the sidelines and inside the offensive huddles, the boasting and "just do your job" complaining when things go wrong.

But on that forlorn field in McDermitt, he was dumbfounded to witness something that rose above the level of a scholastic football game: a team that lost with dignity. He saw untested boys walk through a threshold to become men.

Donston, a supply chain manager at the Nevada Gold Mines, had scouted the game. As part of his homework as referee, he'd watched films of each team's previous contest. And he feared a mismatch of the worst kind.

"We knew Owyhee had a good team with older kids, juniors and seniors," he recalled. "They were just tough-looking, with a 250-pound freshman in a jersey that barely fits."

The Bulldogs had three juniors, the rest freshmen. They were boys, Donston said, who "never played football, lined up against a senior defensive tackle who weighs a hundred pounds more. When the bigger kid bull-rushes him and knocks him three feet into the backfield, a lot of kids just say to themselves, 'Why do I want to do this?'"

He knew the contest was a battle for bragging rights. "As the game went on, I was keeping an eye on the kids," he said. "The kind of success Owyhee was having didn't come every day. You could see the cockiness come out. That's when the chatter started, the trash-talking."

As the Bulldogs fell behind, Donston fought a feeling of dread. "I thought, 'C'mon Owyhee, take your foot off the gas pedal.' Oftentimes I'll say to the winning coach, 'This game's over, you should play the kids who need to play.' Then I looked over at the McDermitt sideline. There weren't any kids. All their kids were already on the field."

After taking big hits, the McDermitt players were slow getting up, so Donston gave them time to gather themselves. But he saw poise in the Bulldogs huddle. "I never heard any of the McDermitt kids say anything derogatory, like 'I want to quit' or 'This sucks,' as you would expect from a bunch of teenagers."

In fact it was the opposite. "They'd say things like 'C'mon man, get your block, we gotta get a first down.' It wasn't older kids barking at younger ones, it was just encouragement, like 'We need you.'"

Donston became a spectator as well as a ref. "I was thinking, 'C'mon, McDermitt, bust one, get one around the corner, and just run.' I was just willing them to score."

Then Enzo made his timely hit. A few players hadn't realized what had just happened, but the older kids did. The younger guys finally caught on, shouting, "Yeah, we scored!"

Over thirty-five years, Donston has known of only one rural player to reach the big time. Chester David "Tuff" Harris, from the Crow Nation in Montana, played in Lodge Grass—known as the Valley of the Chiefs—before going to the University of Montana and being signed by the Miami Dolphins in 2007. He played professional football for five years.

Still, football is not traditionally a Native American sport, he explains. "You see a lot of these kids shooting hoops," he says. "In the fall, most often there's no football to play. The reservations are too isolated for any organized league, so they play basketball."

But when football comes to town, it provides players with a rare, fleeting moment in the public spotlight. "You go to these places and everyone knows there's a football game at 7:00 p.m.," Donston says. "The boys are the pride of the town. Family and friends watch them play. Games at bigger schools that play eleven-man football can be a graveyard sometimes, but not in McDermitt."

It's a tradition that needs to be preserved: "Take that team out of a McDermitt and the town would lose that history. It would destroy the soul of that town. People would lose their *game day.*"

And those young players? "For them it's just fun. They're not usually playing for the league championship or a scholarship. They practice two hours every night, and this is their prize after all that hard work," he said. "When those kids in McDermitt strap on a helmet, every game is their Super Bowl."

After the Bulldogs' loss, Donston couldn't forget about the maturity those boys had shown in such a lopsided defeat. He wrote an email to Superintendent Dave Jensen because he did not want that afternoon to go unnoticed.

My name is Alden Donston and I'm sending you this quick note to share with you my experience with the McDermitt football team this past Friday, he began. *I was an official for their game and all I can say is that McDermitt should be very proud of those eight boys and the way they carry themselves on the football field. Even when the scoreboard was not in their favor, they continued to complement their opponents on their play, help them up after each play and displayed a very positive no-quit attitude.*

It was, frankly, something he'd rarely seen on a high school football field.

In today's sports world this is something that you don't see very often and especially when you're losing, Donston wrote. *They could have folded up the tents and gone home but they kept playing and that showed a lot of class and character. At no time during the game did I hear negative comments towards us as officials, the other team and even to each other.*

These were not average teens. *I know you always hear about the kids when they're bad,* Donston closed his letter, *but sometimes you need to hear about the good also.*

In his eyes McDermitt had won that day.

The flies are winning the battle inside my stuffy bungalow. The two coaches slowly rise from the sagging couch. The spring season is over; another campaign awaits.

Smith knows that these boys will remember what happens for years to come. He coined the phrase "We are who we are" so the boys remember that too.

The line was first uttered by NFL coach Bill Parcells, that "you are what your record says you are," but Smith had turned the intended meaning on its head. Parcells's words were a helmet slap, a way to disparage a talented team that was not winning games. In Parcells's world, the game's final score speaks volumes about a team's identity—far more than any boasting.

But McDermitt is a long way from the NFL sidelines. For Egan and Smith, the idea of "who they are" isn't solely defined by wins but by character and effort. You can lose games and even be beaten badly, but honor still counts for something—and in their eyes it's the biggest lesson that can be learned on a football field.

"I told them in the huddle against Owyhee, 'You guys are here,'" Smith says. "'Other kids at school didn't even come out for the team. You guys had the guts. Richard and I are proud of you guys because you're out here battling.'"

Smith shakes his head. "There were boys in the stands we could have used. They came to watch, but not play. So we let our kids know that they had the heart and guts."

The McDermitt Bulldogs are who they are.

Fig. 10. Assistant football coach Jack Smith poses with gloves containing ashes of his father, Moe. Photograph by Randi Lynn Beach.

11

Everybody told Moe that his son needed a roof and four walls, not the back seat of a station wagon. So in the 1970s the old boxer moved to Spirit Lake, Idaho, a logging town of a thousand souls set deep in the north woods, not far from Coeur d'Alene.

Along with Cummings and ten-year-old Jack was a promising new Carson City fighter named Johnny Cushman. Moe began helping run a bar called the Linger Longer, one of three local taverns. The Linger Longer and Jo's Hole were downtown bookends, with a joint called Park Place wedged in between.

After driving all day, Moe's little band arrived after midnight, passing through thick woods as the winding two-lane road dropped into town. Jack was overwhelmed by the fresh smell of the forest, a scent he'd never experienced as a boy from the desert. The men rolled down the windows and took in deep gulps of air.

"Moe, can you smell that?" Cushman asked.

Then the boxer farted, dousing the car in a methane cloud.

"Cushman!" Moe roared. "Can I enjoy a moment for once?"

"Sorry, Moe," he said as Jack laughed in the back seat.

That first night in town, they came upon a street fight outside one bar, a violent affair that people lined up to watch. It was like the wild West, and it scared the kid. The next evening, as the men left for a few drinks, the boy cried. "Johnny," he pleaded, "don't let my dad get hurt. Don't let anything happen to him."

Cushman got on one knee to calm the boy—like Sonny Liston had once done—then looked over at Moe. "I remember being his age and worrying that you'll lose your dad."

Moe later bought the Park Place saloon and renamed it the White Horse, after the McDermitt tavern where he'd created so many memories. He introduced the Moe burger, a monstrosity with double-meat patties and ham and secret sauce that drew people from across the Washington state line.

The outsiders got into fights with the locals, a rough crowd that included loggers, ranchers, and buckaroos. Many eyeballed Moe's wrestling and boxing pictures displayed at the bar and said, "I think I can take ya, Moe."

Nobody ever did. But Jack worried his aging father would get hurt. "As long as I'm here," Cushman assured the boy, "your dad will not be in another fight."

Jack hugged him then. Good old Johnny.

The boy was about to lose his second dog. One day he walked downtown, followed by Cummings II, a pit bull with fighting experience. Jack spotted another dog and tried to pull Cummings away, but there was no stopping it. The latest brawl on Spirit Lake's main drag drew another crowd.

Moe came running with a chisel to pry the dogs apart. By then Cummings had his foe by the throat, and Moe was trying to pry his jaws open. "Jack, I can't get it," Moe said as the boy loomed close.

The other dog was killed, and Moe soon got rid of the second Cummings. He told Jack he'd found the dog a good home, but Jack now wonders if his father put the dog down. Neither father nor son could live without a dog for long, so Moe brought home a basset hound they named Homer, who quickly became the unofficial mayor of the White Horse tavern.

With his forlorn look Homer even had his own seat by the wood stove, and the drunks had fun with him. But no one ever took Homer's spot.

When Jack was fourteen he fought in a series of smokers. His opponent in the main event was a wiry street fighter named Mike Meadows, known for his toughness. As Moe pulled on his son's gloves, he said, "You can beat him with straight punches."

The bell rang, and Meadows was on him, fists flying, punches landing. At the first bell Donny Temple, Moe's old friend and a veteran trainer, offered more pointers. In the next round, Jack threw short, straight jabs. Just maybe he had a chance.

Then Meadows landed a haymaker, his glove laces raking across Jack's right cornea. Suddenly he saw three fighters there, not one. "I got scared," he says. Temple saw the swelling in Jack's eye and panicked. "I'm stopping this fight," he said, pulling off Jack's headgear. He turned to Moe. "I don't want to chance it."

Moe was irate. He pulled off Jack's gloves, berating him, his face just inches away. "My kid's a quitter," he spat.

"Dad, *he* stopped it," Jack protested. "I didn't."

Moe had once taken a punch that disconnected his eyeball from its socket, ending his career. "I had my eye dangling out of my head, but I kept on fighting," Moe screamed, pointing a thick finger. "Don't you *ever* get into a boxing ring again.'"

He stormed away from the hotshot kid who supposedly couldn't be beat. Two weeks later, Jack had another fight in Coeur d'Alene. Moe stayed home, and Donnie Temple took him instead. The loss to Meadows had angered Jack, and that night he quickly dispatched his opponent.

Afterward Temple drove Jack back to Spirit Lake. The car was quiet. Then Jack asked the older man the question that would forever haunt him.

"Why did you stop the fight?"

The boy knew that Temple was only looking out for him, but his father had wanted him to continue fighting. And Jack never wanted to let his father down.

Temple gripped the steering wheel. "Your dad's from a different generation," he began. "In the 1940s and 50s, they didn't stop fights, even when they should have."

The boy cried then.

He felt caught in the middle, and Moe was unhappy.

Moe was at the White Horse, draped in his white apron, mouthing his cigar. Temple's arm was draped across Jack's shoulder as he set the boxing trophy on the bar.

"Moe, you should have seen him," he said. "Four or five right hands, just like you taught him, and that kid went down."

For a moment, time stood still. Then that telltale grin surfaced on Moe's face. He walked up and hugged his son. Still, Jack knew the damage had been done.

"I never talk about it," Jack said, his voice breaking. "I just think about it. All the time."

He had failed his father. It still hurts.

The White Horse had a mammoth woodstove, and during the winter Moe took Jack out to forage logs and kindling. The old man always brought a shotgun in case they spotted any grouse, which Moe thought was good eating, tender—if maybe a bit gamey.

One day Moe spotted a bird and told Jack to ready the shotgun; the boy would take the shot. As Jack sized up his aim, his father said softly, "Anytime, Jack, anytime."

He didn't pull the trigger. He couldn't. "Anytime, Jack."

Still nothing. The grouse flew off. "What happened?" Moe said.

"Dad, that grouse had a tear in its eye. I didn't want to shoot him."

One thing the two shared was a love for animals. Back at the White Horse, Moe told the story about his "sensitive" son. In the ring, however, his demands remained unyielding. He morphed from concerned father to exacting coach, whose goal was to raise a true fighter.

By high school Jack had filled out and began challenging his father. "Dad, when I turn eighteen," he'd say, "we're putting the gloves on for real." He recalled a winter night on February 3, 1978, when he turned to Moe at dinner. "Dad," he said, "tonight's the night."

Even at forty-eight, Moe was thick and dangerous. The pair had play fought—never with gloves—with the father easily fielding off the incoming blows. At the gym he watched the kid move gracefully around on the mat yelling, "I'm Ali!"

That night, Moe eyed his son. "Yeah, you're eighteen."

"We gloving up, Dad?"

"Yeah, I'm ready."

Moe's new girlfriend, Marsha, twenty years his junior, pulled aside furniture to create a ring in their living room. Gloves laced, the two moved in. Right away, Jack hit his father with a quick right hand. He didn't mean to hit Moe so hard; it was reflexive. "Bam! I hit him with a nice one, and I thought, 'Oh, shit.'"

Moe landed a short hook, and the boy thought, *Is this serious?*

Then the older man began to move in close, taking away the kid's space, Jack recalls, a move Joe Frazier might have tried on Ali. Jack hit his father with another right, this one harder than the first. "In my head, I'm thinking, 'This is getting out of hand.'"

The next thing he recalled was opening his eyes, gazing up at the plaster swirls on the living room ceiling. Moe had knocked him out.

"I mean *out* out." Jack laughs. "*Flat* out."

He never saw the *coup de grâce*, delivered as corporal punishment for being so big-headed. "When I woke up, I thought, 'Why am I looking at the ceiling?'"

Marsha was hovering. "Moe, what did you do? You hurt him!"

Moe stood over his son like Ali looming over the downed Frazier. Not in victory, but concern. Then he saw the boy's eyes flutter. "Nah," Moe announced. "He's alright."

Jack never challenged his father again. "I knew better than that."

Fast forward to the fall of 1982. Moe had sold his Spirit Lake bar and log-ging business to pay a million dollars in back taxes. He'd returned to Reno, Nevada, soon joined by his son, who'd dropped out of college in Boise, Idaho, to pursue a fighting career.

Jack's ego was still his main opponent. He sparred against Frankie "Sugar Man" Davis, one of Reno's hottest welterweights who, unlike Jack, boxed to pay his rent. Sugar Man could go ten rounds with barely a sweat. Jack could go four, tops.

Jack began classes at the University of Nevada, Reno, working as a casino valet as he trained in the gym. Moe tried to keep him grounded. "Get your degree," he said.

Around that time, the national fight promoter Top Rank Boxing came to Reno to stage world title fights. Moe was hired to organize the undercard and got his son odd jobs around the ring. He had a front-row seat to the show.

That's when Colin Jones showed up. A Welshman in his early twenties, Jones fought in the 1976 Olympics in Montreal and later became British and European welterweight champion as a professional. Now he was vying for the world championship welterweight title.

Days before the fight Moe invited his son to have lunch with Jones and his entourage. Quiet and polite, Jones mentioned he was down one sparring partner.

Jack's eyes lit up. "Dad," he whispered, "I'll step in."

Moe spoke up, "My kid can spar. He's pretty good. He spars with Sugar Man all the time." Jones agreed to spar with the kid.

The following afternoon the arena was crawling with reporters; Jones's hometown TV station was there to cover the fight. Jack watched Jones man-handle Sugar Man, his sparring partner, who'd built an 11-0 record as a pro-fessional. There was something lethal to Jones's delivery that day. His punches were designed to do damage.

When his turn came, Jack was ready to go. But Moe yanked off the gloves. "Get out of here," he spit.

Jack looked at his father, dumbfounded. That made Moe even madder. He rarely raised his voice, but now he was yelling. "I don't even want you to change here. Go somewhere else!"

Jack slinked out of the gym unseen. Later he confronted his father.

"You didn't need that," Moe explained. "That guy's whole hometown was there. He was *fighting*. And I was not going to let that guy pummel you like he was doing to Sugar Man. He was making statements. You were next."

As a member of the boxing team at the University of Nevada, Reno, Jack competed in a regional championship against a rising UC Berkeley fighter who traveled with his own entourage. Moe sat ringside. It comforted Jack to know he was there, but it also added an element of pressure. He had to fight like Moe's boy, and he knew it.

Moments into the fight, the Californian hit Jack with a powerful punch he never saw coming. In fighting parlance, he'd had his bell rung. Already he knew he was hurt. The referee gave him a standing eight count.

Jack's mind raced back to that fight as a fourteen-year-old when he'd hurt his eye. But he kept fighting. The Berkeley boxer hit him again. The ref called for another standing eight count. One more and the fight would be over.

"I was hurt," Jack said. "But I was not going down, not with my dad there."

This time when the opponent moved in, Moe's kid threw a reflexive right hand, straight like his dad always taught him. And then another. The Berkeley kid wobbled.

Jack went the distance but lost in a split decision. Then Moe said something he'd never forget. "You showed me something tonight," Moe said. "You came back."

Jack began to talk about that night as a fourteen-year-old. "That's all gone now, Jack," Moe said. "That guy tonight had you beat. But you didn't quit."

For Jack the conversation was freighted with significance. Even though he was finally a man in his father's eyes, he lacked Moe's killer instinct. As both a man and a fighter he was more laid-back. Moe said he took after his mother that way.

"He was just tougher, a natural boxer," Jack says. "I just didn't have that meanness to me to become world champion. I was just a dreamer."

By his early eighties, Moe's health was in full decline. He'd moved back to Idaho with his girlfriend, Marsha, who provided around-the-clock care. By then Jack had graduated from college, had fought as an amateur, and had won two professional fights before an injured finger ended his career.

He'd stepped outside his father's shadow to become a high school athletic instructor and coach. Every summer when Jack paid his customary visit to Idaho, he noticed that Moe was less mobile. His legs and feet swelled. Dementia was setting in.

Still, father and son kept a routine: Looking at old boxing pictures, watching westerns. *Rawhide. Gunsmoke. Have Gun Will Travel.* Every day from 8:00 a.m. to 2:00 a.m. Moe was kept on a strict diet, but Jack made late-night runs to Taco Bell, just like in the old days.

They'd tour old haunts around Spirit Lake. Whenever they walked into the White Horse, the drinkers called out, "It's Moe Smith!" That brought back the crooked old smile. Once, a musician shook Moe's hand. "You gave me my first break," he said.

Jack saw the doubt on his dad's face. "I'm sorry," Moe said. "I don't remember you."

The scene broke Jack's heart. He still had the old photo of Moe when he first opened the White Horse in the early 1970s. Moe was forty-two, and he stood in front of his new saloon, dressed in a white bar apron, the smile beaming. So that day, Jack recreated the shot, placing his aging father in the same spot: Moe and his beloved White Horse bar. Jack's eyes teared as he looked into the camera's viewfinder.

The next time Jack visited, in 2012, Moe had trouble getting into the truck. As hard as he tried, Jack could no longer boost his dad, who couldn't help himself. It was a hot summer day, and Jack made one last push. Moe still weighed 200 pounds and wouldn't budge. Jack feared that if he let go, his father would tumble to the asphalt below.

"In my mind, I'm not letting my dad drop," he recalls. "I would die before that."

He was sweating through his shirt. "Dad," he said, "I can't hold on much longer."

Then the boxing gods got involved. Moe finally slid into the seat. "It was like somebody helped us," Jack said. Then Moe didn't want to get out of the truck. "There's so-and-so," the son would say. "Don't you want to go say hello?"

Moe would wave his hand. That was their last trip.

It was October 2013 when Jack got the call. Moe had just suffered a major stroke. "It's a bad one," his sister Debbie said.

Jack arrived at the Coeur d'Alene hospital at 2:00 a.m. "I'm here, Dad," he said.

Then Moe grabbed his hand and kissed it.

Two weeks later Moe was moved to a nearby hospice. "For twenty days, I got to stare right into his eyes," Jack says. "I talked to him about everything, and he looked right at me."

Jack told his father he'd been recruited for a job in isolated McDermitt. Should he go? "I thought he said yes with his eyes," Jack said.

Donald "Moe" Smith died at 2:00 a.m. on October 22, 2013. "I was screaming at him," Jack says, "telling him that I loved him. I saw his spirit leave."

The memorial service was held in Post Falls, Idaho. In 2004 Jack had attended "Irish Pat" Duncan's funeral in Carson City but hadn't addressed the mourners that day. He listened to others tell stories about the fighter who had helped raise him.

His voice breaking, Jack told the old stories of how Moe had returned to Spirit Lake in 1994 to promote fights at a tribal casino. There were TV commercials and ads with Moe's face, cigar and all, plastered across the sides of buses in nearby Spokane.

It wasn't a world championship, but to father and son, it was.

"Yeah," Moe had said, laughing, "your dad's famous."

"Shaddup, Dad."

"What? So what? I'm on a bus."

"Look at you."

"Knock it off," Moe had said, but Jack knew his father loved the attention.

Jack told the story of his last professional fight, where Moe was ringside, this time with a fighter named Bobo Olson, a former 1950s world middleweight champion.

Jack knocked out his opponent. He climbed down the stairs from the ring, with Moe and Bobo there to greet him. "You got a nice right hand," Bobo said.

The father was beaming. To the son, that smile meant more than anything.

On that day, when he said his last goodbye to his father, he really *was* Crying Jack Smith. And he didn't care who knew it.

12

My landlord stops by one Sunday morning for a chat.

Junior Huttman is seventy-two and has lived around McDermitt for most of his life. He's been a rancher and entrepreneur who has flown small aircraft to help farmers harvest their hay. He still owns a light plane that he keeps in the garage next to my house.

His given name is Howard, like his father's. He calls himself No. 2 but goes by Junior.

Who calls him that?

"Everybody," he says.

Junior pulls up atop his four-wheeler, his usual transportation around town. He likes the buggy because it's fast enough to sneak up on troublemakers like Cowboy Bob. He mostly uses it to run his pack of adopted dogs and check on the houses he and Lorraine rent out around town, including mine.

He takes a seat at the dining room table I have turned into my writing desk. He is whip-smart and politically conservative. In my weeks in McDermitt he turns me onto screeds he insists will change my view of America. When he gets to talking about politics, Lorraine tunes him out. She has no idea what political theories he's absorbing from his computer, and she doesn't want to know.

And after one trip up inside that light plane of his, she won't go anymore.

"Oh, Junior," she says.

On this day Junior is full of gossip. Along with the Covid pandemic, the summer first brought an invasion of Mormon crickets that snapped and popped in a sickening way when you stepped on them. Then came the forest fires and smoke that blanketed the region like a brown fog. Just the week before, eighty-mile-an-hour winds ripped through town, uprooting trees, damaging the old rodeo yard, and making the weather vane atop the ranch house near my bungalow spin like a whirling dervish.

I shake my head and commiserate because I care about Junior and Lorraine. Considering my troubles with some locals, I find myself seeking their approval. If I'm embraced by Lorraine and Junior, maybe it's a sign others in town might do the same.

Fig. 11. Howard "Junior" Huttman poses atop ATV. Photograph by Randi Lynn Beach.

From the beginning they invited me to drop by their house to figure out the town they call home. We drink coffee and eat scrambled eggs and Basque sausage, which Lorraine whips up in the kitchen while Junior sits at the table holding court.

For me they're a rural aunt and uncle, at once beloved and familiar with their easygoing "we've been married forever" banter. Junior doesn't get anything by Lorraine, and, well, she doesn't get much past him either.

The feisty repartee comes from sixty years of marriage and parenting three girls and a boy born within a decade—Heather, Hailey, Ryan, and Olivia.

"We were productive," Lorraine smiles. She's now a grandmother of eleven, with a distinguished splash of gray hair.

"No," Junior says, "you were prolific."

"It was the other way around," Lorraine protests.

"What do you mean the other way around?" Juniors says, giving me a wink. "I used to call her Fertile Myrtle."

Lorraine laughs, then sets him in her gaze.

"What?" he says defensively.

"Nothing, but you're sitting there with your crotch open, and I got a foot right close."

That day at my house, Junior fills in more McDermitt gaps. First off, my little bungalow was built by Lorraine's grandfather in 1917. Some out-of-towner just bought the old White Horse and wants to turn the old tavern into a marijuana motel, a so-called Bud-and-Breakfast.

And that big, orange, truck-chasing dog I'd encountered the night before? Well, his name is Tater, and he's found a way inside the couple's heart, along with a passel of newborns. My landlords collect strays, and I'm just the latest.

The roosters are crowing as Lorraine fires up yellow school bus No. 113, ready for another semester of making her reservation rounds. It's the first day of classes at the McDermitt Combined Schools, and at age seventy-three the veteran driver moves a little more slowly every year.

"Am I ready for this?" she asks. "No."

For years Lorraine has driven a 40-mile reservation loop, where cows and horses throw up roadblocks amid set-back homesteads and abandoned cars, a vista of rural poverty.

She greets each child who climbs on board with a "Good morning!" The sleepy-eyed students are quiet. In the afternoon this same bus, with these same kids, will become a raucous, sugar-fueled energy party.

As she drives, Lorraine scans the landscape because she's here to collect more than schoolchildren. She seeks out neglected dogs that otherwise wouldn't survive for long without a shepherd like her.

In America's small towns, on its farms and ranches, life can be cheap for former pets and feral litters. The long arm of PETA and the Humane Society doesn't often reach this far out, and frustrated folks around McDermitt sometimes run down strange dogs on the road or shoot them on sight when they wander onto their properties.

It can also be tough on the reservation. Right now Lorraine and Junior have four strays at home. There's Tater, Mac, Shuggie, and Tickie, who hops around on three legs. And that passel of cats that Lorraine can't let herself see go hungry.

"Hell, she's got a herd of twenty or thirty cats out back," Junior says one morning inside a living room where big dogs clamor like restless convicts.

"I *do* not," Lorraine says. "There's only maybe fifteen."

"That's why they call you the Cat Lady."

There are so many cats that Lorraine hasn't named them all. She just counts as she lays out their food, "One, two, three . . . I know when somebody's missing," she says.

She tells animal stories like other women her age might brag about grand-kids. Take Tater, for instance. One day on her morning bus route about three years back, a cute little girl climbed aboard. "I got a new puppy!" she exclaimed.

Days later the child confessed, "My daddy doesn't like my puppy." The next day the girl said her new puppy was gone. Lorraine headed home to find Junior on the couch.

"C'mon Junior," she said. "Let's get in the pickup."

"Where we going?"

"Out to the reservation."

"What we doing out there?"

"We're going puppy hunting."

They scoured the roads near the girl's house and finally heard a yelp from an old shed. The puppy's eyes were barely open. Lorraine took the dog home. She sat in the living room, the tiny body lying in her lap like a newborn, cooing as she fed it with an eyedropper, a home remedy concoction of egg yolks, plain yogurt, and canned milk.

They named him Tater, she says, because he looked like a little potato.

It's always been like this—Lorraine saving her strays. There have been lambs, calves, chickens, birds, and even a baby badger. In the 1960s she fed scraps to stray dogs behind the town gas station until a county man in a pickup truck shot the entire dozen of them.

That taught her to be vigilant. Not everybody cares for the downtrodden as she does.

Her heart goes out to varmints like Tickie, who she found in the same shed where she'd rescued Tater. When she got the dog home, she found so many ticks that she and Junior stopped counting. Then Tickie began chasing cars and one day got walloped. After a week of watching the dog drag his front left leg, they paid a vet $100 to amputate it. "Tickie still chases cars," Junior says. "Now he's not fast enough to catch 'em."

For twenty-six years Lorraine worked as the town postmistress and heard about all the animals that needed saving. Like the ten chocolate lab puppies somebody found in the abandoned White Horse. That was fourteen years ago, and Lorraine's son still has one of those dogs. Another adopter says her lab comes into the shower with her.

Pets are like family, Lorraine says.

The dog named Mac once belonged to a motel owner here, and Mac used to dance for him in the front office. After the man had a stroke, his wife ordered him to either give the dog away or shoot him. Instead the manager went to see Lorraine. "Want him?"

"Well, I've already got enough dogs . . . Oh, okay."

Somebody found Shuggie as a puppy inside the old jailhouse, a hundred-year-old abandoned stone structure next to the post office. She says it took Shuggie three years to emerge from her shell. "She was abused, wasn't she?" Lorraine says to the dog, who wags its tail at the sound of its name. "But she's not abused anymore, is she?"

Hardly. Lorraine spends hundreds each month on animal food, along with the "treats." The cats get canned tuna and, when she fears they might have worms, grounds up bits of an unlit cigar in their meal. "You know, to smoke 'em out," she says.

And those dogs? "I give 'em baloney sandwiches at night, without the mustard, of course, and sometimes spaghetti," Lorraine says. "People tell me, you can't feed dogs like that, but right after they're done with their snacks they all run right over to their beds like, 'Okay, we're ready to go to sleep now,' and off they go."

Junior feeds the four dogs Keebler shortbread sandies from the package.

"Junior, don't you dare feed them my Fig Newtons," Lorraine protests.

"They don't like your Fig Newtons," Junior answers.

Then he tosses a Fig Newton to the three-legged dog.

Lorraine has a similar soft spot for the children along her bus route. She knows everyone by name, knows which houses and parents are theirs. I'm along for the ride one day, and I see how she coos from her driver's seat as she passes a mother taking memento photographs of her children at the bus stop on the first day of school.

But Lorraine worries. At stop after stop, where students usually wait, she finds no one. "I guess his mother is taking him to school today," she says. "Or not."

She looks into her rearview mirror at a dozen or so riders. "I guess nobody's coming to school this year," she says. Is it the pandemic? She can't say.

At the next stop, she tells me, "This little girl is just starting school. She's a kindergartener. Good morning!" she says. "I like the way Mommy did your hair."

At the last stop Lorraine sighs. In the past, the bus with room for eighty-four students was filled. Today there are only twenty-nine passengers. (And no stray dogs.)

"There's no young people anymore," she says. "Our little town is dying. When I was young, this was a hopping and bopping kind of place. It's sad, really."

Talk about her animals restores her smile, all those creatures come and gone—like dogs Ringer and Ruff, Nicky and Molly, not to mention those damned cats, a few of whom are crafty enough to turn the house's front door handle and let themselves in.

Lorraine tells about the day she learned that the reservation clinic was offering free spaying and neutering. "I loaded up the station wagon with cats to take them out to the rez to get fixed," she says. "That car was just a meowing machine, cats in the back seats and trunk, cats in cardboard boxes and metal containers."

She laughs. "One escaped, but I managed to catch it."

Another kitten climbed into the clinic's rafters, and it took three men with nets to catch it. "If we aren't just the biggest joke of a little town," she says, "then I don't know what is."

I've done my best to befriend Mac, Shuggie, Tater, and Tickie. But the dogs still bark at me like I'm some stranger or a passing pickup—even the three-legged one.

Meanwhile the cats stick to themselves.

Lorraine Alcorta grew up in a McDermitt markedly different from the alcohol-fueled party Herman Hereford described in his town history.

Her McDermitt was underaged, a place that didn't get telephones until the 1950s, a place where residents didn't have to go to Winnemucca for food;

Fig. 12. Lorraine Huttman with one of her dogs. Photograph by Randi Lynn Beach.

they had cattle and the crops they raised. If they couldn't grow it or raise it, they bought it at the Quinn River Merc.

While the town barflies drank, Lorraine's generation danced at those same saloons. "We square-danced and did the twist when it came in," she says. "Always to live music." She recalls one dance in junior high where a musician played an accordion, with cymbals dangling between his legs and a harmonica in his mouth. He rolled around the Orveda Dance Club on skates, playing oompah music. "We had fun," she says.

She was a second grader when reservation children began attending school in McDermitt. A few years later, Paiutes outnumbered whites, but Lorraine rarely interacted with Native children, and McDermitt residents seldom set foot on the reservation. McDermitt was a segregated place like the rest of America.

Her Basque parents, Bernardo and Emilia, owned the gas station and store on the Oregon side of town and kept a strict eye on their daughter. She had to be home each night by 9:00 p.m., and Bernardo even set an alarm to remind himself.

There wasn't all that much to do, anyway, other than watch the last policeman ever posted in McDermitt, who sat in his vehicle along the highway and never moved—not even if a car whizzed past at 80 miles an hour. The kids called him "Petrified."

In McDermitt in the 1950s, sex was a closeted concept. As a high school freshman, Lorraine waitressed at the State Line Cafe and one day noticed a business card some traveler had left. It had his name on one side and something unspeakable on the other.

"A picture of people having sex," she recalls. "I gasped. That's how it's done? That's *gross*! I had no idea." The next year, one of Lorraine's classmates fainted in biology class when the teacher showed a film on the human reproduction process.

By then Lorraine had met a young boy everybody knew as Junior Huttman. She wasn't exactly impressed. "He was just kind of there," she recalls.

Junior's family had moved to nearby Orovada from Woodland, California, in 1960 and he already hated the place. "The wind would come up, and the whole valley would be a cloud of dust," he says. "You couldn't see your hand in front of your face."

His father ran a crop-dusting business and owned a fleet of small planes. Junior wanted to fly as well, but he preferred commercial planes, not crop dusters. "I told my father that was a crazy man's business. You had to fly right along the ground and under power lines. That's not the occupation I wanted." Junior's father never taught him to fly. He later learned commercial flying on his own.

Lorraine says she met Junior at an eighth-grade dance. He was with his friend Benny Baker, who'd set his sights on her.

"I wasn't there," Junior interrupts.

"Yes, you were! Benny introduced me to you!"

"Oh."

I ask Lorraine what she wore that night.

"You were in pants," Junior says.

"So you remember me then!" Lorraine blurts.

"I didn't want to admit it."

"Whatever," she says. "I danced with Benny all night, anyway."

Benny also walked her home. They came through the back gate of the property I now rent. When a dog barked, Lorraine's grandmother looked out the window. Just then, Benny was kissing her granddaughter. "I don't even think it was on the mouth; he just reached over and kissed my cheek," Lorraine explains. "The next day my grandmother had a talk with me."

Lorraine walks in from the adjacent kitchen, wiping her hands on a cloth. "Did I overcook those eggs?" she asks.

Her mind returns to Benny. "I thought he was cute."

Junior is silent, brooding.

He begins a story about his bachelor days, but Lorraine misses a few words. "What?"

"Bachelor!" he repeats. "Do you need a Roto-Rooter for your ears?"

Talk turns to their first date. "We just got in the same car, riding around," Junior says.

"Junior, don't you remember? It was your mother's car! The one you tried to hide when you asked me out."

"That old Ford Falcon station wagon?" he asks. "Are you kidding me? A boy in high school cruising around in the family car?"

Junior later earned the inside track to Lorraine's attentions through an unlikely intermediary: her strict father. "Older boys in McDermitt wouldn't mess with me; they wouldn't even ask me out," she says.

"Your dad had 'em scared."

"Yeah."

But that didn't stop Lorraine. Waiting tables at the White Horse, she checked out the boys. "I remember one who wouldn't even kiss me, and I know exactly why," she says.

"They probably figured your dad was looking out the window," Junior deadpans.

But the Huttman boy was different; he was the only one who wasn't afraid to come to the family's door. Once, Bernardo rushed outside with a shotgun pointed at the boy's head. "I kept walking," Junior recalls, "and he said, 'Ha! I was just trying to kid you.'"

By then Junior was a successful hurdler for the high school track team. Lorraine's father complimented him after one race. Bernardo liked him. "He started pushing me toward Junior," Lorraine says. "And I was like, 'No! He never talks. I don't even know him. He just struts by. His nose is in the air all the time!'"

She pauses. "Anybody want milk for their coffee? Tickie, get outta here!"

After Lorraine graduated from McDermitt High in 1967, she attended business school in Boise and briefly worked at a bank in Winnemucca. Then she came home. "I never thought of leaving," she says. "This was home. I came home to Mom and Dad."

The two corresponded while Junior attended college at the University of Nevada in Reno for two years, studying geology and education.

"Did we write letters?" Lorraine asks.

"Well, there was a telephone, but I don't remember calling you."

"There weren't cell phones then, so I couldn't have called you either."

When they married, the couple moved into a mobile home on Junior's family farm in Orovada, where they stayed for fifteen years. Then Lorraine began running her parents' service station while Junior flew planes to help farmers with their pest spraying.

Over the years, the couple's children worked in the station store, learning to count out change for customers, making their parents proud. But McDermitt was changing.

Early one morning after a snowfall, Junior found his back door shattered. He followed the tracks to a house where the living room was full of passed-out McDermitt teens who'd stolen several cases of beer and some beef jerky.

Small-town justice took it from there. A judge in Winnemucca made the boys write an apology letter, which was published in the local newspaper, along with their pictures. Each was also directed to give Junior $120 to cover his losses. Then something happened that helped to restore Junior's faith in human nature.

A reservation teen came to the station to admit that he, too, had been involved in the break-in but didn't get caught. He apologized and handed Junior $120 in cash.

Years later the couple sold the station and store. But Junior stays busy. He reports the daily high and low temperatures to the National Weather Service in Winnemucca.

"Where's your recording station?" I ask.

"Right there," he says, pointing out the back window. "That little box."

Lorraine explains how the collection process *really* works: "When it rains or snows, *I'm* the one who has to go there," she says.

When it's cold, Lorraine complains about going out to measure the overnight snowfall. That's when Junior gives in. "Okay," he'll say. "We'll just call it a trace."

We have tortured voices, Lorraine and I, like two coyotes in a gospel choir. We stand inside the tiny Baptist church, belting out the lyrics to "Come, Thou Long Expected Jesus" as traffic speeds past along U.S. Highway 95 on the way to somewhere else.

Lorraine is a volunteer force behind this chapel. I'm a first-timer, here to meet Dave Lewis, the resident pastor at the Quinn River Baptist Fellowship. I'd warned Lorraine to steer clear of me: God might cast down his own lightning bolt as a message to a failed Roman Catholic. But Lorraine is heaven-sent. She stands beside me, looking to see that my hymnal isn't upside-down, as out-of-place as I am here.

Such houses of worship were woven into the region's cultural fabric when the first wagon trains jounced through here, full of rugged individualists en route toward the mighty Pacific and the promise of a better life. It wasn't just Brigham Young and his Mormon pioneers who came in search of the promised land, but priests, ministers, and missionaries, all focused on saving the souls of the Natives who already lived here.

McDermitt's first church was built in the 1940s by Basque Catholics. A Mormon temple opened for awhile, and the former Assembly of God church was rebranded in 2022 by Korean Presbyterians. Then there's the Baptist church, a small white chapel that's been in Lorraine's care for thirty-five years.

In the 1960s, a group of youths showed up and hammered together the little chapel in a few days, Amish-style, its stained glass windows showing images of God in all the colors of the rainbow. As the years passed, Lorraine pitched in to handle the cleaning and yard work, making sure the chapel didn't fall into disrepair.

She asked Junior to tag along, of course. She could have used another pair of hands, but she soon learned that getting him to go anywhere near that chapel was like dragging a bull into the barn.

She quickly found that it wasn't just the chapel that needed watching, but the pastors themselves. Few worthy holy men wanted to come to such a remote place. For years the tiny congregation sent letters to a national Baptist association and would receive the résumés of the available parsons. Lorraine and others reviewed the applications, praying they'd make the right choice.

But not all prayers are answered. In 2006 Pastor Sonny arrived.

The full-faced Alabama transplant raised eyebrows as he uttered inappropriate sexual remarks, banging his fists on the pulpit, angry one day, sullen and distant the next. "We didn't know what to do," Lorraine says. "But nobody had the willpower to stand up to him and say 'This is not acceptable.'"

When Pastor Sonny's wife passed away, he announced that he was looking for a new mate. He told worshippers that he wanted a woman with red hair and even rattled off her preferred measurements, 36-24-36.

Congregants took note. "It was time to get rid of this donkey," Lorraine says. One day Lorraine's daughter called. "Is your pastor a drinker?" she asked. *That and a lot of other things*, Lorraine thought.

"Well, he's been arrested for pulling a gun on somebody in a road rage incident near Reno," Lorraine's daughter continued. "And it's going to be on TV tonight."

That evening Lorraine watched in horror as Pastor Sonny was led into court dressed in a red jail jumpsuit. He'd been charged with assault and carrying a concealed .40 caliber handgun during a run-in with a motorcyclist.

That was it for Pastor Sonny. Soon came a succession of more God-fearing pastors who all eventually moved on. Little McDermitt, this gas stop on the road to somewhere else, couldn't hold on to a Baptist preacher to save its life.

Then Pastor Dave Lewis and his wife, Ashley, arrived in 2016. Both had previously worked in law enforcement; Dave is a former Nevada highway patrolman, and Ashley worked in parole and probation.

At the one service I attended, Dave wears a red flannel shirt—tail out—beneath a black suit coat and pants, the vivid stained-glass window behind his pulpit the color of the sky and the clouds. In his late thirties, standing 6-foot-3 and weighing 285 pounds, he's a bearish man with deep a baritone voice who began growing his chest-length beard the moment he shed his trooper's uniform.

Ashley has her long hair pulled back into a bun, wearing a homespun floral dress as she sits with the couple's five children: four tousled-haired boys (half a Bulldogs football team) and a blonde-haired two-year-old daughter named Haley. Dave uses Bluetooth to trigger an electronic organ backup. His children know the lyrics to all the hymns, and they aren't afraid to call out if their father has cited the wrong page in the hymnal.

The couple's struggles are real. Before they found their faith, they'd almost divorced. Now they live without health insurance and miss big city comforts. Before he quit law enforcement, Dave arrested a parishioner for drunk driving

Fig. 13. Pastor Dave Lewis in the study of his chapel
outside town. Photograph by Randi Lynn Beach.

right after services let out. On the morning I attend, there's only a handful
of us inside the church. Covid has chased away worshippers, especially the
Paiute families Dave tries so hard to attract.

But with Lorraine's help, Dave and Ashley are staying put.

After services, I stop by Lorraine's house for coffee. We agree that our
new goal as Christians is to get stubborn Junior to grace the doors of that
little chapel. But Junior has his own relationship with God and doesn't feel
the need to howl any holy tunes on Sunday mornings to please *his* maker.

But Lorraine does. She loves everything about Pastor Dave and his services,
except her singing voice. And mine.

It's 9:00 a.m. on Labor Day when I walk past the White Horse, once the cra-
ziest place in town when McDermitt had a bigger heartbeat.

Junior and Lorraine are taking me to visit their 1,100-acre spread they
call Rancho Pobre. The place was named by Lorraine's grandfather who
pioneered the land for cattle and sheep more than a century ago. The ranch
is one reason they've remained here after their children left. Now Lorraine
wants to move in full-time, so Junior is clearing space with his bulldozer for
a new modular home.

As I approach their house in town, Junior races by on his four-wheeler. Then it hits me: Where are the dogs? The boys—as Junior calls them. They're usually barking.

Lorraine greets me in the yard with an explanation of the breakout: an hour earlier, Junior had driven off to meet the beekeeper from Boise who keeps more than a hundred hives on the couple's property. For some reason the bees do well in this area, possibly due to the abundance of greasewood, sagebrush, and buckbush.

That's when Tater and Tickie bolted, and Junior, upon his return, was beside himself, circling the neighborhood on a last-minute hound hunt.

"Those two knuckleheads shot out of here like a cannon," Lorraine says of the dogs.

They usually run out to the fields, sniff around, bark at the birds and snakes, do their business, and then come home. But not today, and Junior is worried. "Those are his kids," Lorraine says as two kittens climb a nearby power pole.

Junior returns without the dogs. He worries they've been shot by ranchers who don't take kindly to stray dogs that start chasing their horses and cattle. We hop into the couple's pickup. I'm in the back with Mac the dog.

"He'll get hair all over you," Lorraine warns. "Oh, just look at that hair; we live in the old West. My dad would be turning in his grave if he saw the back seat of this pickup truck."

Junior looks over at his wife. "Lorraine, your dad's in the grave, been there a long time. No need to worry." Junior is thinking about his boys.

We drive several backstreets as Junior keeps his eyes straight, scanning yards and lots for those pesky dogs. "If they're not back by now, there's something wrong," he says like a worried father. "They're not coming back. Somebody put traps out on 'em."

"Oh, Junior," Lorraine says.

For now we suspend our search to head out to the ranch. Four miles north of town, we turn onto a dirt road. Lorraine is quiet now. She relaxes once she's in wilder country. We pull up to a locked gate. "This is Rancho Pobre," she announces. "Poor Ranch."

She hops out to open the padlock. Junior stays behind the wheel. I thought he might be sheepish for not doing the task himself, but he isn't embarrassed at all. "Why do you think I took her out here?" he whispers.

Mac jumps out of the truck cab and takes off like a furry brown-and-white bullet.

"Those two knotheads," Junior says of the missing dogs. "They'd be running here too." There's a wistfulness to his voice. "I doubt they'll come home. I'll be surprised."

Back inside the truck Lorraine explains that her grandfather lived on the ranch while her grandmother lived in town to raise the kids. He might have been lonely at times, but that's just how it was. We ease into a small valley to find a spread of buildings and a water tank that Junior moved out here years ago.

So why do they need another house? Junior points at his wife. At 2,400 square feet the new place might convince her children to move back home to raise their own kids.

"Well, how long are you gonna live in it?" he asks. "Until you kick the bucket?"

"I don't care," Lorraine says.

The money could be better spent on one of those new small planes he's got his eye on.

Junior has already dug culverts and bridges and fixed roofs blown off in storms. But there's always more work. "If I was twenty years younger," he marvels, "the things I'd do."

"Well, I want two new metal gates," Lorraine says. "But it ain't happening."

"Oh, honey."

"Don't give me that honey crap."

Lorraine helped Junior put the new roof on the cabin porch.

"She was my slave labor." Junior winks.

"Well, that project almost led to divorce," Lorraine says. "I've never been yelled at so loud and so often in all my life."

"Honey," Junior says in his defense. "I just didn't want you to get yourself hurt."

The moment the couple arrives at the hacienda, Junior checks a trap he puts out to catch the mice that have taken to chewing things around the cabin. There's a ramp where the mice can walk up to the brim of a little bucket. They nibble at a dab of peanut butter before falling into the standing water below.

Junior opens the container lid to find a dead rat the size of a small cat.

"It's huge!" Lorraine exclaims.

"He *is* a big bugger," Junior says, holding it by the tail.

It's the third rat they've caught after Lorraine found rodent droppings and gnawed wires in the pickup. Well, that takes care of that. Now it's back to the good life.

The couple sit inside the cabin and count their country blessings. Junior bought the place when it was located in town from a Reno dentist who hunted near McDermitt. But professional movers wanted $5,000 and a bunch of permits to relocate the building out to the ranch. So Junior got some cronies together, put wheels under the frame, and just pulled the house out here with his tractor. Now it's a little bit of rural heaven, out under the stars.

"What are you going to do out here?" I ask Lorraine.

"Whatever I feel like," she says.

"Ah, she'll be in hog heaven," Junior says. "She'll be living with me."

"That could be the problem," Lorraine says.

On the way back to town, Junior is quiet, his mind on his boys. When we reach the house, they're still gone. I hop out of the truck, feeling sorry for Junior: He's been robbed of a simple pleasure—the companionship of a good dog or two. Or four.

Then later he telephones me. The boys are back in town. Who knows where they've been?

But they're home now. And so am I.

awaken before dawn, fuel up on gas and coffee, and head south along U.S. 95. The sun is rising over Red Mountain, and long slants of light shoot across a raw landscape, lending the tarmac dew a diamond sparkle. Grazing cows ignore me as I pass.

I'm driving 265 miles southeast to Eureka, a Nevada mining town whose fortunes shine as brightly as the coming dawn compared to dullish McDermitt. In Eureka, mining bolsters the local economy with an enviable tax base that has built numerous edifices, including a state-of-the-art high school football field, the home of the Eureka Vandals.

Home to 1,200 residents, the community was founded by five Civil War–era prospectors who unearthed a rock containing silver-lead ore in a place called Horse Thief Canyon, quickly creating the West's newest boomtown.

Settlers called it Eureka from the same Greek term meaning "I have found it!" and by 1873 the new community became Nevada's second-largest city. The promise of riches lured ten thousand Italian, Basque, Irish, and Chinese immigrant laborers, who were soon joined by itinerant gamblers, hustlers, and hangers-on who crowded into a town with 125 saloons, 25 gambling halls, and a handful of brothels. There were also doctors, lawyers, surveyors, railroad men, and three newspapers. After both fire and flood devastated Eureka in its early years, residents promptly rebuilt grand buildings. The town bloomed once again like a stubborn sagebrush. Many of those buildings remain today, including an ornate opera house that hosts the annual Christmas dinner, the biggest social event in town.

Mining money also supports Eureka's high school sports programs. Completed in 2010, the $1.5 million Grant Crutchley football and track facility, named after a beloved former coach, features a modern athletic center, field lighting, and a synthetic playing surface—all financed by pit operators. Ranch families chipped in as well, proving the claim that Eureka is not actually a mining town but a town *with* mining. Officials pushed for artificial turf, for both easy care and simple pride, to show visitors they were on a special field in a special town.

Down the hill from the football field lies the lavish $14 million Vandal Athletic Center, with a basketball court, an indoor track, and dining facilities, which hosts statewide tournaments. The Vandals are whisked to away games in a bus fit for a rock band, with plush seats, a bathroom, and Wi-Fi hookup, a ride that beats McDermitt's chug-a-lug yellow school bus hands down.

Meanwhile, with school classrooms that are decades old, albeit still in good shape, I wondered about the choice to invest such a fortune into athletics over education. Maybe the thinking is that there's always more mining money where that came from. And who can blame them?

At $200,000, Eureka's annual athletic budget is more than three times that of McDermitt's $60,000 fund. In Eureka Egan sees just what money can buy.

In a few days the high school will host its annual homecoming celebration that includes pep rallies, a bonfire, a nighttime football game, and a snake dance—where students parade through town, cheered by smiling locals and befuddled visitors.

In the kingdom of rural Nevada scholastic football, these Vandals are the moneyed *haves*, the Bulldogs the less fortunate *have-nots*. But I also want to talk with officials at a high school where students are literally the *have-nothings*.

The tiny town of Jackpot, located on the border of Nevada and Idaho, was founded in 1954 after the potato state banned gambling. But Nevada casino operators lacked the generosity of their mining brethren, and the Jackpot High School Jaguars suffered as a result.

Averaging just fifty students in grades 9–12, the school battled underfunding, lack of interest, and a litany of losses. Finally in 2015 the air hissed out of the ball entirely: Jackpot killed its football program. Brian Messmer, the school principal and former assistant football coach laments, "The kids just didn't want to play anymore."

That fact is lost on neither Egan nor Smith, who know their own program could soon join Jackpot on the scholastic scrap heap.

The sun is up now. To reach Eureka, I face a 73-mile stretch to reach Winnemucca, followed by a 90-mile jaunt along Interstate 80, until I head south on Nevada State Route 278, where I go miles without spying another living soul. Only then, on U.S. Highway 50, celebrated for its remoteness, do I finally find Eureka, a place that bills itself as the "Friendliest Town on the Loneliest Road in America."

Suddenly I'm in Vandals country.

At the Owl Club Bar and Steakhouse, there are "Vandals" specials celebrating the team mascot, a stern Viking lookalike with a horned helmet, based on the tribes that sacked Rome in the fifth century. A gas station bears the team's green and yellow colors.

It's all part of a passion that McDermitt once had but lost, slipping from its grasp like so much gold dust.

At the team's afternoon football practice, the youthful Vandals run drills as a cohesive group, calling out mantras like polished U.S. Marine Corps recruits. Superintendent Tate Else and principal Jeff Evans watch the boys like investors sizing up their latest Kentucky Derby two-year-old.

The sturdy Else, a weekend rodeo rider, explains how the homecoming was nearly sabotaged by Covid. Days before, the Owyhee Braves forfeited the scheduled game when a player got sick. The move threatened a Eureka tradition now extinct in many towns, a celebration of high school and all the memories those years evoke.

Eureka founded its basketball program in the 1920s. For a few years during the Great Depression, they became the Bulldogs—and for a short time the Jackrabbits—before reviving the more intimidating Vandal. In 1948, as the school launched a budding football program, victories were few. Two years later the Vandals didn't win a single game "or even come reasonably close," reports the school's yearbook.

"Nevertheless the Vandals can still hold their heads because even though they did not gather the fruits of victory they can never be accused of 'giving up,'" the yearbook proclaims. "No school with Eureka's twenty-plus enrollment can, year after year, compete on equal terms with schools with three and four times that number . . . There is nothing we can do now except come back in '51 with grim determination to win after having had our 'bad year' in 1950."

Ensuing years featured a booster club known as the "Pepperettes," straight from a Norman Rockwell painting, whose mission was to provide a "yelling section" for games and cook dinner for visiting teams.

By 1980, says Rich McKay, a Eureka County commissioner, the annual bonfire was central to the homecoming party, and students would dismantle local outhouses to provide wood for the blaze. "They did it every year," he says, before adding, "Pretty soon you ran out of outhouses."

A decade later, with the snake dance in full swing, downtown bars hid their pool equipment because each year some sticky-fingered student would swipe some pool balls as a prank. "You just carry those memories with you for your whole lifetime," McKay says. "They're such sweet small-town recollections."

The Owyhee forfeit threatened all that. So Else and his staff got on the phone, wheeling and dealing with officials and coaches statewide, calling in favors, seeing what could be done to salvage the weekend.

They got answers from varsity teams from Elko and Battle Mountain, though neither fully committed despite Eureka officials offering to feed them dinner and provide a school bus for the trip. The alternative was unthinkable: either host a homecoming without a football game or resort to an inter-squad scrimmage.

Both teams eventually bowed out. At the last moment Elko's freshman squad agreed to play. The Eureka High School 2021 homecoming and football fiesta were on.

As they patrol the practice field, Vandals head coach Fred Minoletti and assistant Josh Auch resemble deer hunters in flannel vests, blue jeans, and brimmed sports caps. They both played here twenty-five years ago when Auch was quarterback and Minoletti played fullback. Back then few players realized the Vandal team mascot was based on a historical figure infamous for pillaging great cities. "We just saw a warrior," Minoletti says, "a person who does not give up."

Minoletti's father worked for the county roads department. His older brother, Gio, also played Vandals football. When Fred graduated, he went to college at the University of Nevada, Las Vegas and taught in Clark County for six years.

Eureka is no different than most small communities. Graduating seniors yearn to break free of the same old faces, gossip, and nosey neighbors. But what sets the town apart is this: Many people come back. Like the Minoletti boys.

Now forty-three, Fred teaches social studies in the same classroom where he was once a student. For a few seasons Gio helped call the shots on the football and basketball sidelines. In Eureka, coaches aren't only friends but relatives.

Fred went 1-6 in his first year as football coach, so he knows what it's like to lose. He's since won twice as many games as he's lost, fielding teams fed by an endless string of new talent: the sons of miners hired in the local pits.

Auch grew up on a local ranch and later went on to play college football at Minot State University in North Dakota, a team whose mascot, Buckshot the Beaver, was decidedly less threatening than a Vandal. He returned to

Eureka in 2008 for a mining job and soon worked in the high school maintenance department. "I have lots of family here," he says. "I love this town, and I want my kids to be raised here rather than in some big city, because we know what happens there."

Now the pair has teamed up again as Vandals. "Fred asked me to be his assistant," Auch recalls. "And I said, 'You're danged right.'"

Both coaches have sons who play, making Auch roll his eyes. "Even if he is your boy, kids can be real asses," he says. "You can't favor them. Mostly I want to chew his ass out. So Fred and I have a system: he takes care of mine, and I take care of his."

A light snow falls as the Vandals scrimmage. One gives another a chippy shot; the downed boy springs up, yelling, "Kiss my ass!" Auch steps in like a police dog loosed from its patrol car. "I'll kick your ass right off the field. Would you talk that way to your coach? Then don't talk like that to each other."

He continues his tirade. "That's just horseshit. Family doesn't do that. There better not be any more disrespect, or you'll be talking to me. When you go on defense, pay the fuck attention. We don't know if you're on your guy or not when all you're doing is blah, blah, blah. And then you say, 'Coach, I wasn't paying attention.' Well, no shit."

Suddenly he softens. "The only way we're going to get to our ultimate goal is together."

The players don't dare crack a smile. They're as humbled as a fifth-century city that's just fallen victim to a hoard of Vandals.

Later I join a pep rally in the school's old gym, a tiny bandbox with wooden bleachers, located near the main office. The stands are packed with 150 people—gaggles of teens and parents watch toddlers run across the polished court. The team's mascot looks cartoonish in a green horned helmet, furry boots and a skirt, a mask, and a fake beard, fooling no one with any attempts at ferocity.

Principal Jeff Evans looks on. Nearing sixty, he's a martial artist who once taught bilingual education in Las Vegas before moving to several northern Nevada schools. "Eureka is a special place where everybody knows everybody," he says. "I know every kid here, and most of their parents know me."

Later, as Evans gives me a tour of the $14 million Eureka County School District Gymnasium and Recreation Facility, completed in 2014, I feel like an awe-inspired Dorothy in Oz. The building has the town's only elevator and is so lush that the senior prom is held there. But why does a small town require a 42,000-square-foot monument to wealth?

The answer: because they can afford it.

There's a collective will to create something lasting, a place to brag about. "We hosted a regional volleyball tournament that brought coaches from state-wide," Evans says. "Some complained they had to travel way out to central Nevada. I was here when one coach walked in, and I heard him say, 'Now I understand why we're playing in Eureka.'"

The center is a contemporary mix of metal, brick, glass, and concrete, flooded with natural light, sunk into the side of a hill. Reno-based architect Jack Hawkins says he found it odd to design a sports temple in the "geographical center of nowhere."

"They had all this mining money and needed to spend it," he says. "They don't have a lot of community spaces, so building something on that scale is visionary." Hawkins used what he called a "derelict" piece of land with a fifty-foot drop-off that had no other use, wedging the building into the hillside. Like an iceberg, most of the structure is hidden from the eye.

Challenges included harsh central Nevada winters and sheer isolation. Most contractors came from urban areas, and few wanted to spend months in such a small town. But Hawkins hails the results as something that will outlive everyone in town.

Eureka needs such calling cards. While they offer salaries competitive with the state's big cities, the school has lost candidates to a lack of housing and its isolation. Natives who return are more accepting. They know what Eureka has to offer.

Amanda Rosener fled in 2001 after finishing high school. "I was so tired of the drama, where everyone knows what you did before you did it, people saying, 'You kissed Jimmy, didn't you?'" She returned in 2011 to work as a secretary for the school counselor. Rosener has four children, aged seven to thirteen, and she now appreciates that people know her business: "If you have an issue, people find out and support you."

Rich McKay also couldn't wait to leave town. I met the county council-man inside the Eureka courthouse, a building that—like Eureka itself—has changed with the times. The original building was fashioned from a former ice-skating rink donated by a judge shortly after Eureka County was estab-lished in 1873. Like many town buildings it was made of wood, and when a fire three years later ravaged the town, the courthouse was replaced with something more lasting.

Today the elegant red-brick edifice, one of Nevada's best-preserved public spaces, features a front door flanked by two bells imported from Cincinnati and San Francisco. In the second-floor courtroom, the judge's bench and witness box are built from Spanish cedar, providing an Old West flair to trials involving car thefts and drug busts.

McKay grew up on a cattle ranch 40 miles south of town. He played football under legendary coach Grant Crutchley, an all-American at Elko High School before he went to Vietnam, where he served as an army helicopter door gunner who was shot down twice. Coming to Eureka County High School in 1969, Crutchley served as a teacher, principal, athletic director, coach, and activity bus driver until he retired in 1992. His favorite saying: "Win, lose, or draw, as long as you give 100 percent and come out with a good taste in your mouth, that's all that matters." For a kid McKay's age, Crutchley seemed as ancient as that old Eureka courthouse. "He was no-nonsense," McKay says. "If you messed up, he'd give you a slap on your helmet he called 'knowledge knocks.'"

McKay "escaped" in 1982. He says Eureka's biggest exports have always been gold, alfalfa, hay, and its kids. "Either you could work the ranch or starve in the mines," he says. He worked a tech job in San Francisco and each summer brought his wife and three children back to the family ranch. When a good friend committed suicide from pressures at work, McKay reassessed his life. "I went home that night and told my wife, 'We're out of here. Let's take the kids and go.'"

In 2014 the couple purchased the Sundown Lodge and continued the ranch life McKay knew as a boy. But living full-time in Eureka was different than visiting in the good summer weather. There were long winters and an economy tied to mining. McKay soon asked himself whether he'd made a mistake. But he persevered. His children—Alexander, fourteen, and eleven-year-old twins Anna and Lucas—fit in with the rural crowd. Not only that but McKay has relatives here: Vandals coach Fred Minoletti is his nephew. "I'd traveled all over the country, but Eureka is a place you come home to."

Yet no small town is perfect. The pits attract a breed of worker locals know as "tramp miners," young nomads who cram a family of five into a small trailer on the outskirts of town, a life that leads to student truancy and domestic strife. At any time, 30 percent of Eureka students are the children of transient miners, and the town now has its share of drug and alcohol problems. That's where Eureka's homegrown kids come into play. "I've seen local kids reach out to newcomers and help them adjust. But they don't put up with drugs. So many of these miner's sons fit in, and others don't."

Through it all, the Vandals just keep winning.

Brian Messmer has witnessed the death of a rural football program. The former Jackpot High School principal and assistant football coach of the Jackpot Jaguars compares it to the loss of an aging uncle who one day can't get out of bed.

In Jackpot—unlike Eureka—there is no money. With a few casinos and eight hundred residents, athletic funding is just not there. The gambling bosses would kick in a few thousand each year, but it was never enough.

In 1958 Jackpot was called Horse Shu when it was established as an unincorporated community. Located 47 miles south of Twin Falls, Idaho, and its fifty thousand residents, Jackpot has always felt more akin to Idaho than Nevada, where the nearest town, Wells, is more than twice that distance along the Great Basin Highway.

When Messmer arrived in 1993, the school boasted 360 students in grades K–12. By 2021 enrollment had fallen to 125. With rural gaming in decline, many Jackpot residents returned to Twins Falls for opportunities. The number of players dwindled. The losses piled up. Messmer joined a six-man league in Idaho as a way to preserve his teetering program, but Nevada league officials later blocked that participation.

"The kids got their asses handed to them every week," he says. He recalls one game where one Jaguar broke his leg. "I was there on the sidelines. I heard the other team laughing, their coach egging them on," he says. "I had to ride home with that kid. I saw what disgrace does to a boy."

The program's demise touched Messmer as both a father and a coach. In 2013 his son Isaac was a freshman who'd watched older brother, Ben, enjoy four years playing Jaguars football. Now the former team ball boy had a chance to create his own story.

For Messmer, guiding two sons on the football field is the biggest thrill a coach can have. He'd just bought Isaac a new pair of cleats when two players quit the team, forcing him to forfeit the boy's freshman season.

"It sucked," recalls Isaac, now an accountant in Nampa, Idaho. The Jaguars forfeited Isaac's sophomore year as well. In 2015 the program was killed. By then Messer had given up coaching but was still a Jaguar principal and father. The team's equipment sat moldering on shelves, moving beyond its shelf life. "Without a benefactor, it was just impossible for us to get things going again."

Isaac still feels the loss. He'd grown up on the football field, chasing balls, hitting tackling dummies. Mostly he remembers all the losing but also how good it felt when the Jaguars won, how it gave every kid on that bench a sense of hope.

"My brother ended his season with a torn meniscus, so I know football comes with injuries. Who knows if I'd have gotten hurt as well, hitting heads every week? Freaky stuff comes with the game. Still, I wish I'd gotten to play."

Brian Messmer retired in 2022 but continues to drive past that patch of green where people now walk their pets. "Gosh, I miss it," he says. "Those games were just a lot of fun."

The Eureka Vandals are once again under the stadium lights that bounce off the glossy finish of their helmets and accentuate the rich color of the turf, giving the scene a touch of high school football magic.

On the cold October night a few hundred fans wear gloves and wool hats, stamping their feet to keep warm. Girls run the sidelines with flushed cheeks painted in the hometown colors. Little keeps this crowd from celebrating its hometown boys.

The Vandals win the coin toss against the Elko freshmen; they win just about everything on this night. The young kids from another mining town up the road are no match for a Vandals machine that will finish the season 6-1. They will more than double the point totals of their opponents in making the state playoffs for yet another year. The Vandals are simply bigger and more athletic. Within minutes they return an Elko punt for a touchdown, then their quarterback knives through for a 2-point conversion.

"There we go," says a boy in a Vandals-themed jacket, eating from a plate of nachos. The onslaught is on. I imagine being in the Roman Colosseum watching Christians face certain death. This isn't going to be pretty, and I find myself rooting for the Elko boys.

The crowd gasps at a big hit delivered by a Vandal that sends one boy flying. "Ohhhhh."

Three sturdy miners stand side by side. "Would you be afraid to hit a freshman?" one asks his friend. "Hell no!" he says. Then he raises his arms. "Touchdown Vandals!"

I run into eighty-year-old Jim Ithuralde, a Eureka institution. For thirty years he served as the voice of the Vandals, perched up in the press box, his voice echoing off the darkened hills beyond. "I announced kids from Little League through high school, including both of these coaches," he says proudly. He tried to correctly pronounce the name of every player, recalling how an announcer had slaughtered his Basque surname back in high school. "I tried to be as professional as I could. I didn't take sides."

Until the night he was exposed by a live microphone. "Well, that was *bullshit*," he'd said, following a controversial call against the Vandals. "The entire Eureka side got up and applauded me. Still, I apologized to the refs after the game." He retired three years ago. "Thirty years is pretty good," he says. "Time to let younger people step up. But I was proud of all those boys on that field. I still am."

Hours later I'm sitting at the Owl Club Bar, nursing my second pint of Great Basin ale, waiting for the Eureka High School snake dance to wind its way through the tavern. Somebody grabs the cue ball off each of the three pool tables. "They better not touch my Yahtzee game," one drinker warns.

"What was the score of the game anyway?" the bartender asks.

"I don't know," someone answers. "A lot to nothing."

We hear the approaching melee: a line of exuberant youth that starts at the fire station and ends inside a gas station minimart. Then they're upon us, sixty teens in an undulating line, none old enough to drink alcohol here. I turn on my barstool and high-five several rushing past. The boys hit hard; the girls offer a feathery touch. Just like that, they're gone, but you can hear the ruckus continue down the street.

I walk outside to watch the orange light of the bonfire just south of town. The glow reminds me of the smelters that burned here 150 years ago, blackening the skies as men tried to crack the code to extract minerals from this hardened landscape.

On this night the fire is different. It burns with the colors of Vandals' spirit. Eureka has found was Jackpot has lost, a sense of spirit McDermitt feels slipping from its grasp.

14

As a girl, Alice Crutcher rode horses. A half century later she recalls the heady thrill and independence of those outings. Slight and agile, just ninety-five pounds, she galloped hard atop a perceptive, wild-hearted creature that always seemed to know the way.

She and a friend would saddle up in the reservation's predawn chill and race for the mountains that loomed to the east, into the uncompromising blackness from which the sun would rise. With only an apple for lunch, drinking water from streams, the two Paiute girls went where their horses and imaginations took them, returning only at dusk. If her older brothers had taken the family's only saddle, Alice rode bareback. Anything that offered her escape, to enter the respected realm of the antelope and the deer, as her people have done for generations.

"Let's go see what's on the other side," Alice would say. Bolting off, her friend would call back, "I see trees. Let's keep going!"

In the 1960s, before TVs or telephones, reservation life centered around open space. Alice's father, Wesa, a tribal judge and rancher, was a disciplinarian who made sure his three boys and three girls did their chores—care for the horses, sheep, and chickens, cook, iron, and clean—before they could wander off into that great outdoors. At night they ate their dinners together as a family.

The kids called him "the Sarge."

Alice was a tough girl who threw rocks at boys she didn't like. As she got older she still preferred horses to boyfriends. As she did her beadwork and embroidery, her mother, Hazel, counseled her on the way a young Paiute girl should conduct herself—things to do and *not* to do. "You either take the crooked road or the straight road," the Sarge told his daughters. The crooked road meant boyfriends. Alice took the advice to heart: "I wasn't interested in boys. I had plans."

Years later she hands down that parental wisdom to her daughter, granddaughter, and *great*-granddaughters. At seventy-four she's the matriarch of a

Fig. 14. Three strong Paiute women, Martica, Alana,
and Alice Crutcher. Photograph by Randi Lynn Beach.

clan of strong Crutcher women, independent types who've made their own
way, both on the reservation and off.

Even today Alice is quiet and considered, a thin woman with a formidable
presence, one of those old trees on the reservation that will bend but never
break, no matter how hard the wind blows. Alana, her daughter, is bright-
eyed and proud, even a bit boastful compared to her mother's reserve. She's
a rebel and will get into your face if you come too close, like a wild horse
wary of being cornered. Martica, the youngest, is a blend of both women.
Cautious like her grandmother, she carries her mother's colorful flair yet
expresses herself through her artwork and Native dance. She has a quick
smile and laughs a lot.

For all three Crutcher women, men have come and gone. Some stuck
around for years or just months while others died. Some were Native American, others not. Some fathered children before eventually moving on. The
women raised their families mostly on their own, passing down the independence their own mothers taught them.

Alana was the first girl in McDermitt to play tackle football in the town's after-school Little League. Like her mother before her, she grew up standing her ground, taking on the bullies who called her derogatory names. She threw punches and never backed down.

Now forty-nine, the former college homecoming queen still brooks no bullshit. She's broken horses, performed in rodeos, and worked blue-collar jobs more associated with men, from truck driver and detective specializing in sex offenders and criminal profiling to ambulance driver and emergency medical technician. "One thing my grandfather taught me was to not be ashamed of who you are," she says. "You're your own person. And don't ever let anyone tell you anything to make you feel less than that."

Martica, now thirty-one, has for years performed the intricate "fancy shawl dances" at Native American powwows nationwide. She has settled on the reservation to raise her two daughters and works in the McDermitt branch of the Humboldt County Library.

I finally had the opportunity to meet these Crutcher women and hear their stories of self-determination. Alice was wary of me, but following our chance encounter over dinner on the reservation, she at last relented. I meet Alice and Martica at the McDermitt Library, a place that holds significance to both women. Alice once attended grade school in this building where Martica now stocks shelves with a variety of Native American literature and folklore.

There were only two Crutcher women who met with me on this day. Alana, the wild child, lives off the reservation. "Throughout our history, Paiute women have always been strong," says Martica. "They've stood beside their men in the fight." She glances at her grandmother. "And this one? She's tough. Gosh, yeah. She's the definition of a Paiute woman."

Tribal chairwoman Maxine Redstar says Paiute women have traditionally shaped tribal society. Since her great-grandfather became the first tribal chairman in 1936, Redstar is the sixth woman to hold the post. "Our society is matriarchal, period," she says. "If you have a problem, who are you gonna go to? Your mother or your grandmother. Even men who run their own families have strong women next to them."

Redstar remembers her great-grandmother's advice: "Don't be too eager to get married and start a family," the older woman told her. Men are *work*. "You have to feed them; that's your role as wife in our culture," she says. "It's not like you don't need men, you do. But to have them, you also have to take care of them."

Back in the 1960s Alice Crutcher didn't recognize color. When she was in the second grade, tribal children who had previously attended classes on the reservation were allowed to attend the local school. Alice studied among the sons and daughters of white ranchers, Basque farmers, and miners. Her family attended the Latter Day Saints church in town, where segregation was not practiced.

She was lucky to hold on to her language and culture. Alice's older brothers, Clarence and Leonard, were sent to so-called Indian schools, where conditions were deplorable and Paiute children were beaten for speaking their native tongue.

Alice finished the eleventh grade before she dropped out of school. She was young and impetuous, impatient to see the world, even if it was only as far away as Reno and Winnemucca. She was only two credits short of graduation and still laments the fact that she didn't finish what she started. As she tells her story, she sits at a small library table, and the memories of attending classes in this same building remain fresh, her connection to this place still as tight as she once held the reins of her horses.

Alice moved to Winnemucca to live with an aunt. Even the Sarge gave his blessing; she was old enough to make her own decisions. Years later, between boyfriends and marriages and having children, she returned home to the reservation, drawn by ties to both her family and the land.

In McDermitt Alice worked as a maid at the Basque-owned Diamond A Motel, which she later managed; at the post office; and finally, before she retired to concentrate on being a reservation elder, as a waitress at the Say When casino. "This was always home," she says. "No matter where you go, you always come back."

Alice was living in Winnemucca when she met a young Shoshone railroad worker named Thomas. They had a brief romance, and she got pregnant with her first child, Jayson, before returning to McDermitt. A year later she gave birth to Alana, who was fathered by a white kid named Ronnie. They'd gone to school together since the second grade, and Ronnie was familiar and comfortable. When it came to men, Alice always looked first for a good friend, somebody she could trust. "We knew how to make each other laugh. We had a romance, and had one kid."

Alana was born in 1971 when Alice was just twenty-three. She urged her daughter not to be corralled as a woman in a male-dominated society. "There's a big world out there. You can be almost anything," Alice told her.

Alice's marriage to Ronnie would not last. "We were too young," she says. While she never fell in love easily, Alice went on to have three children by three different fathers, and her grown son Jayson and daughter Larina still live nearby. When a relationship ran its course, Alice took flight. "I didn't stay," Alice says. "But I always left on good terms."

A few years later, while working at the Diamond A Motel, Alice met a man named Dennis who built water tanks on the reservation. "He was a Paiute," she says. "And he was handsome." Before long the couple moved to Reno, which, for Alice, was like blasting off to Mars. "I wasn't really wild; I was just always busy," she explains. "I went because I had a boyfriend." She soon found that Reno did not accept Native Americans like people did back in McDermitt. "Reno was bigger, and people saw color there," she says. "When you're born Brown or Black, you can sense it. You can see and feel a person's reaction."

That line brings a laugh from Martica. "That's my grandmother right there," she says. "She's feisty. She's not going to let anyone get one over on her. Same with my mom."

Still, life in Reno was good. Dennis became the love of Alice's life—until the day she returned from a visit back home to McDermitt and found him at home, dead from a heart attack. It was another lesson in Alice's march toward independence. She moved on. "What else could you do?" she says. "You can't get him up again."

By then Alana was already in college. Early on she left the reservation and now rarely returns. One afternoon I reached her by telephone at her home in Elko, and she still recalled the advice the Sarge once gave her. "They're going to try and take things from you out in that world," he had said. "They can take your freedom, the clothes off your back, your land, and your language. But they can never take your mind, your learning, your knowledge."

The words were prophetic. It was the 1980s, and Alana grew up speaking Paiute. For her, English was a second language. She remembers the era before telephones came to the reservation—the time when her grandparents sent her to carry messages to other elders. "I just got on my pony and rode." She laughs.

Alana resolved to carry on her culture, even when McDermitt teachers forbade her from speaking Paiute. "I spoke Paiute then, and I still do. I speak loud and proud. I don't ever hesitate because they will not convince me that it's rude or inappropriate. If I'm going to address someone, I do it in our language."

She followed the path of her maternal uncles. Clarence, the oldest, kept watch on the young girl, "kept me on the straight and narrow." Leonard was another disciplinarian, a horseman who got her into rodeo. Alana could do anything a boy could do in the rodeo arena, on the football field, and in the classroom.

Like her mother she rode horses, often wild mustangs. "If I wanted to go and ride," Alana says, "I had to break my own horse." As a first grader she was already riding steers in the local rodeo. She won awards, but the competition she recalls most came when she tied with a boy for first place for best steer rider.

"It was a boy's event, so he took the buckle, and I got the prize money," she says. "It broke my heart. I wanted that buckle. It meant so much more than the money." In the early 1980s when McDermitt launched its Little League football, Alana was the first to sign up. "I grew up with the boys, and that's what the boys did."

She competed until high school. Back then girls weren't allowed to play beyond the eighth grade. "Would I have played if I could? Hell yes," she says. "I've always been a girl who could take a hit." Alana met her first love on the rodeo grounds, a reservation boy named Sidney. "He was a sharp-looking cowboy, an eye-catcher," she recalls. "It was an on-and-off thing. He was family-oriented, but I had no intention of leading a traditional reservation life. I had told myself, 'I'm not gonna be no housewife.' I had goals of continuing my education."

The break came when Alana, then just eighteen, got pregnant with Martica. There were no fights. Both she and Sidney just went their separate ways. "I was going have that baby but not necessarily the father," Alana says. The idea of raising children on the reservation felt like a prison sentence. Sidney was intent on staying. He worked construction and lived the cowboy life, doing his rodeo events. For him that was enough.

Alana attended college at Haskell Indian Nations University in Lawrence, Kansas. As head basketball cheerleader, she met a player named Vernon, an Indian from Nebraska's Winnebago tribe. They married and had four children, three boys and a girl, now all in their twenties. When asked their ages, Alana laughs. "I don't know. They're all grown now. I don't have to worry about their ages." She also has eight grandchildren.

While in college Alana took classes with an eye toward law enforcement to "follow in my grandpa's footsteps." After graduation she worked for the

Bureau of Indian Affairs and a sheriff's department in Nebraska. She studied nights for her commercial driver's license and began a side gig as a cattle truck driver to make money. Later she trained as an emergency medical technician and drove an ambulance on weekends.

Alana also spent seventeen years in the mining industry, always having to defend herself as a woman. She quit one longtime job after being passed over for a promotion in favor of a male worker with less experience. "The gold mine is a man's world," she says. "You face sexual discrimination every single day. They tell you it's different, that men and women are equal, but it is what it is."

Most recently Alana returned to school to study real estate investment and now owns three properties in Elko. She also works for Delta Air Lines as a grounds crew technician, guiding airplanes as she stands on the tarmac, a job she calls "playing *Top Gun*."

After Vernon died a decade ago, Alana rekindled a relationship with a Paiute-Shoshone man named Steve, another rodeo rider whom she met in high school. She'd always meant to follow Alice and return to the McDermitt as a mentor to a younger generation of Paiutes; it just never worked out. Still, she cites Alice as a role model, a woman left to make her way after her own husband passed away. "My mother never asked for help from anybody. She did it on her own."

And so has Alana. "My relationships did not dictate my life," she says. "My career, my accomplishments, I can say that I did it. I didn't depend on anybody but me."

As a child, Martica Crutcher was poor without even knowing it. When Alana attended college in Nebraska, she left infant Martica behind with Alice, who had returned to the reservation after Dennis's death. For years Martica shuttled between Nebraska and Nevada, where she attended high school. "For me this was *home*."

She and Alice lived in an old family trailer and later moved into the house where Wesa and Hazel raised their own children. "Until that wire burned out," Alice says. Both women laugh.

The old house had one electrical outlet to run heaters in both the living room and bedroom. "That was it," Martica says. "All we had was that one port until that burned out on us. I remember getting up for school in the morning; you could see your breath. The fireplace was barely going. I think

Fig. 15. Martica Crutcher poses on reservation. Photograph by Randi Lynn Beach.

about it now, and I think, 'How did I do that?' But that's what we had, and we were happy."

On winter nights the kids heated up lava rocks used in traditional sweats and wrapped them in a blanket to keep warm. "That's what we had," Martica says again. "Our wood stove, running water for our bathtub, and our toilet. We always had food in the fridge." From an early age Martica learned to sew and do beadwork, and she later helped Alice embroider the traditional Native regalia the young girl wore in her dance routines.

Alice took her granddaughter, then just two years old, to a Native powwow on the University of Nevada campus in Reno. "I made her a little uniform, and when the dancing started, she looked around. She wanted to get out there," Alice recalls. "So I took her out into the circle. We have pictures of it."

Martica fell in love with Native dance routines that brought her closer to her ancestors. As a teenager she performed the so-called "fancy shawl dance" at powwow contests nationwide. Her outfit was ornate and mostly hand-made, employing fully beaded hair clips, wrist cuffs, bracelets, and sequined moccasins. But the swirling athletic dance hinged around the shawl dancers used to mimic butterflies in motion.

As Martica grew older, Alice reinforced the old "crooked and straight road" guidance her father had given her. Whenever they were together, sewing or beading or cooking, she related lessons about how to carry herself as a young woman.

"I was way mellow. Looking back I should have had more fun," says Martica. "I didn't go out drinking. My concentration was on my dancing." By then her mother had remarried and started a second family. Vernon treated Martica as one of his own. "He was my dad," she recalls. In the girl's eyes, the worst crime would have been to hurt her mother or grandmother—or even Vernon. "It wasn't worth hurting their feelings because I loved them so much. You don't hurt those you love."

By the age of fourteen, Martica was a savvy traveler who crossed the nation by plane and train, following the powwow circuit. Alice, however, was not. She'd never taken a train, never flown in an airplane, so when Martica asked if she'd accompany her to an event in Florida, the grandmother hesitated.

"I didn't know how she was going to act," Martica says. Alice was always so strong, but how would she handle *this*, the girl wondered. She looks at her grandmother. "What'd you think when we got on the plane?"

"It was good," Alice deadpans. Martica laughs again. "I was curious," Alice continues. "I was wondering, 'What's gonna happen next?'"

"Well, you got on that plane," Martica says.

"I never had any fear." Alice smiles. "Once you ride a horse into the wilderness as a young girl, a plane is nothing."

At age sixteen, while on a visit to Nebraska, Martica met a boy from the Omaha tribe. Finally a real romance after years of mere crushes. Recalling the day still makes her flush. She was at a carnival when she spotted him. "He was tall, dark, and handsome," she says. "I looked at him once and said to myself, 'He's mine.'"

Alice shakes her head.

"Hey, he was good-looking at *one time*, okay?" Martica says defensively. Even today she won't divulge his name.

The pair kept in touch even after Martica returned to Nevada. Martica's first daughter, Niyla, was born four years later when she was twenty. The Omaha kid came to McDermitt but left abruptly. While they would later have a second daughter, Hazlynn, any hope for a long-term relationship was over. "Rather than stay and support his new family, he left," Martica says. "That cut the cord. We had both decided, 'We're gonna have kids,' but I was the only one who followed through."

When Martica returned full-time to McDermitt, she had trouble fitting in. The reservation can be a closed social circle, and many isolated girls her age didn't know what to make of this young artist who had seen some of the world. "I was small growing up. I was bullied," she says. "I had tiffs with other girls."

But Martica never told Alice. "I knew if I told her, it would be ten times worse for everybody," she says. So she called a meeting with the girls in the principal's office and confronted them. "What's your problem with me?"

The girls left her alone after that, but the episode taught Martica a lesson about reservation life. "With our people, if they don't like you, you're gonna know it. Off the reservation, people might smile in your face and say, 'How are you?' But not here."

Even today Martica still feels judged—as both a woman and a Paiute. Once, attending a fair in Elko with some friends, she dressed in a Native American—style jacket with beads and feathers. Then she noticed the stares of non-Indians in the crowd. "People looked at me like I was the most disgusting thing in the world," she says. "I recall thinking to myself, 'I've never felt so looked down upon in my entire life.' I was used to being in public and having eyes upon me, but not in this way."

Did she stop dancing? "Heck no, why?" she says. "I just grabbed my friends and said, 'Let's go have fun,' but inside I was like . . . wow, it hurt."

In her own way Martica is just as tenacious as her mother and grandmother. She does leatherwork in a shop behind her house. She calls it her "she-shed." It's her creative space where she hand-stitches Native American—themed belts and wallets and carry-ons, all of which she advertises on Facebook.

People ask if Martica is afraid out there after dark. Her answer: "Of course not." Her two daughters will carry on that spirit. Niyla is a straight A student who knows her own mind. And about two-year-old Hazlynn—whose name combines Hazel, her great-grandmother, and Alana Lynn, her grandmother—Martica says, "That girl is something else. She's a spitfire. She'll carry on the chain of strong reservation women."

A lineage that starts with Alice. "She's always been the one to hold up the house," Martica says. "She taught me who I am, how to negotiate the world of men."

Without warning, Alice will take off for the hinterlands on gambling trips to Reno and Winnemucca. "She and her friend will say, 'We're just gonna stay the night.'" Martica laughs. "She'll come home days later, and I'm like, 'Dang, girl. You're wilder than I am.'"

Alice cracks a tiny smile. "We like to go gambling." Without a man in her life, Alice does as she pleases. "I prefer to be alone," she says. "I don't have to clip anybody's toes."

Looking back I ask if the women have bad luck with men.

"No," Alice says. "Not really."

"I'd say I have." Martica laughs again. "My track record isn't that great."

As usual, Grandma Alice has the last word: "Mine all died on me."

Fig. 16. Dancer Niyla Crutcher in motion. Photograph by Randi Lynn Beach.

15

Ever since I arrived in McDermitt, I've had a hard time getting players to open up about themselves. As a journalist, I've interviewed all kinds of people, mostly adults. I grew up in the Eastern suburbs, lived in big cities. But these boys are decidedly Western. Small town. Country. Unlike them I've never played football, never thrown my weight at tackle dummies, or faced down a 240-pound running back.

I notice that the Bulldogs interact with coaches one way and talk amongst themselves in another. On breaks they lie on the grass and joke about girls, pickup trucks, teenage high jinks. Left to themselves, even their postures are different; more slouched, an emerging tribal clan with its own rites.

One day Bailey brags about being chased by a girl as the younger boys listen. "She wants to meet up this weekend," he says. "I said 'I'm busy.'"

"Is she nasty?" one asks.

"No," Bailey says, "just crazy. I don't even go into the feed store anymore because I know she'll be there."

Talk of the future rarely involves college. "I'm going to a trade school," Bailey says, "so I don't have to put up with English and social science classes."

I've never been a parent or even a coach. "How do you reach these kids?" I ask Egan. "How do you ask a question without receiving a blank stare in return?"

He suggests that I'm trying too hard. "They're just kids," he says.

When I was their age, I also shut out adults—teachers, bosses, parish priests. I preferred my own kind, kids my own age, a clan with whom I could be myself, and if I knew them well enough, divulge my doubts and secrets.

Slowly I make breakthroughs. One afternoon Karter approaches *me* to talk. Quiet and polite, his long brown hair tied into a ponytail, he joined the team this fall but has since hurt his leg. He talks about living on a ranch near town and his love of the country life.

The wall between us seems to have fissured, even if just a bit. I am still the outsider, but as a team newcomer, so is he. Maybe that's it.

Days later I pass him outside the locker room. The question lingers on whether he will be eligible to play. "Hey, man," I say in my most casual tone.

"You playing this season?" He dismisses me with a shake of his head. I feel like a quarterback thrown for a decisive loss, ground I may never recover.

Later that afternoon the coaches direct the boys to remove logs and brush from the yard of a retired teacher. Most players ride in Egan's pickup truck to the dump site, but Taylor, the team's star running back, stays behind, quietly raking up the scattered pile. I ask if there's some way we can talk for longer than one-minute bursts between drills or outside the locker room after practice when he's rushing to flee school. Maybe I can visit him at his house. He considers the question for a moment and then nods.

The next day he's waiting for me outside his property on South Reservation Road. He says he can't allow strangers inside the house when his parents are away, so we sit on the porch. I slowly produce my notebook and stare at the blank page, letting the silence linger between us.

Taylor has allowed *some* adults into his inner sanctum, mostly his two coaches, whom he calls Dad when he's in a good mood. Following a break one day at practice, I watch Taylor suddenly jump up, throw his water bottle aside, and give Smith an embrace. One moment, Taylor is moody; the next, he's quiet; the next, he's howling at the moon, but it's still a surprising moment. The other boys know Taylor and Smith train all summer to keep the boy in shape for basketball season. Then, as though the boy realizes he has recognized one parent and not the other, he gives Egan a similar hug.

It's like he's saying thank you for this reprieve from his humdrum rural life, for offering him a place to belong. Nobody says a word as Egan finally blows his whistle.

We sit on his front step on a hot August afternoon. There's a car battery left to rust and two reservation dogs that laze there on the grass. Taylor wears a baseball cap turned backward and red athletic shorts with a Native American insignia. We don't make eye contact, but we stare out toward Red Mountain as this boy tries to answer an adult stranger's probing questions.

He was born in Anchorage, but his parents returned to the reservation when he was four so his father could help care for Taylor's ailing grandfather, a gray-haired elder who spoke Paiute to the boy. But when Taylor tried to practice his native language with his father, Scooby criticized him whenever he misspoke, so he finally gave up.

Taylor pulls no punches about life on the reservation. "Everyone is so miserable here, so negative," he says, throwing a stick for one of the dogs to fetch. In the summer of 2020, during the pandemic, his mother helped him get a job distributing aid to families. "People said, 'How come my kid can't work? You got this job because your mother works at the wellness center,'" he sighs. "They always wanted more than we could give them." He pauses. "There are good people out here too."

Taylor views himself as a Paiute first and an American second. Still, when he graduates he wants to escape the reservation. "I love my family," he says, "but it will be nice to get away from them." He wants to study sports medicine and has set his sights on state schools in Reno and Las Vegas, along with some Native American colleges.

Scooby, he says, is a disciplinarian. He has hit his son when the boy deserved it, but mostly the punishment comes in chores. When Taylor called his older sister a bitch, Scooby imposed his favorite sanction.

"Go pull weeds," he said. Once, when Scooby had had a few drinks on a holiday, he flipped off his son at some offhand remark. When Taylor flipped his father back, Scooby pointed outside. "Go pull weeds."

Taylor first drank alcohol the previous summer, at age sixteen, while on a trip to Lake Tahoe. Some kid handed him a can of Budweiser. "I had three or four. I didn't do it to look cool, and, honestly, I didn't like it. And I'm not going to do it again. I've got too many relatives up in the tribal graveyard who are dead from alcohol."

We sit for a moment in silence. A gust of wind tries to cool off the afternoon heat but fails. I ask direct questions, and Taylor doesn't flinch.

"Are you a virgin?" I ask.

He nods.

"There are different sides to me," he says. "I wear my heart on my sleeve. I can't be myself around girls because I worry they'll call me gay once they see I have feelings." Anyway, it's hard to meet girls on a reservation where most everyone hails from the same clan. "I'm related to the whole school," he says.

Two years ago on a trip to Fallon with the Future Farmers of America club, Taylor met a girl from Owyhee named Josie. When he got home, she began texting him. But something felt wrong. The reservation features a handful of predominant last names: Crutcher. Smart. Hinkey. The girl had one of those.

Taylor asked his aunt if he and the girl were related. She said they were. That did it. "We still talk," he says. "But that's it."

On the reservation, he explains, marriages between cousins are tolerated. But Taylor doesn't see himself being with even the most remote of relatives. "Kids in small towns are content to wait," he says.

His senior year has also been troubled by the deterioration of his bond with his longtime friend Bailey. Lately Bailey and Elijah have pulled pranks with Taylor as their target. Just a few weeks before, they sent him a text with a picture of a guy working at Walmart.

"Future Taylor," it said.

Taylor knows the dig was intended to hurt. When he removed both the boys as social media contacts, it was Bailey's turn to become wounded. "Oh, now you're all butt hurt," he said one day at school. Bailey says they've known each other for so long, it's just natural competition.

But Taylor has made up his mind. He isn't leaving himself open for any more hurtful trash talk. "This is my last year of high school," he says. "And I want it to be good." So he told his father, "Dad, I think I'm gonna ride solo this year."

As he waits for his senior year to begin, Taylor runs. He runs to get in better shape for football and basketball. He runs to get out of the house, to take his mind off an upbringing that makes him feel poor, where his parents must save to survive. He runs to tell himself that he's a Paiute and that he has to make do with what he has. Every day at dusk, he runs up past grazing cattle and the tribal graveyard, a place many Paiutes keep away from because their culture teaches them to "avoid the dark." But as he passes those grave-stones that date back generations, Taylor isn't afraid. He feels good, at peace, as those voices from the past chant his name, praying to the spirits that this Paiute boy will escape the reservation for a larger world.

And then he keeps running.

I meet Scooby one morning for breakfast at the Say When. We arrive as the place opens and watch several Paiutes wander in to take their places at the slot machines.

Scooby's real name is Tetford. His father was a rancher and miner who worked hard all his life. Taylor is his youngest child, and Scooby knows what it's like to be the last of the litter. "Being youngest makes you tougher," he says. "You have to fight."

Scooby played Bulldogs football in the 1980s when McDermitt played in the state championship game twice. Life sped up after that. He joined the army, barely missed Operation Desert Storm, and came home, where he met his wife, Trixie. They moved to Anchorage, Alaska, where her people lived—where Taylor was soon born.

Fig. 17. Young Bulldog with head lowered. Author photo.

Then Scooby made the biggest mistake of his life. To help care for his ailing father, he and his family returned to a place where there aren't any jobs, where Scooby still passes the tombstones of friends and relatives who died from drinking and bad habits. For years he worked as a wildland firefighter. Now fifty-one, he hasn't been able to find a job.

So he concentrates on his son. From the start, Scooby says, Taylor was strong-willed. He'd line up his Hot Wheels toy cars in an immaculate line. If one of his two older sisters moved one out of place, the boy would throw a tantrum. Once, Taylor somehow dug one of his father's fishing hooks into his mouth as he lay on the couch. He put the boy in the car for a rush to the hospital. A mile or so away, the boy pulled out the hook and handed it to his father. "He didn't cry," Scooby says.

He knows he's tough on Taylor. He says his son "didn't have a clue" when he started to play football. He wants him to work on his speed on the basketball court. "He went down to Phoenix to play in some tournament, and I told him, 'Look at those Indian kids run. Those guys are *fast*.'"

I ask Scooby if he's proud of his son. "Yes," he says without hesitation. "He's a good kid. He's a damned good kid."

He's proud of their relationship. "After a game he'll come and kiss me before he kisses his mom. A lot of kids are embarrassed about that stuff. It makes me proud that I raised a kid who walks up and hugs his dad."

I tell him about Taylor's shock at meeting a girl who turned out to be a distant relative. "Yeah, I heard about that through the grapevine," Scooby says. "She was one of my niece's daughters. Taylor is anal. I told him, 'Do whatever you want to do. But you do know that me and your mom are kin.' My grandmother used to say that everyone on the reservation is related."

Days before, Taylor had been caught vaping at school and was suspended for the first three weeks of the basketball season. The sentence is a blow for both father and son, but Scooby blames Taylor, nobody else. He told his son, "That punishment is justified. You know what's right and wrong. That's on you."

Scooby reaches into his pocket for his smartphone. He wants to show me a text exchange he had with Taylor after the vaping incident. At first the boy had made excuses, denying he was at fault. Finally he owned up to his actions.

SCOOBY: *Ok son, do the best you can. There's a lot of bullshit goin on but maintain your own self. Don't be like us old Bulldogs, be a newer better smarter Bulldog. Love you son. Don't fuck up like I did, it's a helluva hole to dig out of. Like right now you're digging out. Don't do that shit. You're way smarter than that. Don't do dumb shit cuz it's easier.*

TAYLOR: *I love you too, dad. I slipped up and made excuses but I'm going to do better. I have been praying for myself and carrying around my arrowhead and things have been going smoothly so far.*

SCOOBY: *You have all that. A thing is right or wrong. You are better than that. You are no dummy. What's going to cost you more misery later?*

TAYLOR: *Yes I am. The only way now is up. I know the difference between right and wrong. Lesson learned. No more vaping now.*

SCOOBY: *That's what I always say. No excuses. Own up to it and carry on. No sense carrying it with you. A good man forgets that shit and becomes better. That's the stuff I would love from you. An awesome being. I know you are and can be.*

TAYLOR: *I don't know why but I tend to be harder on myself, especially when I mess up. It takes me awhile to let things go but I know I can be better than that.*

SCOOBY: *Stay good my son. I'm done.*

The father smiles to himself as he puts the smartphone away, handling it like a sacred artifact he will forever keep close.

Day after day, as the Bulldogs practice in the sweltering late-August heat, no more than six boys at a time show up for the after-school drills. Egan looks at his watch as if he can hear the season looming.

Tick. Tick. Tick.

So far Jaxon has impressed his coaches with his speed and sure hands. Egan doesn't want to get ahead of himself, but if the kid can lose his fluffy chick feathers and grow some talons, he's going to be a real offensive threat.

The players keep an eye on Jaxon as well. One night they sit in a circle on the grass, doing twenty-five sit-ups. "Count 'em together," Egan says.

Bailey turns his head toward Jaxon, who so far has barely uttered a word at practice.

"C'mon, Jaxon, talk," he grunts.

The boy tries, but his voice is still a whisper. "Sixteen! Seventeen! Eighteen!"

It's not enough. Elijah calls out, "Everyone needs to count! You got a voice, use it!"

Egan takes it from there. "I want your voices to echo off that water tower! Call 'em out! Make sure the drinkers at the Say When can hear us!"

They move to leg lifts, and Bailey keeps his eye on Jaxon. All around him other boys are cheating, dropping their feet. "Jaxon," he barks, "get your legs up."

Egan is protective of his freshman. "He's got 'em up."

When Jaxon's helmet doesn't fit, Bailey tightens the straps. "You want that helmet tight," he says, "so when you get hit, your head doesn't rattle."

Jaxon's family attends each practice, shouting encouragement from the bleachers. "Good job, J.P.!" his father yells, using the boy's initials. When Jaxon drops a pass, the voice is there. "What! Why didn't you catch that?"

Egan looks over disapprovingly at the father. "If he was that involved, he would have been out here working with him," he tells Jack. "The field was open all summer."

In one drill, the boys are sluggish during sprints. Egan has seen enough. "You run like that, grandma and grandpa are going to be running right there with ya. C'mon, put a move on grandma!" Then Smith chimes in, "Run! Richard and I could catch you guys! We don't walk anymore. We run. This ain't the golf team!"

The next day Jaxon vanishes. He's in school; he just doesn't show up at practice. Maybe it's the pressure from the other boys, or his father, or the coaches. Who knows?

Egan heard a rumor that Jaxon had told the school counselor that he had liver failure. The counselor looked him in the eye. "Well, that means you're going to be dead in a few days."

Smith saw the boy during his weightlifting class that morning, but as soon as Jaxon saw Egan walk into the gym, he began grabbing his side like a patient in a hospital ward. He told Bailey his liver had just "quit working" and had to be flushed over the weekend.

"Well," Egan says, "he doesn't look jaundiced. I think you'd know."

A few days later at practice, somebody spots a red pickup rumbling down a dirt road behind the field, kicking up a kite tail of dust. Jaxon and his sister ride in the back, laughing, holding on tight. Smith shakes his head. "If you're going to ditch football practice, I don't think you want to go riding around the field in a pickup truck, rubbing it in." He turns to Egan. "He's got a lot of balls being out here."

The truck stops, and Jaxon walks slowly toward the field, his sister trailing. Then, as though she remembers herself, she stops and heads toward the bleachers. Egan approaches the boy.

"How do you feel?"

"I'm still hurting," he says.

"Are you on the football team?"

"Probably not this year. My dad says it's better if I start playing as a sophomore."

Then the boy's resolve seems to weaken. "Once I get this all figured out, I'll be back," he says. He promises to observe practices "so I'm good to go when the time comes."

"Sounds good to me," Egan says as Jaxon wanders away to play catch with his sister.

The next day, however, he's back on the field, wearing his uniform, ready to play. Egan shakes his head when he sees the boy. He needs him in order to have a season. But this has turned into a small-town soap opera.

As it turned out, Muñoz, the principal, had called Jaxon's family. With his father always working, the family decided that, despite his squeamishness, the boy could use some time getting discipline on the football field.

So the decision was made: Jaxon can play. Yet the coaches are leery. "Now he says his liver is just weak, not exactly failing," Smith says. "He's got ten different stories, and none of them match up."

A day later Egan receives an email summoning him to a meeting in the principal's office. Muñoz wants to meet with both Karter and Jaxon to determine whether the team can count on the boys to play football that season.

The pair sit in the office, heads down. Both finally nod, indicating that they are going to play. Later, neither is at practice. Jaxon tells the coaches he has to have blood work done in Winnemucca. Karter wanders the halls like a zombie, the hood of his hoodie pulled down low over his eyes. Smith sits the boy down in his office and talks about the value of being part of something like a football team. The boy won't look at him. Practice starts in a few minutes, and the other boys are already starting to show up, the hoots and challenges echoing through the locker room.

"Put those on," Smith says, pointing at a pair of shoulder pads. "Let's go practice."

Karter pauses, collecting his thoughts. "See you Tuesday," he says, "after Labor Day."

And then he walks out. Decision deferred.

It's been a week now since Taylor and I sat on his front porch and I saw the clouds part over the head of this complex boy. I felt like I'd made a connection to build upon. But that day at school, the storm clouds are back, darker now.

I catch him walking out to the practice field. By now everyone had heard about Karter. They'd given up on Jaxon, but Karter was Taylor's cousin. They had a bond.

"What's wrong with Karter?" I ask.

Taylor shrugs. I hear myself backpedaling, "I know you have your own issues. You can't be worried about everybody else."

"I forgot something," he says, walking away. The drama plays out like a riddle, a small-town sphinx. I see Egan and walk towards him, determined to get an answer.

"What's wrong with Karter?"

"Aw, he's got *girly* problems." He'd seen the boy that day, talking to a girl, and he heard him say. "See ya. I love you."

Now *that* made sense. Maybe I was overthinking all of this. These players were, after all, *teenagers*. First loves can throw any sixteen-year-old into an emotional tailspin. One misinterpreted text, and the walls come crashing down. It wasn't just about my nosiness, but a kid dealing with new emotions.

I feel like a rookie coach who's finally figured out the complex playbook. "I realize something," I tell Egan. "I can't try to be friends with these kids. I have to be patient until they're comfortable enough to talk to me."

That day on the porch with Taylor, I had apologized for my profanity. I felt like I was on a first date, on my guard, explaining away my *f*-bombs.

"It's okay," he said. "Just be yourself."

As practice ends that day, the players collect for a last-minute huddle, all of them staring down at the grass below. Then we see it: a praying mantis perches below them, pincers extended, head nodding as though on a swivel.

"He's a big one," somebody says.

"Do you know what happens when a male praying mantis mates?" I ask, choosing my words carefully. "Afterwards she starts devouring him from top to bottom."

After a moment, baby-faced Jared speaks up. "Now that's what I call giving head."

The boys laugh. So do the coaches. "I was waiting for that," Egan says.

The Bulldogs break their huddle, these elusive boys sweating in the summer's heat.

16

After a few forlorn years coaching basketball in outlying Owyhee, Dave Kunneman eventually snapped from the long winters and too many nights in. That's when he went AWOL, headed for the hills, and became something of a rural Nevada coaching legend.

It was the late 1970s, and Kunneman took his underrated team to the division finals in Reno, where the plucky bunch walked away with the trophy. Before boarding their creaky yellow school bus for the 500-mile ride home, the team stopped at a casino for a buffet dinner.

But Kunneman never made it back on the bus, sealing his nickname among sportswriters as "Kooky." "I don't know if he got drunk or had a revelation inside that casino that he wasn't going back to Owyhee," says veteran Reno journalist Ray Hagar.

The coach later called Hagar with an explanation. "The last thing he said was we hadn't heard the last of Coach Kunneman," Hagar recalls, "which was the last time we ever heard of him."

That's the kind of story Hagar delights in recounting about those crazy early days of Nevada's eight-man football and its improbable characters—the screwball coaches, cantankerous referees, and high school kids who all seemed built from solid oak.

Hagar remembers descriptions of the tortuous bus drives the teams took to reach roughhewn sandlots of dirt and crabgrass. They were exhausting trips along two-lane roads that stretched into infinity, just to play a high school football game out in the asteroid belt of rural Nevada.

Hagar loved football. The Reno native played offensive guard for the eleven-man Bishop Manogue Miners. At the University of Nevada, Reno, Hagar also played football and, in his last two years, returned to coach his old high school team.

In 1977, soon after he graduated from journalism school, Hagar's career launched him out into the state's unheralded outback. As the new prep reporter for the Evening Gazette and the Nevada State Journal, he covered eight-man football in towns like Wells, Beatty, Alamo, and McDermitt, talking with coaches and players on teams with such as fanciful mascots as the Muckers, Railroaders, and Tarantulas.

He recalls the bizarre characters he met with a sense of wistful romanticism.

The memories create sepia-toned snapshots of high school football in 1970s Nevada when the state's population was one-tenth of today's three million. That amounted to a whole lot of nowhere. Today the vast, unpeopled landscape still demands the nation's longest drives to contests between satellite communities so widespread that they have no business sharing a league of any kind.

Even though the schools are now more tightly knit geographically—with four distinct regions—teams like the McDermitt Bulldogs still meet before dawn for away games, as they did in Hagar's day, and spend hours on the road, for all kinds of sports, from eight-man football to track and field to girls' volleyball.

In Hagar's era many rural high school teams were led by young, inexperienced coaches, recent college graduates hungry for bigger opportunities. The result was often a decided culture shock. Hagar never worried about kids who never knew anything but a small town with more cows than people; it was the young coaches from bigger cities who languished in those backwater burgs who kept him up nights.

They were mysterious strangers left to find their way among cliquish boys and their families. Some connected with the community, won games, and prospered. Others, feeling like desperate lifers whose jailers had thrown away their paperwork, fled after a few losing seasons.

In many towns there was absolutely nothing to do. One coach told Hagar about life in Wells, a mining town with a few hundred blue-collar families. Sunday nights were so desolate, with nothing on TV, that he couldn't wait to go to school the next day just to have something to relieve the boredom.

Yet some coaches thrived. Louis Matthew "Sonny" Lubick, a kid from Butte, Montana, spent two years in a stagecoach stop in a town on the outskirts of Death Valley. Between 1960 and 1962 Lubick coached every sport for the Beatty Hornets, from boys' flag football to girls' basketball, and he even drove the bus to away games. Now eighty-five, he still recalls the school superintendent's pitch to get him to take the job. "He said they were *real* close to Las Vegas and that 'the roses bloom all year round.'"

The twenty-two-year-old bachelor sometimes hit the Las Vegas Strip—a two-hour drive each way—but mostly stayed in Beatty where he shared an apartment with Roy Georgoff, another young coach, and looked for those blooming roses. Lubick recalls that first year before the school built a gymnasium when the basketball teams played outdoors. "The wind," he says, "was our home court advantage."

In Beatty coaches were celebrities. Mothers delivered cookies, and Lubick joined the Lions Club to help the town grow and prosper. "People listened to what we had to say," he recalls. "Maybe it was because we both came from someplace else."

In 1962 Lubick returned to Butte and later coached collegiate football in Montana, Miami, and Colorado, becoming a heralded Division 1 coach. In 1994 he was named *Sports Illustrated*'s National Coach of the Year after his Colorado State squad finished 10-2 and went to the Holiday Bowl.

Even now, though, Lubick keeps in touch with players from his Beatty days, and in 1997 he spoke at the high school graduation. "That place and its people gave me my first chance," he says. "They helped shape me."

But not every rural Nevada coach was Sonny Lubick. One Utah coach took a job sight unseen in the remote town of Gabbs. As he and his family crested a rise in the brown rock and scrub brush along Nevada State Route 361, the town came into view, looking like a lunar way station, isolated and lonely. The end of the world.

"When the coach's wife saw the town, she started to cry," Hagar says. "Broke into tears right there in the passenger seat."

Longtime Nevada journalist Guy Clifton played football in Gabbs back then. "We were looking forward to him being there," he recalls. The players even helped the family unload their trailer. But the next day the coach didn't show up for practice. The family reloaded the truck overnight and had vamoosed by dawn.

For players in those god-awful towns, eight-man football provided a break from farm chores. When times were good and there were enough participants, they were competitive, sometimes even outstanding. Other years not so much. But here's the thing: With such a small roster, every kid played. Nobody rode the bench, and that means a lot to teenagers seeking an identity.

Still, for the Gabbs players, the spider-themed team mascot often brought derision. Virginia City, whose mascot was a Mucker—or roughhewn miner— even had a cheer about the Tarantulas: "*Itsy-bitsy spider crawled up the water spout. Along came the Mucker and wiped the spider out!*"

Bus rides to away games that seemed like interminable trips to outer space brought an unexpected bonus. They provided moments of freewheeling male bonding, which were almost as important as the games themselves.

Once, Beatty's team drove ten hours to Owyhee only to find that the referees had not shown up. "They didn't want to cancel the game," Clifton says, "so men from the stands filled in for the refs." After the game they still had to ride another 457 miles to get back home, something you got used to in rural Nevada.

"We created our own fun," Clifton says. The boys played poker and sang songs. One kid introduced Clifton to the western fiction of Louis L'Amour, which he devoured from his seat. As the miles passed, the players dreamed of the buffets that awaited them when that bus finally stopped.

For Clifton there was no temptation to act up, not while Earl Lee was driving the bus. The local Assembly of God church pastor and school maintenance man had the biggest hands Clifton had ever seen. "He taught us the importance of a firm handshake. He'd take your palm in his and crush it; those mitts were that big."

The journeys even involved the world's oldest profession: on a trip for an away track meet, Beatty High's new diesel bus fouled a piston, and Coach John Lisle told his athletes to stay put while he went to use the pay phone.

But the boys didn't stay put.

One player had heard about a nearby brothel and led a search party. When Lisle learned where they had gone, he panicked. Moments later his players straggled back. "The day's only redeeming value," he recalls, "is that the local madam refused to let those boys inside."

The rural Nevada boys were outsized characters in their own rights, strong young heifers who would lead their eight-man teams to victory year after year. Hagar recalls Ralph Nuti from a farming family in Smith Valley. At 6-foot-4 and 230 pounds, Nuti was a big, gentle kid, a devout Christian who played religious music in his car. Still, after football practices, the parents of teammates would call the house and implore his father not to let Ralph rough up their child at practice.

For many Nevada sportswriters, covering small-town sports meant writing about pathos, and not just from painful losses but from tragedy and death.

Former Reno reporter John Trent remembers a 1989 visit to Owyhee as the toughest assignment of his career. Billy "Black Eagle" Manning, just sixteen, was a standout athlete for the eight-man Braves, a player who everyone believed had a future off the reservation, out in the bigger world of organized football.

Then he suffered a hard hit, helmet to helmet, a freak play that took his life and changed his legacy. He'd suffered a subdural hematoma, a buildup of blood on the surface of the brain, and Trent drove out for the player's memorial service "to write about Billy," he says. Trent witnessed a heartbroken town gather to bury one of its boys. He recalls how Billy's father, Leroy, a tribal councilman, saw through his grief to sit down with a stranger.

Trent says it was just about the bravest thing he'd ever seen a man do. "I sat in the kitchen as Leroy told me about his boy." Now he's eulogized not for his field exploits but for being one of the last Nevada eight-man players to die from a blow he suffered during a game.

But isolation and unemployment now plague almost every small Nevada town. "'The mine closed,' that [phrase] pretty much sums up a lot of these places," says Don Cox, author of *Stories from the Sagebrush: Celebrating Northern Nevada at the Millennium.*

And when the mine closes, that changes everything. "People leave, and the place just doesn't recover. It closes the book on a town."

It's been a battle for survival for nearly a century.

You can blame the Great Depression for the birth of six-man football, a scaled-down cousin of the original that would later help spawn the eight-man game. It premiered on the sports pages of Nebraska's *Lincoln Journal Star* on September 21, 1934.

It was a Friday, the kickoff of another weekend of the University of Nebraska's Cornhusker football, and appetites among sports fans were whetted. America was in the throes of a 20 percent unemployment rate, and people needed a distraction. "Stage First Six-Man Game at Hebron," read the headline about a new game that "contains most of the features of the regulation game but is claimed to be less dangerous and more spectacular."

Six-man was the brainchild of Stephen E. Epler, a high school teacher from tiny Chester, Nebraska, who focused his master's thesis in education at the University of Nebraska on tackling a problem then faced by many smaller schools.

Across the Midwest, enrollments were steadily shrinking as families migrated to California for work, causing schools to shut down athletics programs for lack of money and boys to play. Many were so undermanned that they were demoralized by schools with a larger student base. Epler envisioned a more democratic game with teams comprised six athletes competing on smaller fields.

On September 27, 1934, a dozen boys from the state's Little Blue Conference took to the field at the Hebron athletic gridiron in tiny Hebron, Nebraska, the seat of Thayer County, for America's first six-man high school football game.

The teams were each a compilation of two schools, with blended names to match. The six boys from Belvidere and Alexandria high schools became the so-called "Belvalex" team, while the six players from Hardy and the nearby town of Chester called themselves, appropriately, the "Hard-Chests."

More than one thousand fans turned out to watch a 19–19 tie, which the *Lincoln Evening Journal* described as "exceptionally fast and interesting from the first shrill of the whistle, which officially inaugurated the new game, to the final crack of the gun."

The athletes loved the new version of the sport they'd grown up playing. "It's a real game," said Hard-Chest player G. E. Van Winkle. "I'm crazy to play more."

Epler, eventually known as the father of six-man football, returned to Chester in 1993, on the sixtieth anniversary of the sport he invented. Then eighty-two, he told the *Los Angeles Times* that his creation enabled young men to "stay at their own schools and . . . have all the bands and the pep rallies just like the big schools."

By the start of World War II, more schools in Nebraska played the six-man game than the eleven-man version. At its height in 1951, six-man football was played in 2,463 schools in forty-eight states.

Eight-man football owes its start to a Depression-era technicality. On November 7, 1935, in the tiny, wooded village of Schoolcraft, Michigan, two eleven-man teams were set to meet, but, just days before, the Schoolcraft coach called his counterpart at Marcellus High to say his team had too many injuries to play.

The two coaches hatched a plan: Why not compete with just eight boys? They modified a few rules on the fly and kicked off. Unfortunately for Schoolcraft, they were shut out 27–0. Marcellus also won a rematch a week later, this time 26–12.

Eventually other small schools followed suit, and by 1960, eight-man was the chosen variation for teams that could not field eleven boys. Today eight-man football continues to thrive nationwide. In 2019, according to a survey by the National Federation of State High School Associations (NFHS), some 1,030,000 students played some version of organized football. Eleven-man teams led the way with 14,167 teams, consisting of about a million players. Another 37,000 were divided between other variations of the game, with 21,310 playing eight-man and 5,536 playing the six-man game.

And the numbers keep growing. Check any local paper from Maine to Montana and you'll find stories about high schools opting for eight-man football. "Student enrollments are shrinking at smaller schools," said Bob Colgate, the NFHS director of sports and sports medicine. "Coaches don't have the numbers to play eleven-man anymore."

In Nevada, rural schools began playing eight-man ball in 1963 after introducing six-man squads two decades before. In 2022 no school played six-man football, but twenty-one teams statewide still played adrenaline-fueled eight-man contests where the last team with the ball often wins the game.

Some, like the McDermitt Bulldogs, lose far more than they win. But at least for now, the kids keep showing up.

For years many joked that Ray Hagar covered hapless matches out in "cow county" between the "farmers and the ranchers." Now seventy, he still holds a reverence for those gutsy rural characters with exotic native names like Junior Horse and Lionel Flapping Eagle. Rural people took high school sports seriously. If you flubbed a detail on how far some kid had thrown the shot put at a rural track meet, you heard about it and so did your boss. Folks didn't so much *read* the paper; they *studied* it.

Decades ago Hagar learned firsthand the importance of his work. He stopped for a beer in rural Smith Valley and saw that the owner of the CG Bar kept the sports pages of the *Reno Gazette-Journal*, with its box scores and game coverage, chained to a table so no one would steal them. "You had to keep my stories chained up." He laughs. "Football brought rural Nevada together and still does."

As long as the mine doesn't close.

Fig. 18. Coach Richard Egan in his office. Photograph by Randi Lynn Beach.

17

Richard Egan tells stories about his early days playing football, when he was even younger than his Bulldogs are today—tales that brim with details of a wondrous, impressionable age.

As he talks, he's standing on the McDermitt playing field while his athletes run laps, the few moments when he and Smith can relax and swap tales. Something has triggered a memory of his boyhood in Owyhee and the Duck Valley Indian Reservation, a place so much like McDermitt.

When he was just eleven, Egan played on a Little League team called the Duck Valley Chiefs. There were two coaches. Ross Harney was a big Paiute-Shoshone who worked as a hospital EMT; the other was a white guy named John Anderson, the town's recreation director. Egan respected both men. He didn't see color in his coaches.

He wore No. 32. Everyone called him Dickie back then.

"You're the Juice," Harney told him.

"I didn't even know who O. J. Simpson was." Egan laughs now.

The team didn't win many games. "We got killed," he says. "I don't think we even scored." The coaches bribed players to show up. Egan and his teammates were taken to movies after each away game, an outing that included ice cream and candy. "It worked," he recalls. "We loved it."

There were other motivations. "I still have my trophy," he says.

"Was it a participation trophy?" Smith asks.

"Yep," Egan says. "Everybody got one."

He doesn't recall any tough talk from either coach. "They weren't barkers or screamers," he says. "We were a bunch of little kids. If we thought we were being barked at, we'd quit."

Then Egan sighs. "High school was different."

His coach there was a hulk named Bill Roberts, a non-Native whose big 6-foot-4 body was like a barrel you take over Niagara Falls. He swung his arms to the side as he walked as though to keep up his momentum. And he barked. A lot.

By then Egan played end on both offense and defense, but the grit it took to succeed in football did not come naturally. Growing up he'd always had a protector to make sure he never got hurt: his older sister, Nancy. "I wasn't a tough kid," he recalls. "If I ever got threatened, all I did was tell Nancy, and she took care of it."

The family was poor like most in Owyhee. Egan's father, Willard, a Paiute-Shoshone, worked as a buckaroo on the Riddle ranch outside town, where he lived in a house with his wife, Delia, and their growing family. Each spring, Richard's paternal grandfather, Hubert, camped out on isolated Marys Creek to keep the tribe's water supply free of beaver dams, pulling away the sticks and branches the animals dragged up to start their projects. Egan recalls how the elder lived a nineteenth-century existence, alone in a rudimentary shack, rolling his own cigarettes, burying the meat for his meals in a makeshift root cellar covered with old bedsprings so the cows couldn't get at it.

Late in her pregnancy with Egan's brother, Sherwin, Delia went into labor one afternoon on the outlying ranch. Her husband had gone to collect wood, and she was alone. When the school bus finally arrived with Nancy, Delia hopped aboard carrying Richard, a one-year-old in diapers, and told the old driver, Mr. Peterson, of her predicament. Peterson rushed to the home of Nancy's grandparents, where Delia handed Richard to Nancy and sent the two inside before the bus continued into town, with Delia doubled over in pain.

Nancy recalls holding Richard in her arms, watching the bus depart. She felt abandoned even though her two uncles had arrived to watch her. Then she tripped on the diaper bag and both she and her brother fell to the gravel. Both began crying, oblivious to their mother's agony. But there was nothing they could do anyway. A few days later Delia returned to the ranch with the baby, and life got even harder.

Years later Delia became a school custodian and told her kids not to bother her for rides while she was at work. She bought each a bicycle, a yellow Western Flyer 10-speed. After that, Egan was always atop his bike. He learned to fix flats, oil his chain, and true up his wheels. From home he rode 5 miles into town and then 5 miles in the other direction to visit his four grandparents. He made jaunts along mostly deserted roads. Some were paved, others not. The passing landscape was unfenced, the wind in his face and the skies above massive and blue, giving a young boy a sense of freedom, wide open spaces, and big dreams.

Eventually Egan stepped out of Nancy's shadow. He grew independent and toughened his body by playing football in the snow with his cousins, the boys wearing puffy, fiber-filled jackets to provide insulation from both the cold and the body slams.

Yet a dark family force confronted the boy. Egan's father, Willard, was abusive and beat Delia when he drank. As a teenager, Egan stepped in to protect his mother, standing up to his father as his mother slipped out the back door. Nancy was not physically strong enough; it had to be him. "During the night, nobody really slept," he says, especially when his father was out drinking. The boy lay in bed, eyes open, waiting for the encounter. "I was on my toes. Every little sound, I got up to check it out."

In high school he started for the school's eleven-man football team. By his junior year, however, Nancy had left for college, and he'd tired of the egos among his teammates. He told his parents he wanted to return to McDermitt where the family had lived for two years when Egan was small. They only played eight-man there, but he didn't care. Late in the summer of 1981, he moved in with his uncle, Dennis Smartt, and his family on the reservation, so he'd be eligible to attend school.

Dennis headed up a woodland firefighting crew and led the tribe's food distribution effort. On weekends Dennis's son, Duwayne, and Egan were put to work handing out grocery staples. Years later Dennis would follow his father's path to become a respected Paiute holy man. Back then it was Dennis's morning routine that made an impression on Egan. He still remembers how his uncle played the song "Detroit City" by the country singer Bobby Bare. The song was a lament, a cry of loneliness, about a young man far from home who misses the land and his parents and the girl he left behind—with that mournful refrain, "*I wanna go home. I wanna go home. Oh, how I wanna go home.*"

Each time the music stopped, Dennis would lift the needle and start the song again, and soon enough it became Egan's alarm clock. But the boy wasn't lonely, and he did not want to go home. He wanted to play Bulldogs football.

One day Dennis took Egan to meet football coach John Moddrell, but Moddrell's wife, Deena, said her husband was having drinks at the Desert Inn bar. Four decades later Egan recalls walking into that saloon and shaking the hand of his lifelong mentor, a man who would become more than a coach, whose gentle voice and pragmatic game plan still plays out in his mind every time he takes to the football field.

Perched on his stool, Moddrell sized up the newcomer and his taut, football-ready body, a kid just as tall as he was. Then he swiveled back toward the bar and, as the story goes, told his cronies, "We're going to win a championship this year."

Moddrell's tenure in McDermitt began as a fluke Hail Mary pass. Late in the summer of 1979 the team's head football coach quit to take a job dealing cards at a casino in Reno. The departure left the school principal in a bind. Principal Jerry Rockstad was having breakfast at the café inside the Say When, drowning his sorrows in bacon grease and caffeine, when he spilled his predicament to bookkeeper Pat Stinton.

What was he going to tell the players? Hell, what was he going to tell their *parents*?

Stinton listened intently. Her son-in-law had just graduated from Boise State University; he was a smart kid who'd worked on the training squads at various Boise State teams and was looking for work. At the time, Moddrell was working at a Firestone plant in Boise as he sent out resumes for any kind of job that would get him out of retreading tires. He didn't have high hopes.

Then his phone rang on a Sunday morning. It was Jerry Rockstad, and Moddrell listened to the job pitch. The position was far from perfect: teach six science and physical education classes a day and coach football at a high school in his wife's hometown. The annual pay was $11,000. Although McDermitt was 200 miles from Boise, the couple could live with Moddrell's in-laws and save some money.

Moddrell took the job, but when he blew the whistle at the first practice, the new coach realized just what he'd signed up for: only seven players had shown up to compete on an eight-man squad. Still, he knew the talent was out there, and he knew where to find it: the Fort McDermitt Paiute-Shoshone reservation.

One afternoon Moddrell drove out onto the sixteen-thousand-acre reservation with Edmo Bitt, one of his players. They knocked on doors, waiting in the sun for Native elders to present themselves—mostly grandmothers who were happy to see Moddrell—and hear his pitch on the importance of playing high school football, how it could help shape boys as students and, later, as men. "You got the attention of players by showing respect to the elders," Moddrell recalls. "They were happy to see me come out, made sure I had a cup of coffee and a few homemade cookies." The campaign supplied the team with nearly a dozen new players, fresh clay for this new coach to begin molding.

The Bulldogs lost their opening game by a wide margin—Moddrell's first harsh lesson in rural coaching: like in poker, you play the hand you're dealt. "John would come home shaking his head," Deena recalls. "He'd say 'My God, I have players who don't even know their positions.' He had to go out onto the field in practice and say, 'This is where you stand. This is what you're going to do.'"

That first season the Bulldogs lost seven of eight games, with their only victory coming in the very last league contest and at the expense of the Lund Mustangs, who'd traveled a whopping 377 miles for the game. The final score was 12–8, and Moddrell recalls walking off the field, giddy from victory. He yelled out to Jerry Rockstad, "Will that get me another contract for next year?"

The elation didn't last long. The Bulldogs had scheduled a final non-league game against a reform school team in distant Las Vegas. Grant Crutchley, the hard-nosed Eureka coach, warned Moddrell not to play the game. The drive was too damned long, he said, the opposition too tough. But the coach and his boys went anyway. They lost 78–0. On the long twelve-hour drive home, the bus was silent, the players slouched with their heads down. "What's wrong?" Moddrell asked. It was only one game.

It wasn't the lopsided loss that had his players glum, he soon realized, but the reality that the season was over. There would be no more practices or games, no more camaraderie. "It wasn't that they'd just got their butts handed to them," the coach recalls. "They were down because the whole adventure was over."

That's when Moddrell realized that he'd tapped into something—in that town and among those players. There was a spark there, a smoldering ember that, with care, he could turn into a full-blown fire.

McDermitt had tasted success years before and was hungry for another winning team. Central to it all was Claude Reeves Field, which Moddrell considered one of the best football fields in the state: green as a Kentucky lawn, well-fertilized, and irrigated, an oasis. He began taping every game— video records used to decipher team weaknesses. Every Monday afternoon he'd rally his players in his classroom, and Deena would deliver a case of soda so the boys could watch game film and guzzle soft drinks. They called it the rootie-tootie hour.

At home Moddrell continued to obsess over his search for answers, and he circulated the film among Bulldogs boosters he called the Blue Smurfs. He also encouraged players to drop by his house at any hour, for any reason.

Many came from single-parent homes. Some drank too much, which became a problem not only then but later in life. Bad habits developed early were the first rogue winds of the coming hurricane.

A boy might lose a parent to suicide, a brother to a drowning, or a friend to some senseless car crash in a deadly mixture of speed and alcohol. "At least once a year," Deena says, "John would come home and say, 'One of my boys is having trouble and is going to come stay with us tonight.'"

One summer night when Moddrell was away, a player showed up at 11:00 p.m.

"Is coach here?" he asked tentatively.

When told he wasn't, the boy stammered, "Well, is it okay if I stay the night?"

Alone with her infant son, Deena swung open the door. "I showed him where the bedroom was and made him breakfast the next morning," she says. Before the start of one home game, Deena entered Moddrell's classroom to find the coach and his players all down on one knee. "John always gathered his players to pray that no one got hurt. Then he sent them out to have fun."

Two years after he arrived in McDermitt, Moddrell still felt like there was one missing piece to complete a "shoot-the-moon type of team." Then he sat on a barstool and shook hands with a young transfer named Richard Egan.

That 1982 season was something magical for Moddrell and his two star players—offensive end Egan and quarterback Nick Wilkinson. The Bulldogs would later win another championship in 1984, then finish runner-up in 1985 and 1987, before the McDermitt Mine closed and it all collapsed, but there was nothing like that first year when everything clicked from the very first practice snap.

Before each home game Moddrell directed his thirty players to run onto the field as a unit, a ritual designed to intimidate the visiting team. Back then Wilkinson was a 5-foot-10 junior "who weighed a buck-fifty-five." He still has memories of those afternoons. "I remember the cool fall air," says Wilkinson, now a south Oregon rancher. "We'd run along the pavement, and our cleats made a clattering noise all the way to the field. We'd clap our hands, pound our shoulder pads and knees in a war chant."

"Who's tough? We're tough! How tough? Damned tough!"

Then the public address announcer would introduce each boy as the cheerleaders jumped and the Bulldog mascot prowled the sidelines. Following each win, the players would whoop and beat on their lockers, a racket that should have carried back out onto the field, but the fan celebrations and all those blaring car horns usually drowned it out.

Two years before, as a 130-pound freshman, Wilkinson faced a defining moment as a Bulldog. In the first scrimmage against the Crane Mustangs, he played defensive end and lined up against a kid named Clint Singer, a 6-foot-6, 260-pound brute who would go on to play four years at Oregon State. At the first snap Singer stuck a huge paw on Wilkinson's helmet and mashed his face into the dirt. The freshman ran back to the sidelines with so much mud caked on his mask he couldn't see.

"You gotta get tougher," Moddrell said.

Singer took it easier on the kid until the Mustang coach gave him hell from the sidelines. "You gotta play this kid like he's your size," he yelled. "If you want to play Division 1, you can't worry about hurting him." After that, Wilkinson recalls, "he beat the shit out of me." But Wilkinson made Moddrell proud; he'd stuck it out and passed the test.

In the '82 season opener, the Bulldogs won at home against the Jordan Valley Mustangs, with help from a team booster. Jess Jaca, a Basque who owned a McDermitt trucking firm, snuck by the visitor's practice while on a road trip and copied down the defensive schemes the Oregon boys would run. The Bulldogs scored in every quarter, holding the Mustangs without a point in a 32–0 victory.

In the second game the Bulldogs traveled to Oregon to take on the Adrian Antelopes, comprised of the lumbering sons of farmers, many 6-foot-2 and over 200 pounds. Egan, at 6-foot-1 and 195 pounds, was the biggest Bulldog. So Moddrell evened the odds with a sleight of hand. The Bulldogs received the second-half kickoff and ran toward their own sidelines. On the first play from scrimmage, Moddrell instructed Egan to linger by his coaches, camouflaged by his own team. On the snap Egan sprinted toward the end zone, and Wilkinson hit him with a pass that fooled the Antelope boys. Egan broke four tackles on a 60-yard touchdown romp. The Bulldogs won 22–0.

Wilkinson still marvels at Egan's pluck. "Richard was dirty-tough, and I mean that as a compliment. For him it was full contact all the time. Kids dreaded scrimmaging against him because he always brought the heat. If you weren't watching, he'd put your head on a swivel. You were going to get hit—hit hard and hit mean." As a senior, Egan had one season to establish himself as the Bulldog to beat. He followed Moddrell's advice to treat every practice like a championship game, and that meant hitting hard. He recalls the league contest when he injured an opposing player named Erwin Mix. Egan hit him low after he went up for a catch, and Mix hit the ground howling, his leg broken.

Decades later the two met at a sports event. "I thought that was a cheap hit," Mix said, his ego still smarting. Egan disagreed. "No," he said, "you were up in the air, and I drove you right into the ground. My shoulder pads hit your legs, and I wrapped you up. I just planted you. I didn't try to hurt you." It wasn't the only time Egan broke bones. "I wasn't a dirty player, but I *was* a team captain and thought everyone had to go through me," he says. "I don't think I ever let up. I didn't pick on the younger ones, but I went after the older boys. I got my hits in."

The next two Bulldog games were won by unlikely forfeits. The Lee Vining Tigers canceled after a groundskeeper had spread too much limestone powder on the football field the previous week and it burned the skin of several boys. Next several Coleville Wolves got sick after their team bus broke down and exhaust leaked inside. Now 4–0, the Bulldogs got cocky. "We weren't gonna let anybody score on us," Wilkinson says.

They beat Dayton 58–0. The Dust Devils came from a larger school that played eleven-man football, and word got out that their coach had guaranteed a victory. "When we heard that, it got us all fired up," Egan recalls. They played eight-man that day, and in one early play, Egan ran the ball from a T formation from the opponent's 15-yard line. He hit a defenseman and knocked him back 5 yards. But Egan slipped on the wet turf and landed on his head in the end zone. "I was dizzy," he recalls. On the sidelines Moddrell reached into his pocket for smelling salts and brought the boy back to his senses. Then he sent him back in to play defense. The kid Egan had plowed over on the goal later pleaded, "Please don't hit me so hard again."

The Bulldogs spoke Paiute on the line so opponents couldn't pick up their schemes, including the so-called *pieba* hit. Taken from a Paiute phrase that means "sissy," the play involved one Bulldog striking a ball carrier high, the other low, finishing the kid off.

Then came the game against Eureka where nothing worked.

The Vandals led 6–0 at the half, the only time any team had scored that season on the Bulldogs. On one play, as Egan readied to punt, he thought he saw Moddrell swing out his right leg, a sign for a fake kick and a long downfield pass. At the snap, when Egan moved right to throw the ball, Moddrell held his head in horror. "No, Richard! I said punt!" Egan hit a Bulldog named Omar Horn for a touchdown, but back on the sidelines Moddrell was still upset. The play could have ended in disaster, he insisted.

"Well, we scored," Richard told his coach defensively.

The Bulldogs scored 32 successive points to win 32–6.

The next week they were tied at zero with the Pyramid Lake Lakers, a fellow Paiute team. "It was a big game for bragging rights, Native versus Native," Egan recalls. "Back then games were different. No smartphones or laptops. We traveled together like a bunch of buzzing bees in a hive. No contact with the other team. No talking to friends. No social media. It was two enemy camps."

Bulldog mistakes sent Moddrell into an uncharacteristic rage. "He went after us," Wilkinson recalls. "It was a real ass-chewing." Beating the Lakers meant an automatic playoff berth, and the Bulldogs were blowing it. "I told them, 'Are you guys serious? Get your act together. Jesus Christ, we've worked too hard to squander our whole season,'" Moddrell recalls.

The ploy worked. Minutes later the Bulldogs led 24–0. That's when the entire offensive line walked over and asked Moddrell, "Is that good enough for you, coach?" They won 58–6.

The rest of the season stayed on script: even busted Bulldog plays led to touchdowns.

In the end, for the first time in a decade, the Bulldogs brought home the championship trophy. In their final regular season home game, they led the Gabbs Tarantulas 12–0 at halftime. When Gabbs scored a late touchdown, McDermitt only prevailed after a late interception that allowed them to run out the clock. "It was pretty scary," Moddrell says. Later, with both teams in line at a buffet dinner, one Bulldog told the coach there was a band scheduled to play that evening at the community hall to celebrate the undefeated season.

The news stunned Moddrell like a *pieba* hit. In McDermitt you needed to schedule a band *well* in advance. None of the parents had told him, and he was glad he didn't know. "That would have scared the crap out of me," he says. "It's like guaranteeing a win."

Maybe it was a curse. The Bulldogs won the trophy that season and enjoyed a few more years of success but eventually vanished from the playoff picture. A long history of winning turned to losing.

When Egan graduated in 1983, he'd already made a footprint in the adult world. His new wife, Lori, whom he met at a high school party, was pregnant with their first son, Lowell, and Egan was determined to lead a cowboy life.

He got hired on for the haying season at the Lucky 7 Ranch, where Cowboy Bob later worked. For five long years Egan labored seven days a week, sunup to sundown, until they brought the cows down from the high pasture in October. Then heartbreak hit like a stampede. First his father committed suicide, shooting himself in the head. Egan found out while he was out pushing cattle near Disaster Peak. Lori's father and the ranch manager drove 40 miles to give him the news. He slumped in his saddle, overcome by a sudden heaviness, then rode to the ranch, picked up Lori, and headed for Owyhee. He learned that his father had been depressed and that relatives had advised him to reach out to Richard, but he never did. "I love my dad," Richard says now. "I was so heartbroken for a long time."

A few years later his brothers, Sherwin and Willard, were both killed. One died in a car wreck, the other in an unsolved case of suspected murder. The deaths sobered up the young cowboy whose dreams of youth had emptied out like the now-closed mines.

By 1989 Egan was fixing fences in his sleep. By then Lori had begun driving a school bus in McDermitt, and Egan decided to join her. In 1990 he returned to the place of his boyhood exploits as a groundskeeper and bus driver. "It felt good to be back at the school," he says. It wasn't long before he returned to the football sidelines as Moddrell's assistant. By then he and Lori had two more children. Their son Lindsey was born in 1991, and a daughter, Ashley, came the following year.

It was a heady time to be in McDermitt. In 1991 McDermitt Mine officials financed a new high school football and track field. Mining money paid for a walkie-talkie system that Moddrell used to communicate with staffers up in the field's press box during games, and it helped raise $1,500 to send the senior class on a spring trip to Disneyland.

But nothing lasts forever. Star quarterbacks graduate, winning streaks end, and mining minerals are depleted from the ground. When the quarry closed in 1992, workers vanished, as did the facility operators and their deep pockets. From that point on, both the town and its football team were on their own.

By then both Bulldogs football coaches had left the team. When Moddrell stepped down to take a new job as school vice principal, Egan reluctantly followed to concentrate on his family. It was a painful time for both men.

For years, eventually as principal, Moddrell bent to political pressures that dictated he spend more time in meetings and less time on the football field. A few years later, in 2006, when he returned as coach, he felt revitalized. "When I saw those players every day, it reminded me why I'd gotten into coaching in the first place."

When he eventually retired, Moddrell didn't want to go. "I was heartbroken," he says. He recalls those crazy boys and their uneven skill sets, from the kids who struggled to even compete on the level of a tiny high school to those boys who dreamed bigger. Over the years he's gone to countless weddings—and far too many funerals—of his former players: "I just hope I left a mark on their lives."

Moddrell's final departure devastated the program. Nick Wilkinson's son, Hyland, was playing Bulldogs football the year Moddrell was replaced by a less-experienced coach. The rancher drove up to Oregon to watch his son play an away game and was shocked by what he saw. The Bulldogs were shellacked 72–0, and on the long drive home the boy said he didn't know why he was even playing football. "It was tough to see your son take a butt-kicking and admit he didn't know what he was doing, didn't even know where to start," Wilkinson says.

He advised his son to forget about the score. "If the scoreboard wasn't important," Hyland responded, "they wouldn't put it there." Wilkinson knew things would not improve. "I'd never told my kids they could quit something once they'd started it, but I was afraid for his health," he says. "He was like me as a kid, all bone and no meat. So I said, 'I won't hold it against you if you don't go back. I don't think you're learning anything here, and you're going to get hurt.'"

The boy never played another game.

After leaving football in 1992, Egan coached basketball during the four years his son Lowell played. "Not many fathers get that opportunity," he says. After graduation Lowell returned to McDermitt to teach high school math. He became his father's assistant, and the long car rides to scout opponents solidified the father-son bond.

Lowell later took over as the coach of the basketball team. Today, at thirty-eight, he's an assistant coach for the Salt Lake City Stars, the G League development team for the NBA's Utah Jazz. Lowell recalls his dedication as a boy, how he worked out in the gym at all hours, often with his father there rebounding his shots and firing them back for another three-point launch. "Both my dad and I are quiet," Lowell says. "There came a time when we knew what each other was thinking without having to say it. And when words needed to be said, they meant something."

For years after he stepped down as Moddrell's assistant coach, Richard Egan had yearned to return to football but didn't know how. Then came 2010 when the football team had another head coach opening. He was running the game clock during a home contest when the new principal, Don Almquist, leaned over.

"We're gonna have an opening in football. Interested?"

Egan knew that a culture of losing had descended over Bulldogs football, a program with too few players who were always gassed by the third quarter. But he loved the team, and he loved the town. So he took the leap.

Egan is behind the wheel of his rattling 2016 Chevy pickup, the truck's 135,000 hard, rural miles having taken their toll. He's touring Owyhee, his hometown, a place the outside world has largely avoided.

Even though Egan left forty years ago, the memories remain. The old hospital where both he and Nancy were born is boarded up, replaced by a new facility just up the hill. The original tribal office and gym remain, their nineteenth-century rock masonry now faded and crumbling. Egan pulls up to the main house where his mother lived until she died in 2016. He comes here several times a year to maintain the five-acre property, mow the lawn, and check the brands on the forty head of cattle his sister runs nearby. Nancy is now CEO of the Duck Valley Shoshone-Paiute tribe and has her own home nearby, but the family house remains as a shrine of sorts, a connection to simpler times.

There's something Egan wants to show me. He walks out behind the main house, wading through waist-high weeds and overhanging branches that cause him to duck and sidestep. Finally he arrives at the place where he and his siblings grew up: a lopsided single-wide trailer with a collapsed roof, a teetering old shack that sinks into the ground, retaken by the weeds and undergrowth and too much time abandoned.

Boyhood images flood his thoughts—the pecking chickens that wandered the yard, each morning gifting the family with fresh eggs. And all those glorious sunrises as the boys came and visited the coops to claim their prizes. "We had a basketball court out here," Egan says, pointing to a dirt expanse nearby. There were two hoops, forty feet apart, supported by sturdy poles

Fig. 19. Coach Egan at rest. Photograph by Randi Lynn Beach.

harvested from mountaintop wood, with backboards fashioned out of ply-wood. "We played full court," he adds. "Nancy and all of us."

Back then the Egan place was the last of a line of small spreads, and the children explored an endless landscape of rocky ground and sagebrush. Along with any one of their two dozen cousins, they chased calves and squatted close by as their father milked the cows. Richard was so young he referred to the cows as "black wows."

The afternoon is warm, and Egan begins to sweat as he picks his way through the thicket. For the first time in four decades, he sizes up the bare-existence trailer that looks like something out of Appalachian coal country with a patchwork of add-ons his mother built by hand as her family grew, including a kitchen extension and an extra bedroom. He peers through a window, now clouded and cobwebbed, and he spies one of the yellow bikes his mother had bought each of the kids. He goes quiet.

"Sometimes I'm ashamed to show people how I was brought up." Back then Egan and his brothers would head up to the mountains to cut wood for the hearth. "Eventually we got heat, but I used to feel embarrassed of my life. But that's the way things were back then." Early on he brought Lori up here to meet his family so she'd know what she was getting into. "I told her how poor we were," he says. "She accepted it."

Egan has put on nearly a hundred pounds since he first left here as a teenager. His body is still muscular, but now there's weariness to his gait. Who knows, maybe it was this rural poverty that drove him away from Owyhee, a kid escaping his humility in the hope of something better. Maybe that's why he hit those other boys so furiously on the football field, summoning the aggression he felt when he stepped between his mother and his abusive father. Maybe he was just showing the world that he was something more than just a poor Indian kid from a reservation in the middle of somewhere.

I mention Abraham Lincoln, saying it's not where you start that matters, but where you end up. He nods. We notice Nancy's horse, Ginger, just over the fence, and Egan tells me of the time when he first rode her saddle, but it was loose, and stubborn Ginger threw him. But Egan dusted himself off and got back into the saddle like he always does.

The siblings' care for their mother's house and the old trailer helps preserve a bond forged when they were children—when Nancy held her brother's hand and tried to wave off a hostile world. For Egan it's also a way to reconnect with a distant part of himself. "I like coming back," he says. "But my life is in McDermitt. My family is there."

The year before, he'd brought his grandson, Andres, to connect this place to a new generation. The boy's father, Lindsey, works as a Humboldt County sheriff's deputy based out of Winnemucca. Egan's daughter, Ashley, is a nurse in Elko. The first time the boy and his grandfather came to Owyhee, Egan was tired from the long drive, but Andres went right out to the yard.

"Grandpa, let's get busy right now. I'll start picking up these branches over here."

"I wanted to rest," Egan says, "but he was supervising me."

He also took the boy to the family graveyard miles from town where all four grandparents are buried, along with his parents and two brothers. As Egan pulled weeds around the gravestone, the boy wandered.

"Grandpa," Andres finally said. "There sure are a lot of Egans buried here."

Egan isn't sure he's going to join them. Four decades have brought an attachment to another place. Years ago Egan even surrendered his Owyhee Shoshone-Paiute membership to join the McDermitt tribe. It was the last vestiges of a boy's life slipping away into manhood, the admission paid to move from one border town to another.

In Owyhee we drive down Dog Street where Egan once swam in the canal on summer afternoons, easing past the mountain of bottles discarded by the town's winos. We see piles of cordwood stacked like tepees in the Native way, and we pass the house where one of Egan's grandfathers lived, the site of so many family gatherings. He slows at the football field, the one without lights, where a boy first took part in the sport that would soon center his life. That was before Coach John Moddrell's voice echoed in his mind: "Play every practice like it's a championship game."

From the passenger seat I watch as Egan returns the wave of a passing driver. "I don't know who that was," he says. "They wave, and I wave." Now only the elders remember him. He points to things that weren't there when he was young, amazed at the new fences that now mar the horizon and divide the sagebrush.

For a moment it seems he's back on that yellow Western Flyer, peddling hard, the wind in his face, blue skies as comforting as heaven, before the deaths of his father and brothers, when he was a boy who didn't know that hurt or heartbreak or boundaries even existed to be broken.

Fig. 20. Scholar Thierry Veyrié at the old Fort
McDermit. Photograph by Randi Lynn Beach.

18

I pull my station wagon just off a narrow road outside town and sit in silence. Harley Jackson, a mixed Paiute and Nez Perce artist, is in the back seat. Riding shotgun is Thierry Veyrié, the anthropologist who has researched the Native oral histories of this land and its original people and who has become my Paiute cultural interpreter.

It's late on a Sunday afternoon, and we squint into a weakening sun that casts long shadows over the rock walls of a small canyon. We hear the rustle of the wind, a mercurial force that has shaped this landscape for eons and will continue to do so long after we're gone. Nearby are the abandoned ruins of two mercury mines gouged into a forlorn hilltop, fickle enterprises that once provided an economic bedrock on which residents here could raise families, including young boys who wanted to play high school football as McDermitt Bulldogs.

But Veyrié wants to discuss a local history even more calamitous than mining. During the turbulent 1860s, westward-bound wagon trains packed with white settlers converged upon the region with a destructive force that seemed to rival nature itself. The newcomers drove off the big game that the Paiutes and other tribes had depended on for their survival. The intrusion led to bloodshed and war, and this small canyon played a part in that history. We're at the site of a decisive skirmish between Paiute warriors and U.S. soldiers during the Snake War of the 1860s that would define future battles and provide the name of the nearby military fort and, eventually, the town itself.

Jackson jumps from the car. He's a lithe man about fifty, and on the ride over he had engaged in battle with the backseat safety belt, which clanged when disengaged while the vehicle was in motion. Every mile or so I'd hear it and then look back to see Jackson without his belt, gazing out the window. He's served time in prison and now chafes at such manmade restraints.

Once outside, he searches for small rocks to fashion into arrowheads as Veyrié and I walk on. "This is McDermitt Canyon," the scholar says. He'd been shown the place years ago by his mentor, Dennis Smartt, the Paiute storyteller—and Richard Egan's uncle—to help him comprehend the Paiute victory that once took place here.

The son of a French nuclear physicist, Veyrié has long been drawn to the study of indigenous cultures. While in high school, he worked summers as a buckaroo on an Oregon ranch and fell in love with the sweep and dusty antiquity of central Nevada's Great Basin, part of the traditional lands of the Northern Paiute tribe. Since 2013 when he began his doctoral work in anthropology on the culture and history of the Fort McDermitt Paiute-Shoshone reservation, Veyrié has established himself as one of the town's many obtuse characters. He's a romantic figure, seemingly out of place in this unadorned Western town, dressed in blue jeans, a cowboy hat pulled low over his eyes. He's a regular on the reservation and has spent months in McDermitt's tiny library, located just across from the Say When casino.

At the onset of his research, residents even collected money to help the cash-strapped scholar afford the gas to return to school in Indiana. Now thirty-one, he is a new breed of anthropologist, one who hasn't stuck around just long enough to glean his data and insight before hurrying back to his university hub.

Veyrié has spent years studying the difficult Paiute language, a tool that offers him a more profound insight into the tribe's culture. He has helped Paiute elders write down old stories that were once only repeated orally— tales about Native folklore and the rewards and struggles of Paiute life. Some residents have adopted him as family.

Even after he submitted his doctoral dissertation in 2021, Veyrié has stayed on to help shape the Paiute's future and keep its dying language alive. Working as the language and traditional culture manager for the nearby Burns Paiute Tribe, he oversees a language immersion program for Native children. On weekends he drives 150 miles from Burns, excursions that include driving Jackson into the hills east of the reservation to scout for wood, rocks, and other resources for his art projects. Veyrié has also used his research skills to apply for federal grants to help fund numerous tribal cultural projects.

Still, Veyrié has learned the limits of a white foreigner operating within a tribal culture historically suspicious of outsiders. "I have to remember," he says, "that I'm still considered a foreigner here."

We stare out into the quiet canyon as Jackson adds an interpretation of the spot's historical value. "This is where my grandfather shot General McDermit in the neck with an arrow," he says. "He shot him right here."

I glance at Veyrié. Did Jackson mean *great*-grandfather or great-*great*-grandfather? The time sequence doesn't add up. The scholar stares off into the afternoon.

"They never did like us after that because the Indians killed McDermit, and he was a big man," Jackson continues. "They mistreated us and sent us off to boarding schools where we learned how to box so when we got out and those cowboys didn't like us and talked shit to us, we'd say 'C'mon with it, then.' We'd fight because we could scrap."

For Jackson and other Paiutes, the history of this place has indelibly shaped their culture. On August 7, 1865, Cavalry Lieutenant Colonel Charles McDermit, the commanding officer of the military's nascent Nevada district, was, in fact, ambushed by two Paiute warriors hidden in the brush. The clash took place as the U.S. military and an emerging army of volunteer white settlers faced off against the Northern Paiute, Bannock, and Western Shoshone bands who populated a broad swath of Oregon, Idaho, and northern Nevada.

On the day of his death, McDermit led soldiers on a mission to track Indian war parties, including one commanded by an elusive chief by the name of Black Rock Tom. The soldiers had ridden north through the canyon earlier that day on their way to Disaster Peak a few miles to the north, but Black Rock Tom had once again evaded them.

On the return journey McDermit had dispatched scouts to the canyon hilltops and was riding twenty feet ahead of a corporal and several other men when he was ambushed. "There was a very confused series of shots, but in the exchange McDermit fell down," Veyrié says. He offers no details of whether the Paiutes shot arrows or fired guns, careful not to contradict Jackson's account.

A mortally wounded McDermit died within hours. The men returned his body to a settlement then known as Camp 33, located along the Quinn River, where a lieutenant wrote to his commanders suggesting that the outpost be remade into a military post, bearing the name of their fallen commander. In his doctoral dissertation Veyrié cites "General Order No. 2" issued at McDermit's funeral at nearby Fort Churchill, headquarters of the Nevada district. The commander, it reads, "while in the noble performance of his duty, gallantly leading a portion of his command through a wilderness infested by savage foe, was shot and killed by hostile Indians."

In a footnote Veyrié's research also delves into a small but significant detail: how McDermit's last name, originally spelled with one *t*, morphed into the present-day spelling, a version used by both the town and the nearby reservation.

"It was a clerical mistake, a typo," Veyrié says. Near the turn of the twentieth century when the fort was finally abandoned, a U.S. army lieutenant, Peter Leary, wrote to affluent benefactors in Boston for donations to help renovate the old Fort McDermit into the site of an Indian school to be run by the U.S. Department of the Interior. "He was the first one to spell it with two *t*'s," Veyrié says, the error adding to the long list of often atrocious misspellings that were among the accepted vagaries of an era when not everyone was a spelling bee winner.

Far more than providing minutia, Veyrié's research interprets the broader effects of McDermit's death, which unleashed a new spasm of violence by settlers and soldiers seeking vengeance against the Paiutes. "The killing of McDermit was an epitomizing event," Veyrié says. "Everything that happened afterwards can be traced back to the events at this canyon."

The scholar interprets decades of frontier violence through the prisms of both white and Native American cultures. Using his broadening fluency in the vanishing Paiute language, he weighs established Anglo records with that of Native oral histories. The result is a historical record that reflects *both* sides of the conflict.

For example, even as McDermit was seen as a martyr by whites, Veyrié explains, the canyon where he died has become a local symbol of resistance, a place of celebration, "because it was the site of a Paiute victory, really."

Jackson points to a place where he once took part in the revelry. "That was main party ground," he says. "When I was sixteen, we came out here and drank whiskey."

Veyrié laughs. "All those tribal elders still alive today were probably out there partying with you," he says.

The moment not only captures a foreign scholar's quest to erase barriers but says a lot about McDermitt's rich cultural kaleidoscope. We walk back to the car, and I notice how sun-bleached Veyrié's cowboy hat has become—a badge of honor in a foreign land.

Veyrié is no stranger to violent culture clashes: He was a teenager living in the Paris suburbs when race-related riots broke out in 2005. The unrest, driven by high unemployment and police brutality in blue-collar neighborhoods dominated by North African and sub-Saharan immigrants, saw the burning of cars and public buildings.

The turmoil was a regular topic at the dinner table at Veyrié's home where his father, Pierre, a widely traveled nuclear scientist who worked with weapons for the French government, wasn't shy about expressing his opinions. "There was a dynamic of paternal dominance," recalls Veyrié, who learned how to listen before speaking, training that would later serve his anthropology. "Being the youngest of three sons, I always acknowledged my inferiority in any talk. But I learned to argue and debate."

In high school Veyrié was a loner who never concentrated on girls or sports. "I've always felt like an odd duck, but I've always accepted it," he said. "It's relevant to my career because it's part of my position as an anthropologist, someone who's not entirely in and not entirely out." His interest in social science came when he visited a friend's Native home in Senegal, where he spent time among the Jola tribe and witnessed their monthlong *bukut* ceremonies during which young boys were indoctrinated into manhood. He returned to France hungry to learn more about how isolated cultures sanction the personal development of their young.

At age sixty, Pierre wasn't happy about his son's career direction. He accepted the fact that atomic science wasn't his son's strong suit and that he would not be following in his footsteps. Yet he didn't believe anthropology offered enough structure, and the father steered his son toward a career as a high school teacher.

Yet Veyrié had already decided upon his life's mission: to use anthropology as a way to help repair his father's murky legacy as a weapons-based atomic scientist. "I wanted to imitate my father's achievements," he says, "but in a way that was building community instead of potentially destroying it."

Like with his older brothers, Veyrié's mother, Geneviéve, who would later become a social worker, encouraged him to spend summers studying abroad. When Veyrié chose to work on a ranch in the American West, Geneviéve contacted friends in Burns, Oregon, whom she'd met through her own interest in Native ceremonies. At seventeen, Veyrié began a decade-long internship at a ranch 150 miles north of the Oregon-Nevada line, returning each summer to ride the range as a buckaroo. He was drawn to the difficulty of the work, rising before dawn to face the elements, and he became known among other ranch cowboys as "Frenchman Terry."

On visits to Nevada's Great Basin National Park, Veyrié marveled at the natural grandeur that heightened his passion for the region. "It was a landscape different from anything I'd ever seen," he says. "I grew up a city boy in France, which is a lush country. Out on the basin there are no trees, no limit to how far the eye can see. I felt dizzy just looking at the immensity of that barren place."

While studying for his master's degree in Paris, Veyrié met Raymond J. DeMallie, a visiting U.S. professor from Indiana University and a renowned anthropologist of the American plains. DeMallie was friends with historian and theologian Vine Deloria Jr., whose book *Custer Died for Your Sins* became a kind of manifesto for Native American rights. Published in 1969, when young Indians in white-run schools were punished for speaking their own language, the book advocated that Native Americans be allowed to retain their tribal society in the modern world.

Deloria argued that tribal members weren't cardboard relics, fodder for churches, or self-serving crusaders, and held his most vitriol for what he called "anthros"—the anthropologists. "Into each life, it is said, some rain must fall," he writes. "Some people have bad horoscopes, others take tips on the stock market . . . But Indians have been cursed above all other people in history. Indians have anthropologists."

Veyrié knew his field's reputation among many tribes. Historically the work had involved excavating spiritual artifacts and even human remains curated for display in some far-off museum. Most social anthropologists saw their job not as creating relationships but as writing books. Veyrié's goal was to become an accepted member of the reservation, and he was determined to treat his study subjects as real people, not as organisms floating in some sociological petri dish.

After an anthropology professor in France wrote to DeMallie on his behalf, Veyrié was invited to visit the American Indian Studies Research Institute at Indiana University, which DeMallie cofounded. Veyrié considered the institute, located in a two-story limestone house on the Bloomington campus, a perfect fit. He pursued a discipline of anthropology known as ethnohistory, studying cultures through written documents and oral histories, which, for Veyrié, meant telling a balanced, culturally sensitive historical account that included the Paiute point of view.

"I wanted to work on Native cultures in a way that was supported by the tribes themselves, to figure out how I could conduct research that would be accepted by the community because I wanted that relationship to continue," he says. To do that among the Paiutes, he needed a guide "to follow me closely and chew me up enough times so that I would develop my own understanding of my surroundings."

Then he got lucky: he met Dennis Smartt.

Veyrié first encountered his future mentor unloading a pickup truck in a parking lot in Burns, Oregon. It was the summer of 2012, and he was working as a buckaroo during a break from his studies back in France. He'd volunteered at an Indian culture camp in town where Smartt was presenting Paiute oral histories. Since it would be another year before Veyrié would meet Raymond DeMallie, he still had little clue his studies would concentrate here or that this eloquent, dark-eyed Paiute elder would help to galvanize his work.

"I was fascinated that Dennis was fluent in an endangered language," he says. "There aren't many people who can still speak Paiute." Not only that, Smartt was schooled in the tradition of Paiute storytelling—known as *nadigwianna* or "telling each other." He spoke poetically, using imagery to resonate with both human listeners and the spirits, the living and the dead. In his late sixties Smartt projected a quiet intensity as he presided over affairs requiring spiritual authority. He died in 2020, so it's impossible to know what he thought of this inquisitive white foreigner who spoke English with a distinct French accent. But he agreed when Veyrié asked if he could visit the elder at his home on the Fort McDermitt Paiute-Shoshone reservation.

The relationship started slowly, with Smartt likely conflicted between his mentoring instincts and his tribe's general distrust of white interlopers such as anthropologists. For his part, Veyrié wanted Smartt's perspective on Paiute histories published by fellow white scholars. On that first drive into the McDermitt reservation, Veyrié witnessed a scene of sobering poverty distinctly foreign to his upbringing, including signs promoting suicide prevention programs to cope with staggering drug and alcohol problems. "For me, as an outsider, it was difficult to relate to what I was seeing."

At their first meeting, the pair talked for hours. And it was no surprise to Veyrié that the elder's accounts of his tribe's clashes with the U.S. military and white settlers differed greatly from the scholarly history. Smartt explained how Paiutes dealt with both a painful past and a difficult present, the hard reservation life of violence and abuse: rather than rely on modern social programs, they sought more ancient ways—the retelling of parables and spiritual ceremonies.

In time Veyrié came to comprehend the complexities of Paiute culture, how many reservation residents chose to live in the moment and resist making any investment in the future. "The seasonal cycle of the Paiute is one where every year you go get traditional food and return to where you spend your winter," Veyrié says. "That's the engine of the culture, growing older by the season." On the reservation, he says, "Most people are not concerned with buying a house because one is provided, or they live with family. There aren't many role models with successful careers or reasons to look into the future and say, 'I want to do that so I can better myself and my community.'"

When Veyrié eventually met DeMallie in Paris, the elder anthropologist was impressed by the student's budding relationship with a veteran storyteller like Smartt. By then Veyrié had already settled into the rhythm of reservation life. In those days he spent most of his time with Smartt, a man prone to reflection.

"He liked to dream on things," Veyrié recalls. "If you asked him a question about the language or a ceremony, he took days to sleep over it. He lived by a different rhythm, not one of immediacy. With important decisions, he waited to vet his actions spiritually." Rather than retell his stories individually to Veyrié, the mystic preferred to have his protégé accompany him to presentations where the audience could share its own insights. Early on, the pair arranged a storytelling festival on the reservation, during which Veyrié suspected that a parable the elder told involving the starving wolf and the sage hen, a tale of predator and prey, targeted him. Was Veyrié the hungry wolf, a feared visitor? Or a sage hen, a naive admirer ripe for exploitation? The student considered himself neither.

In private, Smartt imposed a strict regimen upon Veyrié like an old martial arts expert guiding a young fighter. Rule one: no sex. He didn't want a relationship with a Paiute woman to cloud Veyrié's vision and, perhaps worse, upset tribal members. "I thought, 'Well, I can do that.'" Veyrié laughs. "I'm experienced at being a loner." He was also tasked with driving his pickup into the mountains to haul back spring water that Smartt used as medicine in spiritual ceremonies. Once, Veyrié forgot to tie down the containers, and one cracked. All the water leaked out on his return.

Not acceptable, said the mentor.

Then Veyrié unknowingly broke a tacit agreement to deliver firewood exclusively to Smartt in exchange for his oral stories. He usually bought the wood in Burns and trucked it down to the reservation. One day he shared some cut logs with other community elders, whom Smartt had encouraged him to get to know.

Again, not *acceptable.*

"By delivering wood to others, I had broken my word," Veyrié recalls. "And on the reservation, one's word is important." By then Veyrié was camping in Smartt's backyard as a way to remain close to his mentor. Now the elder suggested he rent space someplace else, and he declined to accept payment for his Paiute instruction. Being paid for his expertise was like selling his own language. "And that," Veyrié says, "is a line he would never cross."

The two kept in touch while Veyrié was away at school, but the scholar felt a new and unmistakable emotional distance. "Dennis was my gatekeeper," he says. "Our relationship wasn't always easy. He was ornery sometimes, but I was faithful to him. He was the first one I saw when I arrived on the reservation and the last one before I left."

It was a bitter lesson on the shifting personal landscapes of a reservation where unforeseen events could swallow a relationship whole, not only between Native residents but especially when a white outsider is involved.

Now Veyrié had a problem: Who would teach him Paiute?

One day in 2013 he walked into the senior center on the McDermitt reservation and met Norma Tom, who was having lunch with other female seniors. At that point Veyrié already possessed an arcane insight into Paiute women. For his master's degree thesis he'd examined the gestures among genders in aboriginal cultures, focusing on Paiute femininity. He found that while men favored piercing gestures used with handling spears and other weapons, women used motions derived from digging and scraping while hoeing crops and treating animal hides. It wasn't much of a calling card, but Veyrié hoped his scholarship would appeal to these women.

For Tom, such interest in her culture was a revelation. While the Fort McDermitt Paiute-Shoshone reservation contains the nation's largest collection of Paiute speakers, the language is disappearing and desperately needs to be preserved. Yet not *one* of her two children, six grandchildren, or three great-grandchildren could speak the language, with traditional storytelling sessions superseded by smartphones and TV. Still, at age seventy, she speaks the language at home, hoping the words—like ambient background

Fig. 21. Thierry Veyrié around town. Photograph by Randi Lynn Beach.

music—will eventually resonate among a new generation. "It bothers me that our language is dying," she says. "I was amazed that this foreigner wanted to learn. Nobody else did."

The relationship benefited both sides. Veyrié recorded oral histories to explore how Paiutes traditionally interpreted their complex battles with white society. In return he helped elders transform those stories into a written form. For the first time many Paiutes could see their language as well as hear it. Not long before, Veyrié had met Boise State University linguistic professor Tim Thornes, who had written his doctoral dissertation on Northern Paiute texts. Veyrié pored over the dissertation but didn't yet have the conceptual tools to follow it.

Yet with Tom's help he cracked the code. Sentence by sentence, using Thornes's work as a guide, Veyrié painstakingly transposed the tales handed down by Tom's ancestors into written script. "It was a question of effort," Veyrié says. "If you put in the work, you can learn this difficult language. If you think you're entitled to those skills, you won't catch on." Here was a foreigner willing to work hard to accomplish something even Tom's own extended family could not. An unlikely friendship formed. "I'm going to adopt you," Tom told him. She calls Veyrié her nephew. He calls her Auntie. On his visits Tom still cooks him his favorite dish—biscuits and gravy—and offers advice about life and women. Still, whenever he's within earshot, she uses slang to joke with fellow Paiute elders—to mask their private gossip or women's talk.

One day, however, Veyrié remarked, "I know what you're saying."

"We were trying to hide it," Tom blushed. Her teaching efforts were bearing fruit. There would be no more secrets around *this* Paiute language student.

Still, residents gossiped about how Tom was tutoring this stranger as though she was giving away secrets or selling off family heirlooms. "Don't tell this white guy anything," they warned. Tribal chairwoman Maxine Redstar says many Paiute traditionalists resent the French scholar. "The most adamant ones say you don't reveal everything about yourself, especially to a white man," she says. "Even if he's doing something even our own people aren't doing: making an effort to retain the language and the culture."

For nearly a decade Veyrié has played by reservation rules. Following the Paiute concept of community and charity as a rite of passage, he donated his first month's salary to elders in both Burns and McDermitt. It's his way to heed Vine Deloria Jr.'s manifesto *Custer Died for Your Sins* to give back to a society from which he drew knowledge. "I want a reciprocal relationship," he says.

His relationship with Jackson is a good example. He's not concerned that the artist's stories don't ring true, like the claim that his grandfather shot an arrow that killed McDermit. "Whether they're true or not is irrelevant," he says. "I want to understand Harley's view of the world." Some in town may ridicule Jackson's version of McDermit's death, but not Veyrié.

He listens.

After our time in McDermitt Canyon on that October afternoon, we visit another legacy of white expansionism here: the site of old Fort McDermit.

These days the grounds are hardly a fortress, with no towering wooden walls, no sniper slats for sentries, and no huge lumbering gate like you see in old Hollywood movies. We stand on the old parade grounds surrounded by a rectangle of adobe, brick, and wooden buildings in various stages of decay, including a tiny jail, barracks, and an old hospital. Occupied for twenty-four years, the longest-active fort in Nevada was demilitarized in 1889 when the last commanding officer departed. Its care transferred to the Department of the Interior, ending a legacy of war and manifest destiny.

Today the old military commander's office serves as a rebuilt tribal headquarters. Reservation activists talk of refurbishing an adjacent white-washed structure—believed to be among northern Nevada's earliest original buildings—that once served as the enlisted men's cafeteria. Last used in the 1970s as a tribal senior center, the building, activists say, is the future site of an interpretative center and museum. "It's not an innocent history embodied here, but one of colonization and the invasion of the Paiute people," Veyrié says. "Yet maybe something good can be done here."

Veyrié filled out paperwork to register the building on the National Register of Historic Places. The McDermitt reservation doesn't have a tribal preservation office to certify the application, so the scholar launched a drive to create one. The efforts brought backlash: a white man should just leave things alone, many say. "In theory it's none of my business," he says. "But it's good to push for things."

As the sun grazes the horizon and cows low in the distance, Jackson reaches into his pocket for a piece of obsidian he plans to fashion into an arrowhead. He believes in the safeguarding of old things, like rocks and historical buildings. "I'd like to see this place preserved," he says.

Veyrié is determined to press on, inspired by his late mentors—Dennis Smartt, Ray DeMallie, and his father, Pierre, who died of congestive heart failure in 2019. In the end Pierre was proud of his son. Maybe in some small way, Veyrié is reinterpreting his father's work by helping sustain one isolated tribal society in a world under threat of weaponized atomic science.

Like Jackson, he wants to see it all preserved—the building, the language, and the ancient Paiute culture as well. "But I'm just a foreigner," he says.

With the sun gone now, Veyrié senses a change in the wind and says it's time to go.

He listens.

Fig. 22. Niyla Crutcher in motion. Photograph by Randi Lynn Beach.

19

Late in the fall of 1998, Wilson Wewa Jr. and his father, Jazzy, made a six-hour drive across northern Nevada to deliver urgent news to clan members in distant Owyhee.

Then forty-two, Wewa was executive director of the museum and cultural center for the Pyramid Lake Paiute Tribe based near the town of Nixon. He'd recently received a letter from the Smithsonian Museum: as it turned out, remains belonging to Chief Egan, a revered ancestor and leader of a band of Northern Paiute Indians, had for years been stored within the Washington museum's historical archives.

In 1989 Congress passed the National Museum of the American Indian Act, which required the Smithsonian to repatriate its vast collection of human remains, including those of Chief Egan, which for generations had languished on a dusty shelf in the nation's capital, thousands of miles from the leader's homeland. A year later the Native American Graves Protection and Repatriation Act mandated that federally funded institutions return all 200,000 Indian remains held in collections around the country.

But the return of the body had been glacially slow, delayed by both politics and bureaucracy. Nearly a decade passed before Smithsonian officials finally sent letters to Paiute tribes in California, Nevada, Oregon, and Idaho in an attempt to locate Chief Egan's direct descendants.

One was sent to Wilson Wewa Jr.'s tribe.

Written on Smithsonian stationary by a caseworker named Paula Molloy, the letter explained that the institution was repatriating Native American remains "culturally affiliated to the Paiute" from its vast collection. "Enclosed are copies of . . . documents relating to the remains of Chief Egan and his brother-in-law Charlie . . . who died with him on the battlefield on 14 July 1878," it read. "In reviewing these records, I find that Chief Egan's skull was also taken from the battlefield" after medical officers reported "seeing Chief Egan's headless body on the field sometime after battle."

The news was as bitter as chewing dandelions. From the stories told by tribal elders, Wewa's generation knew that Egan was killed in 1878 in southeastern Oregon during the so-called Bannock War amid yet another wave of white migration into their native homeland. Yet no account ever mentioned what had happened to Egan's body.

The revelation reopened an old wound. For more than a century, Egan's skull, along with Charlie's, had been kept by the U.S. government as a trophy of sorts.

With the disclosure too urgent for a telephone call, Wewa drove to Owyhee to inform the chief's oldest living kin, Hubert Egan, the slain leader's great-grandson and Nancy and Richard Egan's grandfather. The whole clan knew Hubert as a self-reliant elder who sometimes inhabited a solitary shack where he guarded against the beavers building dams along isolated Marys Creek.

For two days Wewa and his father sat solemnly with Hubert at his home in Miller Creek, just outside of Owyhee. Speaking in Paiute, surrounded by a handful of Egan's descendants—including Nancy, now a college-educated woman and local tribal administrator—they discussed how to proceed.

They all knew the many historical insults made to Native American culture by white society—all the broken treaties, herding tribes onto reservations and suppressing their language. Now those painful indignities were being dragged into the present—the desecration of the body of a revered tribal elder and hero.

A government report noted how holes had been drilled into Egan's skull, his jaw wired for proposed display. "A sense of shock filled the room," Nancy recalls. "I had to sit and process what I had just read."

The family discussed who should coordinate the return of both the chief and his brother-in-law Charlie for a proper burial—a complicated challenge involving a blizzard of paperwork to negotiate the labyrinth of federal bureaucracy.

In the end Hubert's eldest daughter, Phyllis, chose her niece, Nancy, for the job. The young tribal administrator had lived with her grandfather as a girl and had learned to speak Paiute from listening to his stories about the sage chief who faced upheaval, war, and starvation. But Hubert never mentioned the mutilation of the chief's body.

Now the family learned the hard truth. This was a human being, after all, a cherished ancestor. But according to the reports, Egan's remains had been treated like some random arrowhead found on the ground. "I read parts to my grandfather," Nancy recalls, "and sometimes he would weep."

Nancy also faced a looming deadline. Her grandfather was already ninety-seven and consigned to a wheelchair. "We just had to get this done as quickly as we could," she says. "It was a race to bring those remains home while he was still with us."

Nancy had once wanted to leave Owyhee as her brother Richard had. She planned to join the army, but Hubert disapproved. After all, his great-grandfather was killed at the hands of U.S. soldiers. Maybe he didn't want her to join a force that had brought such a legacy of pain. But Nancy was young then; she didn't think about that. "All I wanted to be was independent," she says.

Now she was tasked with a new mission that was as urgent as it was personal: arrange to bring Chief Egan home for burial.

The return of Chief Egan's remains would be a first step toward closure. But it also rekindled a rising sense of outrage. "Who gave *you* permission to do this to his body in the first place?" she wanted to ask officials. Now she was collecting documentation for the return of sacred remains that were theirs in the first place. "It just left me with a feeling of disgust."

Her disgust would focus not only on the U.S. government but later on her own Native American people.

The chief's Paiute name was "Ezich'guegah," pronounced *e-hee-gant*, the owner of the blanket, protector of his people, but the whites shortened it to an anglicized word: Egan. He was born in the 1830s not as a Paiute but to a Cayuse tribe in the foothills of the Blue Mountains in northeast Oregon.

Early on, the camp was raided by hostile warriors. The adults were slaughtered and the children kidnapped, and Egan was taken in by Weiser Indians, a group of Northern Shoshone people. He eventually married the sister of the Paiute Chief Shenkah, whom he joined in numerous skirmishes against the U.S. Cavalry and encroaching white settlers. "He was raised as one of our people," Wewa says. "He became renowned as a hunter and a warrior and eventually became a chief."

Egan was a contemporary of Sarah Winnemucca, the daughter of Northern Paiute leader Chief Winnemucca, who became a controversial author, activist, and educator. While serving as a translator to various U.S. military leaders, Sarah collaborated with Egan to spread the word about the mistreatment of the Northern Paiutes.

The list of grievances was long.

In his 2022 book *Northern Paiutes of the Malheur: High Desert Reckoning in Oregon Country*, historian David H. Wilson Jr. writes of how the Paiutes saw their homeland co-opted by white invaders, steam by stream, valley by valley. "For their farms they took the best land . . . blocking Paiutes from the sites where they had long gathered grass seed, caught fish, and killed wildfowl," he writes. "To build houses, barns, fences, sluices, and bridges, the newcomers felled forests in a land of few trees, depriving Paiutes of ponderosa pine nuts and destroying habitat for deer, rabbit, quail, and grouse. Fields where Paiutes had gathered the roots of sego lily, wild onion, biscuitroot, and yampah were now fenced, trampled, and fouled by cattle."

When half-starved Paiute bands resorted to raiding cattle from white settlements, the newcomers retaliated, summoning the U.S. Cavalry to protect their interests. The inequities led to bloodshed known as the Snake War. Collectively called "Snake Indians" by whites, the Northern Paiute, Bannock, and Western Shoshone bands were eventually defeated by U.S. Army forces led by Brigadier General George Crook. Egan was captured and surrendered his arms. The young chief, with few other options, decided to live in peace.

Egan led his followers to Fort McDermit, where he would meet Sarah Winnemucca. In her book, *Life Among the Paiutes*, she later made a case that all Paiutes could live in peace with white settlers. "If the Indians have any guarantee that they can secure a permanent home on their own native soil," she wrote, "and that our white neighbors can be kept from encroaching on our rights, after having a reasonable share of ground allotted to us as our own, and giving us the required advantages of learning, I warrant that the savage (as he is called today) will be a thrifty and law-abiding member of the community."

In 1873 Egan and his band took the opportunity to prove just that, returning to southeastern Oregon to settle on the Malheur Indian Reservation. The group included his wife, Sally, her brother Charlie, their adopted daughter, Mattie (daughter of the slain Shenkah), and their teenage son, Honey—Nancy and Richard Egan's great-great-grandfather. At Malheur, Indian agent Major Samuel Parrish assisted Egan and his followers in making the transition to farming, lessening their contact with settlers. Parrish told the Natives that they would be paid for their work and actually own the land they tilled and the crops they harvested. Under Egan's guidance for the next three years, the group grew corn, potatoes, squashes, onions, and turnips.

Meanwhile the whites saw something uniquely distinguished about Egan. While no photograph exists of the leader, army commanders noted his imposing presence. General Oliver Otis Howard, who first encountered the chief during a visit to Malheur, later wrote "how superior Egan was to the others. He had on an ordinary farmer's suit of light linen duck, with a leather belt around his waist, a sheath holding a sheath-knife by his side," he noted. "He wore a straw hat that he removed when he spoke to me. He had all the features of a full-blooded Indian but wore no braid or ornament. His hair, parted in the middle, was cut short at the neck. His pleasant face and resonant voice were mainly used that morning in praising Major Parrish."

But in May of 1876 Parrish was replaced by William Reinhart, who had a vastly different idea about the Indians' role in determining their own future. Reinhart reversed policies advocated by Parrish, and relations with the tribes at Malheur quickly soured.

Reinhart slashed the rations given to Paiutes on the reservation, cuts that he later admitted reduced them to "half-fed paupers." Sarah Winnemucca also saw Reinhart physically attack several Paiutes, including a man who had failed to respond quickly enough to an order and a boy whom Reinhart grabbed by the ear and threw to the ground. Reinhart told Winnemucca that the boy had laughed at his directive, but Winnemucca explained that the child simply had not understood him.

Egan eventually confronted Reinhart. "Did the government tell you to come here and drive us off this reservation?" he asked. "Did the Big Father say, 'Go and kill us all off' so you can have our land? Did he tell you to pull our children's ears off and put handcuffs on them and carry a pistol to shoot us with? We want to know how the government came by this land. Is the government mightier than our Spirit-Father, or is he our Spirit-Father? Oh, what have we done that he is to take all from us that he has given us?"

In protest of Reinhart's tactics, Egan and his band left the reservation in 1878. That same month, the so-called Bannock Uprising broke out. The Bannocks were a warlike people feared by other tribes, including many Paiutes.

The Bannocks, either by choice or force, hoped to bring Egan into their ranks. A Bannock war party descended on Egan's camp at a place called Steens Mountain in southeastern Oregon. While some Paiutes there opted for war, Egan did not, telling the Bannocks, "Why do you come here among us to bring war to our fireside? Go away. We have done nothing. We are at peace. Why should you bring the soldiers upon us? You have made war, and now you come among my people to bring war on them. My people will be killed."

Egan's role in the conflict would be mischaracterized by the military and the American press, which painted him as a savage combatant on the "warpath," leading his people to hostilities and massacres. But the press had long oversimplified Native American motives. Not all tribes—which usually operated in small traveling bands—were united in any one cause, including the Bannock Uprising, and there is no evidence to show that Egan acted among hostile tribes.

In late June, weeks after Egan had left the Malheur reservation, the military, led by Colonel Orlando Robbins and a band of Idaho militiamen, attacked an Indian encampment at Silver Creek, Oregon. Riding atop his horse, Egan was shot in the wrist, chest, and groin. Historians have tried to pierce the fog of battle that day, with some concluding that Egan was either trying to escape or surrender rather than fight. "What the Bannocks stood for was anathema to Egan," Wilson argues. "It was entirely in character for him to do his best to escape from them. It would have been entirely out of character for him to fight in their cause."

As fellow Paiutes dragged Egan from the scene, he lay weak and dying, his left arm shattered near the elbow, wrapped in splints and bandages, bound to his chest.

With Robbins and U.S. soldiers in pursuit, the Paiute band went on the run. At a place called Emigrant Springs, Egan and his followers were attacked by a party of Umatillas, who were loyal to U.S. forces. Egan and a dozen others were killed, including Egan's brother-in-law Charlie.

Precisely what happened next is unclear. Some historians believe that the Umatillas cut off the leader's head and presented it to the U.S. soldiers as proof of his death, denying him a burial and uprooting Egan from his place in the world. Others believe that army surgeon Jenkins "John" Fitzgerald beheaded the slain leader. Either way the gesture marked the beginning of the end of tribal resistance. "Egan's death was a tragedy to the Paiutes that led to the disintegration of their world," Veyrié says, "because this was the last real war. After that there was no more resistance."

At the time, U.S. Army doctors were studying Native American remains in an effort to demonstrate that the skulls of whites were larger and the race therefore superior. They amassed a collection of three thousand Native American remains to "prove" their spurious claims, including the skulls of Egan and Charlie.

They were first deposited at the Army Medical Museum, housed in the former Ford's Theater, the site of Lincoln's assassination, where they were displayed along with the bones of John Wilkes Booth. But rather than use

Egan's skull for "research," the U.S. Army used his remains as evidence of its battlefield mastery. "The army's prowess was accentuated all the more if the skull was that of a chief, like Egan," Wilson argues, "drained of his savagery and exhibited for the world to see, not unlike a scalp dangling from a warrior's belt."

Nancy Egan agrees. The military, frustrated by a decades-long Native American insurrection, saw the remains as a souvenir. "To them, Chief Egan was a defiant activist," she says. "In order to scatter and demoralize the masses, they had to conquer him in a very public way. He was their target." The body of a peaceful Native American leader became a spoil of war.

For generations Egan's skull was kept at the Army Medical Museum as a tourist curiosity before being sent to the Smithsonian where it was stored away like some common trinket, utterly forgotten, its location unknown to the Paiutes.

Now, after 121 years in exile, Chief Egan was coming home.

On that spring morning in 1999, Erman Smartt felt like a visitor from another planet, vulnerable and far from home. Before that day he had always stayed close to his home on the Fort McDermitt Paiute-Shoshone Reservation.

Smartt had never flown on a plane, let alone travel 2,300 miles across the country to Washington, the capital of the white man—a city whose very name commanded fear and respect among his ancestors. Now he was an emissary to a mission of grave importance to his people: to escort the coveted remains back home to southern Oregon.

He boarded a commercial flight in Boise, Idaho, with his wife, Angela, and a fellow tribal representative, Dean Adams, and sat in the back where he felt safer. Now he stood stiffly in a small windowless room in Washington's Smithsonian Museum, witnessing all that was left of his ancestors.

Before Smartt, the remains of Chief Egan and Charlie were gently laid out on a table covered with white buckskin—just two skulls, really.

He was afraid. "When I went in there and I saw all those skulls on the table, I felt like, 'I'm not wanted here.' But the spirit came to me. This was something I had to do."

Smartt cupped a Paiute prayer bowl—a pale pink seashell—and nervously blew into it, allowing the embers of cedar and sage inside to crackle and pop, the purifying smoke drifting dreamlike across the room.

Fig. 23. Niyla Crutcher on the reservation. Photograph by Randi Lynn Beach.

Two decades later Smartt sits across from me, inside the kitchen of relatives on the reservation. As his grandchildren run about the living room, he describes how he was in his thirties that day, dressed in a white turtleneck and black vest, his long black hair neatly braided beneath a wide-brimmed, hand-beaded hat.

In Washington he heard the comments: "Hey, there's an Indian. He's got long braids."

"I hung on to my old lady that whole day," Smartt recalls. "I stuck to her. 'Don't leave my side,' I told her. When it was all done, I turned to her and said, 'Thank you.'"

Wewa, a spiritual figure, had originally planned to handle the return. But waylaid by tribal budget hearings, he sent Smartt and Adams. Yet Wewa remained central to the ceremony. During a telephone call twenty-two years later, Wewa detailed how he'd sent the buckskins, sage, prayer bowl, and cedar boxes provided by Egan's ancestors.

That day, from a speakerphone on a nearby table, Wewa's voice filled the tiny room. Reporter Courtenay Thompson of the *Portland Oregonian*—the same newspaper that had once labeled Egan "rebellious" and helped shape white beliefs about the Bannock Uprising—sat in and took notes about Egan's journey home.

"Okay, now I'm going to sing the song, the burial song," Wewa said that day. "I'm going to do that the best I can over the telephone."

In a voice both clear and strong, like the past brought to the present, he sang a Paiute purification prayer over a muted drumbeat. When he finished, the remains were carefully packed for the long journey back to Oregon.

The three Paiutes then boarded a return flight to Boise, from which they would make the trip's final leg, a 200-mile drive to Burns, Oregon, for the burial. Smartt recalls holding on tightly to the precious cargo, the skulls wrapped in buckskin inside the cedar boxes, housed in two gray, archival cardboard containers.

He was nervous. Wewa had not provided specific guidance on how to carry his cargo to avoid disturbing their spirits. Sitting in the kitchen, amid the ruckus of children, Smartt calls the day the most important of his life. "We kept the remains by our side on the plane the whole way back," he says. "We were not going to let them out of our sight."

When the party landed in Boise, Adams placed the packages in the back seat of his car, and a four-vehicle procession—led by a tribal police car—began the three-hour drive through a landscape that turned evermore familiar, soon crossing the Snake River into Oregon, marking the final return of a great Paiute leader.

Two decades later Smartt remains humbled by his role. "There's no pride. I don't think that way," he says softly. "I represented the elders. I did the bidding of their prayers."

One autumn afternoon in 2021 I sat with Richard and Nancy Egan in the living room of their mother's Owyhee home as Nancy sorted through her yellowing files. Richard knows his older sister made the return of Chief Egan's remains happen, knows that she is the one who still speaks the language, the one with the organizational skills.

Richard had first encountered the great leader who bore his last name as a boy while reading the book *Owyhee Trails: The West's Forgotten Corner by Ellis Lucia.* But he never made the connection and never asked his elders about his family history. He'd once understood Paiute but later lost his fluency in the language and, unlike Nancy, didn't have access to the elder's stories. It wasn't until Nancy informed him of the efforts to finally bring home their ancestor's hijacked remains that he remembered the passages from that book and his long-lost childish innocence.

Nancy gave him a diagram of the family tree that shows how Chief Egan's son, Honey, grew to raise a son, Herbert, who grew to raise his own son, Hubert, Richard's grandfather. Richard keeps the chart by his bedside. Each night as he turns out the light, it helps launch his dreams into a heritage that leads directly to him.

Still, Chief Egan himself remains shrouded in mystery to his ancestors. "I wish there was a picture so I could better visualize him," Richard says. "To understand who he was. I know that when it came to battle, he was there to protect his people."

Nancy had handled all correspondence with Paula Molloy, the Smithsonian's repatriation officer. Elders decided that, once the remains were released, Chief Egan and Charlie would be buried together in a small tribal cemetery outside Burns, near the former Malheur reservation where the leader once worked the land to help feed his people.

"This was the area where Chief Egan was," Nancy says. "He only moved to McDermitt through force. This was home to him." Even today there's a street named for the chief in central Burns, where the name Egan is spoken with respect.

A late April date was chosen for the interment, when the southern Oregon ground was thawed after another harsh winter. Nancy and Richard planned to have both Hubert and their grandmother, Elaine, chauffeured to Burns for the ceremony. Once there Richard would attend to Hubert, and Nancy would care for Elaine.

But it was not to be. Elaine died two months before the ceremony, months before her ninetieth birthday. No records remained of her birth date, but she had chosen November 26 for her official birth date, the day *after* Americans celebrate their own Thanksgiving. Her death underscored the urgency to ensure that Hubert made the 325-mile journey to Burns. "It was devastating to lose her, like we were dealing with dual deaths," Nancy says, "Chief Egan and then our grandmother."

After the remains arrived by plane in Boise and the procession crossed into Oregon, the vehicles stopped near the Malheur reservation for an initial meeting with the family. Wewa blessed those present with burning sage, spreading the cloud of smoke that quickly enveloped the solemn ceremony.

Hubert sat quietly in his wheelchair. "I had told him what was going on," Nancy explains, "that we were going to meet the remains. He cried again after that."

Wewa spoke about how whites forced his Paiute ancestors to scatter across Idaho, Nevada, and Oregon until they were finally rallied by leaders like Chief Egan. As he talked, geese called from the open desert landscape in the distance.

"It really gets me in here," Wewa said, touching his heart, "for one of our leaders to come home. Our people shouldn't have to be in a box or displayed on a shelf. They are somebody. They had a name and spirit. When we sing and pray tonight, his spirit will be at rest and at peace, to go where the rest of our people go."

The mourners later gathered on the Burns Paiute Reservation, where two tepees housed the remains to lie in state overnight. A fire burned into the following day, a signal that a revered elder was making his final journey, the blaze tended by Paiute elders like Dennis Smartt, Erman's uncle and a holy man. To allow that fire to extinguish would have been considered a sacrilege, and there had already been enough of that. Only after the remains were buried would the flames be allowed to die.

After dark, Wewa motioned for Hubert to be wheeled close to the tepees. The elder wore a cap and glasses, his sweater covered by a blanket adorned with Native designs to protect him from the chill. Richard stood nearby, dressed in a flannel shirt, cap, and wide cowboy belt buckle. Scores of people gathered around the fire, performing the sacred round dance. Nancy held her grandfather's hand, leaning close to speak to him "in the language," Paiute.

"Here's cedar in front of you," Nancy told Hubert, gently removing his cap. Then her grandfather reached out and pulled the purifying smoke toward him, tapping his head in the firelight as Richard and Nancy Egan looked on.

Hubert Egan cried once again when he woke up on that burial morning.

After staying overnight in the Arrowhead Hotel in Burns, the family was now ready for the solemn day to come. Nancy had made good on her promise to make sure her grandfather witnessed the return of Chief Egan to traditional tribal lands so he could finally go to that place where her people go.

Nancy was glad her brother was there as well, this man whose hand she'd held so tightly when he was a child. The already close bond they shared had grown even stronger. Together they felt like the remaining nucleus of the Egans left on earth—Richard pushing Hubert in his chair, Nancy walking alongside, leaning in to comfort the elder, again speaking "in the language."

Around noon they gathered on the ceremonial grounds where the tepees sat and the campfire burned. That's when Nancy spotted them. A half dozen Umatillas, including a Cayuse chief, had arrived from their southern Oregon reservation. While all were welcome there, Nancy was still surprised to see the Umatillas.

She had not expected to feel anger that day, yet there it was. She had read accounts of how Chief Egan had been killed by the Umatillas, his body mutilated and handed over to the white leaders. "Because of your ancestors is why we're here," she recalls thinking. "How dare you."

It was like a killer's family showing up at the victim's funeral, and it felt wrong. Then came a gentle breeze, a wisp of air seemingly out of nowhere. "It came from the chief, that was my sense," Nancy recalls. "He was saying, 'Calm yourself.'"

Wewa stepped forward and greeted Armand Minthorn, a Umatilla spiritual leader, joking that he should have known the Umatillas were coming because the weather had turned stormy. Minthorn asked if he could sing a ceremonial song. The tepee was so crowded that not everyone could fit inside to encircle the remains.

As Minthorn sang, Nancy closed her eyes. She couldn't watch. And then, like the wind before it, another sound brought a sense of warmth. She opened her eyes to see a Umatilla ringing a bell. All at once, a light rain began to fall, the drops landing in feathery finger rolls atop the tepee. Through the open door, a shaft of sunlight shone through, illuminating only Minthorn. Again Nancy felt the chief's presence. "Then it was like, 'It's okay.' That was the message."

Nancy now watched how her grandfather took it all in. "All his stories, as you got older, became more repetitive, but you never got tired of them," she says. "In the end it was doing something for Grandpa, what in his heart he felt needed to be done. Knowing that he had lived long enough to see this happen."

Mourners joined hands for one more dance. As reporter Courtenay Thompson wrote, "Some wear regalia, moccasins, shawls; others wear suits, like the linen shirts Chief Egan once wore. Teenagers shuffle in baggy jeans; grandmothers are wrapped in blankets; a father cradles his baby son. In the center, by the still-burning bonfire, Chief Egan's great-grandson listens from his wheelchair, his white cowboy hat tipped low over his face."

And with that, they were one tribe, one people, together feeling their collective loss. Hubert would die two years later. But on this day he was there, a witness and bridge to the past.

I'm standing atop a bluff on the Burns Paiute Reservation. It's late October, and the sun is out, the tattered edges of an aged American flag flapping in a swelling breeze.

In this isolated cemetery of a hundred Paiute graves, I have come to find Chief Egan.

I have permission to be here from both Richard and Nancy. Still, this burial ground on sovereign tribal land rarely sees white visitors, and I feel like an intruder. Even Thierry Veyrié isn't comfortable that I am here. The day before, I visited him at his tribal office. We stepped outside, and, without pointing, he only reluctantly offered directions on how to reach this spot. I can't blame him.

Now I walk past rows of graves, grouped by family, the remains of U.S. veterans who fought in World War II, Korea, Iraq, and Afghanistan. I take no pictures or notes but dictate my thoughts into a small recorder by my side. I keep an eye out for approaching vehicles, a telltale dust trail on the dirt road leading to this hilltop place.

Inside the barbed-wire fence, a small wooden building lies on its side as though blown over by an angry wind. But now the wind has suddenly calmed, leaving only stillness.

Along with soldiers, uncles, and grandmothers, children are buried here. Toy trucks and stuffed animals adorn the graves. On the marker of a child who died at the tender age of six months are the words, "Granny loves you."

Another marker reads, "Thank you Creator for sharing him with us." And a stone crowded with decorations hints at the remains buried here: "Beloved wife, mother, sister, grandmother, great grandmother, master basket weaver, teacher and friend."

I finally reach the easternmost edge of the graveyard, along the barbed-wire fence, overlooking pastureland below. That's where I find it: a spot not unlike a precipice where a leader might stand, among his people but set apart, if only just so.

The grave is unmarked, formed by a thick concrete slab, eight feet by eight feet, an obelisk of red rocks and a clutch of purple flowers at the center. As Wewa later explained, "We didn't want Chief Egan to suffer any more indignity and disrespect by having somebody dig up the remains and claim they had his skull."

As I stand at the grave, I offer a silent apology to this leader and his brother-in-law, Chief Egan and Charlie, for what had befallen them. Wewa wants an official government apology "for everything it took from our people, for the grave robbing, and the boarding schools. White Americans would not allow that to happen to white kids."

Can modern men account for the sins of their forefathers? In the end Nancy and Richard say it does not matter. They know the blood of their people was wrongfully shed on this land. Nancy has visited the spot, now privately owned, where Chief Egan was mortally wounded, as a way to cope with the past.

For his part, Richard now identifies as a name carrier of this former leader. White ranch families around McDermitt sometimes boast of being third or fourth generation. Richard has them all beat; he's a walking lineage of his tribe's right to remain on this land. "I'm just proud of the name Egan," he says. Regarding the family tree that hangs beside his bed, he adds, "Before I close my eyes, I say to myself, 'This is my place in the world. This is who I come from.'"

It's nearly noon, and I have a long drive back to McDermitt. The silence weighs on me as I stand at Chief Egan's grave. Yet there is no subtle message from those at rest here, no warm breeze, no shaft of light.

Those things are not meant for me.

20

One evening Frank Hill hustles his five-year-old son, Landon, around the high school track as McDermitt's football Little Leaguers share the practice field with the varsity Bulldogs.

Hill is bushy-bearded, wild-eyed, and full of adrenaline. He wears a farm cap, a flannel shirt, and an old pair of blue jeans as he dashes back and forth across the field, doing sprints, kicking the football high in the air, as children practice all around him.

He's crazy Frank Hill, yesterday's Bulldog, and on this green grass of boyhood is the place where he lived out his best days before all the rest came.

It's the first time he's been back in a decade.

"Been awhile," he says.

Hill played offensive wide receiver and defensive end for the Bulldogs. In his junior season, in 2010, the team went 4-5, which, at the time for this underachieving program, was like winning the Super Bowl, Preakness, and the NBA championship combined. Egan was named the league's coach of the year.

"We were good," Hill says.

After he graduated, Hill worked in the mines and as a diesel mechanic before settling for ranch labor out near Kings River. Along the way he got married, fell into trouble with the law, and ended up in jail for a time. Small stuff, he says, like smoking pot and stealing a bottle of whiskey from a store shelf.

He's delighted to be back here. You can see it in his posture, in that laugh, and in the way he runs on the grass. Egan sees Hill and smiles. Coaches don't remember every player. Some kids just don't stand out. Then they get older, and fatter, and when you run into them at some bar, a wedding, or a restaurant, it can be hard to place them. Smith has a secret to help him remember: He listens to his voice, he tells me. While bodies may age, voices stay the same.

But there's no forgetting Frank Hill. He ate up the turf, scored touchdowns, and then tipped his head back and laughed

Back in the day Egan designed a play especially for him. On the call of "turtle," Hill shot straight out for the end zone, running hard like a wild horse, fearless, not even looking up until the ball settled into his hands.

Crazy Frank Hill.

As Egan's team runs laps around the field, Hill approaches, slapping his old coach hard on his broad shoulders.

"I saw you," Egan says. "With that long beard, I thought you were Santa Claus."

Hill spins a football on his fingertips, telling Egan that he and his wife now have seven children between them. But Hill says he still plays fast and loose.

"You have to be quick," Egan says, "to stay ahead of the cops."

Hill blushes. "I haven't always done that."

"I know," the coach says. "I heard."

Hill steals glances at this older man whose approval he once sought. Years ago he'd wanted Egan's advice on such boyhood blunders as getting caught sneaking into his high school girlfriend's motel room on a school outing.

Now he's twenty-seven, no kid anymore. He goes on the offensive.

"You've gotten fat, Egan," Hill says. "Look at that gut, leading you around."

"You, too." The coach laughs, but both men know he's lying.

"Remember that old drill we did?" Hill asks.

Then he fires the football at Egan, who reaches out to grab it, dropping his water bottle on the grass. The ball sputters away. Hill smiles, having gotten the upper hand.

Egan retrieves the ball and fires it back, hard. Hill grabs it with one hand.

They continue, back and forth, a boy turned man challenging his old mentor, until Hill finally drops one.

But the coach now has new protégés, and he walks off toward the huddle. Suddenly there's Frank Hill, yesterday's Bulldog, standing alone on his field of memories.

Dogs on three! One-two-three Dogs!

As the last week in August plays out, the McDermitt Bulldogs are a sagging, depleted bunch, a football team fumbling for an identity—and enough boys to make a team. There's always a reason one player or another fails to show. A lost dog, a spat with a girlfriend, or, like Maverick, one mysterious AWOL after another.

Egan can't afford to lose any of them. One day when Maverick shows up late, the coach walks over to the boy. "McDermitt needs you," he says within earshot of the others. "These boys need you."

"McDermitt doesn't need me," Maverick replies. "If I can just get two more kids to come out here and play, I can quit."

Egan ignores him. "Remember your dads and grandfathers and uncles were here, just like you," he says. "Go look at their yearbook photos, the looks on their faces. You gotta be excited to be here."

The boys continue to fall like toy soldiers, complaining of phantom injuries or anything that comes to mind. "Man, it's hot," Enzo says. "We need some air-conditioning."

"Don't complain about the heat," Egan snaps. "Soon we're going to be playing in the rain and sleet that comes sideways. Then you'll want that heat back again."

He turns to Smith. "Same shit, different practice."

Is it even worth it, I ask? Worrying all year? Designing plays just to produce another team of out-of-shape softies not only lacking the will to win but to even play?

"Some coaches, if they're not winning, won't stick around," Egan says. "But I'm not going to give up on these kids. As long as they come out, I'm gonna work with them."

Meanwhile the malevolent tension between Bulldog seniors Taylor and Bailey builds with each practice. After Bailey's texting prank, taunting that Taylor would spend his life working at Walmart, there's been an uncomfortable silence between the boys.

One afternoon Bailey gave his ball cap to a younger kid in the school hallway who used it to run over and take a swipe at Taylor, making several boys laugh. Not exactly a Mike Tyson punch, but it was enough to get the attention of a boy already fed up with the antics of a scrawny kid he's known since grade school.

Their aggression unmasked, the two boys now glare at each other. Bailey whispers with the big boy Elijah. The coaches have seen this act before.

"Bailey stirs the pot," Smith says, "and then gets Elijah to step in."

Taylor tells Egan that Bailey and Elijah have been texting each other all day, probably about him, making him feel like the odd man out.

"That's not right," Egan says. "We're like a ladies drama league here."

Taylor is brimming with adrenaline on his three laps before the start of practice. He beats the others by far, running up to the coaches breathless, psyching himself up. "Big dogs don't roll in packs," he says.

He lets out an animal sound, something like a wolf's howl. "Argh!"

The boys team up for a tackling drill. Egan instructs them to come off the line and go for their opponent's knees—but not actually tackle them; those drills will come later. This exercise is just for form.

"Can we tackle?" Taylor pleads.

Egan nods his consent. Knowing that the winner will likely emerge as team leader, he wants the two boys to settle their score. "One needs to step up and say 'This is *my* team,'" Egan says. "Everything and everybody goes through me."

On the very next play, Bailey slams Taylor to the ground.

"You okay?" he taunts.

Moments later the coaches stress the importance of diet to get into opening-day shape. "Stay away from the greasy stuff," Egan says.

"Like Taylor's forehead," Bailey snipes.

Taylor suggests that running every day is the best way to lose weight.

"Shut up, Taylor," Bailey says. "You don't know anything."

When the players ram a tackling sled, Bailey sees Taylor watching him.

"What's your name?" he says.

"Fuck you," Taylor retorts. "Go tackle a dummy."

"I'm gonna tackle you."

"Do it then."

"When you're not looking, I will," Bailey says.

The coaches call a break, and Bailey and Elijah head off toward the bathroom.

"See?" Taylor says. "Those two even go to the bathroom together."

He tips his head and howls like a dog. "Big dogs don't roll to the bathroom in packs."

Each time Bailey and Taylor face off, the hits carry an air of menace. When Bailey performs a textbook tackle, his rival jumps up.

"Good job," Taylor says and pats him on the shoulder pad. Almost at once, the air pressure drops. After taking another hit, Taylor shakes Bailey's hand. Is this a subtle shift in battle tactics or a genuine breakthrough? Neither coach can tell.

While the two seniors may have called a truce, the others are still sleepwalking.

"We don't want last season," Egan barks, recalling the opener against Eureka.

"To be honest, you looked like a bunch of pussies that first game. Those guys weren't that good, but you made 'em look like an NFL squad."

The boys grow quiet. He has their attention.

"But you know what? You're gonna get knocked down. And when you do, you get back up. Some of you guys, I could make a grilled cheese sandwich by the time you get up. Show us that you're not gonna let some other kid own you. Because I'm not seeing it."

But a coach can only rant so much. Eventually the players have to take over. And that day, they do. Slowly a subtle camaraderie emerges as though the boys realize they better become a team.

They give shoulder pad whacks after a hard tackle and speak up to rally slackers. No one is more vocal than Elijah. "You guys are dogging it!" he spits after one drill. "I'm the biggest, heaviest guy on this team. There's no way I should be beating you smaller guys down the field. Have some self-respect."

Enzo gets the worst of his wrath. He's the team's smallest player, yet in the past he's shown some grit. On one play against the Eureka Vandals, a beefy 240-pound Vandal running back barnstormed down the sidelines. Only Enzo stood in his way.

"I was afraid for him, to be honest," Egan says. "I wanted to call out, 'Hit him low! Try to trip him up!' But it happened so fast."

Enzo froze.

"The guy with the ball just ran over him as though he wasn't even there," Egan says. "It was like a cartoon. Like the Wile E. Coyote after an explosion. He was just lying there, flat, one with the ground."

But the little Bulldog got up, staggering and shaken. And he didn't complain.

Still, Elijah dogs Enzo. "Hit that bag!" he yells. "It's not a person. Don't be afraid of it!" After another weak hit, Elijah quips, "Hey Enzo, at least take her out to dinner first!"

Then Elijah teams up with Enzo for a blocking drill, which calls for players to clash at the whistle. No tackling, only pushing, like two sumo wrestlers establishing ground.

Elijah moves Enzo around like a paperweight. After one hard hit, tears well in the younger boy's eyes.

"Watch out," Egan warns Elijah. "He'll quit." The coach is worried about Enzo's mother, a single parent who works the graveyard shift at the Carl's Junior in Winnemucca. "She's tough. She'll be here, all over me, not you."

As the players walk off the field, Elijah trots up behind Enzo and offers a big-brother embrace. "Sorry I hit you so hard back there," he says.

The next day the team hits the blocking sled to test their strength at the line of scrimmage—not yielding, always pushing forward. The blue human-shaped pads feature images of faces and helmets so the boys can focus their aggression.

The seniors go first. With Elijah leading the way, they move the sleds down the field, grunting as they go. "I'm a Bulldog!" Taylor yells. "Grrr. I need to get fired up!"

When the underclassmen take over, the four-man sled hardly moves.

"Stay low!" Elijah yells. "Pump your legs! Let's go!"

Egan joins in. "Push that Dodge truck down the road," he says.

Then they start doing monkey rolls, where three players take turns diving over the other on the ground. It's up and down, bodies thudding as they hit the turf.

The seniors get their rhythm, and the coaches are pleased. When the younger ones try, their monkey roll resembles "hear no evil, see no evil, and speak no evil."

"Shit," Maverick says. "I'm done."

"No, you're not," Elijah says. "Not until he blows the whistle."

In the final practice before Labor Day, Bailey suggests that the team do the "nutcracker drill," where two boys lie on their backs, head-to-head. The coach drops the ball into the hands of one, who must jump up and get past his surging opponent.

Taylor and Bailey jump down, ready to have at one another. Bailey gets the ball and slides by Taylor. The two fist-bump. Then Taylor faces Elijah, who hits the smaller boy with a sickening thud. He falls, then rises slowly.

After practice Egan tells Taylor he's glad he and Bailey have worked out their aggression. Then he mentions Elijah's big hit. "I felt sorry for ya," he says. "I thought, 'There's my big dog, on his back, staring at the sky.'"

A few days later Taylor delivers the news: he may have suffered a concussion. "My head aches," he says. "Loud noises bother me."

He'll have to sit out practice as he awaits the results of a CT scan. Everyone knows the injury came from Elijah's hit. As the others run their laps, Taylor stands with the two coaches. "Taylor, we need to get you back out here," Egan says.

For Taylor, who has trained for months, running long-distance, readying for his last season to show the world his skills, the injury is particularly heartbreaking.

He's on the brink of joining Crazy Frank Hill as a former Bulldog, and all too soon.

Fig. 24. Little League coach Ryan Murrah on field. Photograph by Randi Lynn Beach.

21

On that summer evening in 2019, Art Subori felt the fresh breeze of change blow into his hometown. The McDermitt High School field was overrun with an explosion of community support. The bleachers brimmed with parents, and a line of pickup trucks kicked up a cloud of dust as they arrived in the dirt-and-gravel parking lot.

It wasn't a game for McDermitt's varsity Bulldogs, but an old tradition rekindled: the revival of the long-dormant youth football program that Subori believes might help address many of the social problems that plague this isolated community.

Little League football starts kids off as kindergartners, so they can play flag football and learn coordination. As they grow older, competing through the eighth grade, they learn fundamentals so that by high school they already know how to don shoulder pads and crouch into a three-point stance.

In a town where the nearest movie theater is an hour away, the football league helps get lethargic kids off the couch, Subori explains, and it gives young athletes something to do as they wait for another winter basketball season. For others it distracts them from the reservation's lawless badassery that goes on all around them.

Subori, a thirty-eight-year-old former Bulldog who worked at the tribal wellness center, was just a kid when the first Little League folded in 1989.

Back then Todd Murrah, the star running back of the 1973 Bulldog team, was the piston driving the effort. But Murrah got busy running the Say When casino, and the will to keep youth football alive waned. The Little League's demise, Subori says, partly explains why the Bulldogs haven't been back to the league playoffs in three decades. Sure, the mine's closing robbed the town of players, but Little League had offered critical support, and when it left, the varsity program's success scattered like a dropped deck of cards. Subori wanted to bring it back.

He recognized the challenge. McDermitt had no equipment or uniforms. Even worse, there wasn't any willpower to get them. On the reservation the attitude had become one of defeat. Why start a league? Nobody will show up anyway. We'll only fail. Again.

He called his friend Brad, the youth director in Winnemucca, a prime rival in McDermitt's first era of Little League, and Brad threw the town a lifeline. He got them into a local league, providing pads, helmets, and jerseys. Subori helped form a planning committee. "The biggest hurdle," he says, "was showing people we could do it."

Few families could afford $100 football cleats, so Subori solicited hand-me-downs and went door-to-door soliciting donations from local businesses. The reservation's marijuana-growing operation donated $2,500. The high school offered use of the field. Subori used his own money to plug the remaining holes in the league's long list of needs.

"I remember driving around town with my car full of water jugs, kicking tees, tackling dummies, footballs rings," Subori says. "Where else could I leave them?"

Subori posted fliers around town. "You're a big boy," he'd tell reservation kids. "You might not be fast enough to play basketball, but you can excel as a lineman on the football field."

Scores of players and their parents showed up that first night. "People said 'Wow, this really can happen,'" Subori says. "They posted pictures of their kids in uniform on Facebook and said 'I didn't know my son had this in him. He loves this.'"

Many players were girls who'd never imagined playing football. During the second half of one game, Subori turned to Everr Crutcher, whose father Ardel lived on the reservation. Subori wanted everyone to play. But Everr was afraid.

"Do I have to do this?" she asked. "I'm going to get hurt."

"Go on," Subori said. "You've got your pads on. Give it a try."

Everr ran back to the sidelines after the first set of downs. "You're right, it doesn't hurt," she said. "Can I go out again?"

Subori smiled. "Yes, you can."

Subori's fire attracted parents who wanted to volunteer.

Coaching Little League, he told them, was an expression of community: you get a chance to guide your own kids and your neighbor's as well. Little League was the key to McDermitt's future, he said, a seed that could empower not only the varsity Bulldogs but the town itself.

"We can't count on the mines anymore," Subori said. "We have to count on ourselves."

Fig. 25. Player Isabella Murrah on game day. Photograph by Randi Lynn Beach.

One volunteer already had McDermitt football in his DNA. Like his father, Ryan Murrah was a former Bulldog. Now twenty-nine, he wanted to pass the game on to his own children. He showed up with his son, Dante, and his daughter, Isabella, and Subori tasked him with coaching the flag football team.

After the exploits of his father, Ryan's own Bulldog career had been a disappointment. He recalls Todd as an absentee father, too busy to be a mentor, working almost around-the-clock at the Say When and then coaching other people's sons.

Ryan was fourteen when his mother died in a car crash. After that, he and his older sister were pretty much on their own. Even today a certain distance lingers between father and son. Perhaps both feel like they've let the other down.

Ryan weighed 245 pounds when he joined the Bulldogs as a freshman. He played with Crazy Frank Hill, whose dad had also been a Bulldog standout. Both boys wanted to emulate their fathers. "I didn't want to be a lineman, but that's where they put me," Ryan recalls. "I wanted to run the ball like Dad did, but I was too fat."

Ryan's dream to recreate his father's on-field magic vanished. "It was a whole different world," he says. "I watched game film from my dad's day. It was the dirtiest football I'd ever seen. I wasn't made that way."

For Ryan there was scant more success after football. He worked as a mine driller and garbage collector before returning to McDermitt in 2016 to take a job at the wellness center where Subori worked.

But after the first year, Subori took a job in a casino in Glendale, Arizona. The opportunity was too good to pass up, but he felt a pang of guilt. "I didn't want people to think this was just another false start on the reservation, because that had happened too many times," Subori recalls. "They had something good and then it was taken away from them."

So Ryan stepped up to take his place.

On a fall evening in 2021, Ryan realizes the scope of the task. Lurking once again is the shadow of his father, who never lost a game in eight years of Little League coaching. Ryan's job is to turn toddlers into Bulldogs. He's both drill sergeant and babysitter because many of his players are still in kindergarten, including his son Malcolm.

One young boy runs up to a tackle bag and stops, reaching out almost in a handshake. Ryan can't help but smile, gently showing the boy how to embrace the bag and use his weight to topple it forward.

During one early scrimmage, Todd Murrah rolls across the sidelines on a four-wheeler. He's curious to see his old league in action. Father and son make eye contact as Ryan shouts directives to his players. "I never did say much on the sidelines; the kids can't hear ya anyway," Todd tells me. "If I did yell, I was usually chewing them out, not saying 'Good job.'"

Ryan is too busy bringing order to chaos. Players cry after tackles. When a sacked quarterback is ushered to the sidelines, Ryan worries about a concussion. "If he gets googly-eyed," Ryan says, "call an ambulance."

Ryan later limps off with a painful charley horse. He was showing a young player how to hit, and he tried to jump out of the way, but the boy's helmet crashed into his thigh. "I taught him to hit low," Ryan says. "He was only doing what he was told."

On the sidelines, a mentoring moment is taking place.

Volunteer Ardel Crutcher, whom everyone calls Chuck, is barking at a twelve-year-old who'd made a half-hearted effort to hit a runner low, as he'd been taught in practice.

"You wanted that playing time, and you got it," Ardel says, leaning in close. "Are you going to show us something? What are you made of?"

It's tough love, a coach trying to reach a player, coaxing him to face his fear of failure. In a way, Ardel is talking to himself.

At age forty-five, he's a compact man whose own character was forged on this field. The discipline of playing Little League and Bulldog football provided a respite from the hard life on the reservation where, by age fourteen, Ardel was already drinking regularly. After high school he worked manual labor jobs, a time marked by sweat and aching muscles, a time when a beer or two to wind down after a hard day's work was almost necessary.

There were bad choices—jail time and eight years without work—all of it outside the lines of the familiar world of youth football, the one place where Ardel learned to think for himself and remain in control.

Now coaching Little League football has offered Ardel a reprise of his football days through the exploits of his own children. His eldest, thirteen-year-old Warrick, played quarterback until a recent injury. His younger son, Desmund, already a big boy at age ten, wants to learn as well. At eleven, his daughter, Everr, has set her sights on playing varsity football and joining a handful of girls to do so statewide.

She wears No. 61, the same number as her father once did. All three kids wanted to wear it, but Everr was persistent. "She wouldn't let up," Ardel says.

Ardel and his kids live with his mother on the property where he grew up, which feels like defeat. "I try not to be a deadbeat dad," he says. "You feel like you're letting your family down. Failure became my teacher."

Fig. 26. Everr Crutcher on game day. Photograph by Randi Lynn Beach.

Maybe coaching can clean the slate from decades of too many failed opportunities. Now the aging former player has returned to the sport he loves. He wants to make a difference, right wrongs, become a role model for his community.

But most of all, for himself.

Ardel had strict parents. Anthony and Idel Crutcher played tough cops against the temptations their four kids faced. The family owned a three-bedroom trailer that sometimes housed sixteen people—if all the cousins were counted.

On the reservation, Anthony said, you never turned away a family member in need.

As a boy, Ardel would rise before dawn, hop behind the wheel of an old pickup with a manual transmission, and drive his uncles out to his grandfather's spread to feed and care for the cattle. "Just keep the wheel straight," the men directed, "and turn when we tell you to." Then he'd drive home, take a quick shower to wash off the whiff of hay and manure, and catch the bus to school.

Then Anthony Crutcher took a machinist job in Winnemucca and wasn't around to shadow the boy. Eventually Ardel succumbed to peer pressure while still in grade school. "I didn't want to go down that route because I had to deal with my dad," Ardel recalls, "He'd be on me, asking, 'Why'd you do this?' You had to listen to your parents."

But he didn't listen. He'd show up someplace on his bike, ready to join the party. "Hurry up," the boys said, "take a puff; take a drink." By ninth grade Ardel was taking pot to school, hiding baggies in his locker.

One day he went to watch his cousin, Omar, practice football with the Bulldogs, and what he saw amazed him. He saw kids drenched in sweat, pushing themselves. On breaks they encircled a pipe that jutted from the ground, each waiting their turn to quench their thirst. "They drank like bulls," Ardel says. "I said, 'Man, that's cool. I'm gonna play football.'"

He played Little League in the last years before it folded. He mimicked Omar and went all out. He wasn't the biggest kid on the field, but he tried to play like Omar through the four years of his varsity career.

By graduation Ardel set a singular goal: get out of McDermitt. He talked of becoming an army sniper, but when the recruiter showed up with the enlistment paperwork, Ardel had already gone AWOL with a bottle of beer and an excuse.

He later became a wildland firefighter, a seasonal job battling the blazes that ravage the region each summer. The routine was grueling: he'd barely finish fighting one fire when he and his crew would be summoned to the next, sometimes in another state.

Ardel made $18,000 in his first six months of work, money he quickly spent back on the reservation, drinking and partying. When the money ran out, there was always the next fire season to make some more.

Each new blaze brought its own version of hell. Grassfires charged up hillsides like flame-throwing soldiers. At night it was like somebody turned out the lights and you could see the redness, eerie and spooky and deadly. It was the stuff of nightmares.

"I was eighteen years old and thinking, 'Shit, what did I get myself into?'" But Ardel stuck with it. He showed up at every fire like it was another Bulldog practice, his coaches telling him, "Just get in there. Do your best. You'll survive."

One spring Ardel went south to Winnemucca and stayed with his older sister, Tanya, and her two boys while taking firefighting classes at a local college. He'd return home each evening to find his nephews on the computer.

He didn't know the first thing about cyberspace, but the boys showed him this marvelous realm where you could meet people from your living room couch. His sister logged him into a Native American chatroom.

At first Ardel's typing was labored, and by the time he had composed his thoughts, his connection had moved on. "Uncle, we can help you," his nephews said. "We can write for you. Just tell us what to say."

The arrangement was a revelation. Ardel couldn't wait to get back on the Internet. One night he met Emmalee Thompson, a Sioux Indian from South Dakota.

"You got a number I could call you at?" she typed.

When they got on the phone she said, "I just wanted to see if you were real or somebody just playing."

"Nah," Ardel said. "I'm for real."

She kept calling.

Then Ardel nearly died fighting a fire. He recalls topping a hill in the Idaho wilderness when he lost communication with his crew. He ran through fields of burning pine and sagebrush until he was rescued. He'd already survived two other close calls. "The third time is the charm," he told himself. "I'm out."

Ardel took a drilling job in Elko, where Emmalee joined him. He worked on a surface drilling rig beside an old-timer with a surly, knife-sharp attitude toward young Native American hires. The old guy sat on his rig, barking orders to the men scurrying around him hefting twenty-foot rods twelve hours a day, trudging up and down the pits.

Some days, amid soaring summer heat, Ardel felt like he'd returned to the scorching nightmares of his firefighting days.

He thought about quitting. Maybe he'd just return to the reservation like so many other Paiutes did. That's when the old man would start with his vitriol, shouting down from this rig, demoralizing words deployed as weapons.

"C'mon, you fucking blanket ass," he'd yell. "You fucking wagon burner."

At first the comments angered Ardel, then they made him work harder. "He was trying to motivate me," he says. "If it wasn't for him, I probably would have just quit that job and never accomplished what I did. In a way, that angry old man saved me."

The trade got under Ardel's skin. For years he trained men who'd never set foot inside a mine before. He mentored new hires like one of his old coaches on the football field, and bosses tried to promote him, but he declined. Maybe it felt too much like success.

Ardel still drank too much. As he and Emmalee had three kids together, his work took him on the road for months at a time. Ten years after they met, the couple split. Emmalee moved back to South Dakota, while Ardel took custody of the children.

Ardel sits at the kitchen table as his mother watches TV. Warrick is in his bedroom, door closed, the sound of rap playing low on the radio. The family's dozen cats peer in through a back window that offers a solitary view of the reservation.

This is the life you lead when you've gone eight years without work. You hang out and drink coffee, captive to your own thoughts.

Ardel speaks slowly as he describes his return to McDermitt in 2013. Work was hard to find, and he couldn't keep the work he found. Working as a security guard, he was drunk the day he rammed his van into a car carrying a mother and daughter. "I was ten sheets to the wind," he says. "Once you make that call, you can't do nothing for it. I'm just glad I didn't hurt those people."

A bar fight in McDermitt earned him a month in jail. At his sentencing, the judge's warning was sobering—like an oncoming wildfire. "Mr. Crutcher," she said, "the next time I see you here in my court, you better pack your suitcase and your toothbrush because I'm going toss you away for a long time."

Meanwhile he made sobriety a full-time job, living on money from his family, but he admits "the fence drops sometimes." One night, after three years without a drink, he got a late-night call from an old party buddy.

"What are you doing?" his friend asked.

"Nothing. Just watching TV."

"I'm coming over to pick you up."

Fig. 27. Young Bulldog in pensive mood on bleachers. Photograph by Randi Lynn Beach.

When Ardel hopped into the car, he saw that his friend had a beer popped open.

"Hey, you want a beer?"

"Nah, I'm cool. I been clean for awhile."

The two drove through a darkness so profound you could imagine a time before electric lights. At the old Cordero Mine site, the friend shut off the car engine. He confessed that he'd been depressed and had considered taking his own life.

The revelation struck Ardel somewhere deep inside. Here was an old friend who, like him, was struggling. He snapped open a beer. "It loosened me up," he says. "We talked all night. I told him that killing himself would leave behind people who cared about him, like me."

The friend never took his life, but, for his troubles, Ardel fell off the wagon and has since struggled to climb back on. He stays motivated by the thought that most of his former party friends "are either in jail, prison, or up there in that cemetery."

In 2019 he heard that Subori was restarting the town Little League. The idea hit him like a drop of rain in the desert. *This could be something positive in my life*, he thought. His kids took it from there. "Hey Dad," they asked, "do you think you could help us learn to play football?"

Could he? Hell yes, he could.

Once on the field, Ardel's depression lifted like the fog. "He started smiling," Subori recalls. "Football gave him something to look forward to."

The gig reminded Ardel of his mining days. "I figured that if I could train those guys like that—underground—maybe I could help teach kids to play football," he says.

One day a player was walking during laps, ready to give up. Ardel ran to his side, urging another step, and then another. "Ardel did not want that boy to quit," Subori recalls. "His mother told me he started throwing a football around the house. It was a breakthrough. Ardel showed him how not to give up."

For a former Bulldog who himself had almost quit, redemption loomed.

In the fall of 2021 Ardel learned that his son, Warrick, was in trouble in school.

There were accusations of pot found on campus. Ardel rushed to the main office. He insisted that his boy wasn't involved. Voices rose.

That's when the security guard struck the blow: Ardel wasn't even listed on the school's paperwork as a member of Warrick's family. The guard asked whether Ardel should even be there in the first place.

Was he even the boy's father?

Ardel sped off. The pain stabbed. The concept of Warrick not being his biological son was unthinkable. "I *may* be his father, but just the thought threw me into that world, asking difficult questions, wondering whether if he really *was* my son."

When the boy was born, he'd been working nonstop, leaving Emmalee on her own. His mind reeled. As far as he knew, there had been no paternity test. And he hadn't spoken to Warrick's mother in years.

After the clash with the school cop, Ardel went looking for firewood "up top" on a ridge near Red Mountain that overlooks the entire reservation.

For generations Paiutes have come here seeking inspiration. Many say that if you look hard enough, you can make out the images of seven chiefs in the craggy peaks near the top. "It's like going to God's house up there," Ardel says.

He took a dirt road east that switchbacked over rocks sharp enough to slash tires. He shifted into low gear, and at the top he pulled off the trail and just sat there, thinking: his life was so much more complicated than when he came to this place as a boy.

He *was* Warrick's father, he finally decided. He didn't need a paternity test to know that. He'd raised the boy. Like his own father always said, only a man steps up to take care of business, even if it may not be his duty.

But had he been paying enough attention to the boy? Was Warrick becoming just like him, tempted by peer pressure? He decided to take a step back from coaching. Before you mentor other kids, he told himself, you've got to start with your own.

"Maybe my own son had been crying out for help while I was trying to be both a coach *and* a dad." He pledged to redeem himself as a father, then consider the future.

As dusk descended he heard a sound from the sagebrush. He squinted and made out two red eyes, spinning around. There was buckskin, dark matter, and a tail.

He turned on the lights and saw a wild horse, solitary, content in its own world, something wild and beautiful. He made eye contact with the horse before it passed from its grazing and then ambled away.

Maybe this was a message: he could only do what he could do. He was a good father, just like his own dad.

That's when Ardel started the truck and headed back down the mountain, leaving behind the power of the seven chiefs with a new resolve to make things right.

22

One day, to everyone's surprise, all eight Bulldog players show up for practice. Sure, Taylor can't play, but he's here. So is Jaxon the mysterious freshman and the mercurial Karter, who has apparently put his girlfriend problems behind him.

They are finally a team. Egan decides that it's time for some fathering.

"Listen up," he says. "You guys are young men, and we're trying to get you started for a life after football when you leave home on your own. Right now you don't have to make any decisions for yourselves. Your bills are paid; your meals are free. But it won't always be that way. You'll have to go out and provide for yourself. I never went to college. I spent seven years working as a buckaroo on a ranch. But that was enough for me. You'll have to make those same decisions."

These boys rarely see this side of their coach.

"I'm glad we have eight players today," Egan continues. "But we have to have eight every day. You know those other teams are working hard. Jogging around this field is not going to get you into shape. You've got to run. You've got to push one another. You've got to be strong."

The scene feels like a deathbed patient rising for one final moment of lucidity before the inevitable. Then it happens.

During school the next day, Jaxon once again says he's quitting the team, this time for good. Bailey and Elijah try to reason with him, pulling him aside in front of his locker.

Then Smith takes his turn. He summons the freshman to his office, located just off the locker room. As an athletics instructor, Smith merits this tiny windowed room with a shower in back to organize his day and collect his thoughts. As groundskeeper, Egan is relegated to a shed out back where he keeps his tools.

This is the place, Smith's office, where the off-field business gets done. The office walls are lined by basketball photos—though none of the football team. The coach is angry now. No more babysitting. "You go tell Coach Egan to his face you're not going to play," he says.

The boy refuses to answer.

Just before practice, several players dressed in their uniforms walk into Smith's office. "Are we going to have a season or aren't we?" they ask.

Smith says he doesn't know and tells them to take the field. Then Egan makes the long walk out to practice, past the weed-strewn Claude Reeves Field where he had excelled as a boy. The players crowd around their head coach as he stands beneath one set of goalposts. When he begins speaking, somebody impulsively blurts out a question.

"Let him talk!" Elijah yells.

Egan has just learned of a possible game that weekend in Coleville, just over the California line. It's an opportunity to add another contest to an otherwise bare-bones four-game season. League rules require players to attend ten practices to qualify to play. But Taylor's CT scan results are not due until the end of the week. And now Jaxon says he has quit for good. Even if the boy agrees to return, Egan says, he's still short on practice sessions.

For everything to work, Jaxon will have to attend every practice this week. Now the freshman is nowhere to be found. They're running out of time.

"All he does is give us the runaround," Bailey says. "Yes, no, I don't know." Egan's face is drawn out like he's been punched.

"I can't force Jaxon to play," he says. "I don't know what to tell you guys. I just do not want to fold a season that means so much for you seniors. It bugs the heck out of me that it's coming down to a freshman who's making the decision for us. It shouldn't be that way. It's not fair to you guys."

Then Lane, usually quiet, speaks up. Even with negative overall passing yardage last season, he holds out hope that a good showing as senior quarterback will attract college scouts. "This is our last chance," he says. "I don't think someone Jaxon's age understands that we can never get this season back again once it's gone."

Lane pauses. "Let's go to his house."

The meeting threatens to turn into a mob. Dressed in their uniforms, the boys want to gather on the boy's doorstep. All they're missing are the lit torches.

Smith won't have it. "That would be strong-arming the kid," he says.

"We won't tell him he *has* to play," Lane says. "We just want an honest answer. We want him to tell all of us right to our faces."

Nobody says anything. A long-distance trucker downshifts as he enters town out on U.S. 95. A cloud of gnats hangs over the boys' helmets.

"Then let's call him," Lane suggests.

"He doesn't have a cell phone," Elijah answers.

"It just doesn't seem like he has the heart," Smith says.

"Then he never should have signed up," Bailey says.

"What's frustrating," Lane adds, "is that he just keeps running away from us. He's got a football in his hands all day at school, but then he won't show up to practice."

The coaches walk away to huddle, leaving the boys on their own.

Taylor stands between players who lounge on the grass or sit on their helmets.

"Guys, this team is going to shit right now," he begins. "Heck, we're McDermitt. Kids don't want to practice. They don't want to be forced to play."

"That's no excuse," Lane interrupts. "McDermitt is the best opportunity all of us here have to play. If you go to a big school, you never even get into the game because you're usually not good enough to get on the field. You practice all week, sit on the bench come game time, and then you go home."

"But here you get to play," Bailey adds.

Lane continues. "You get to start, even after slacking a little all week."

"Or slack a lot," says Maverick.

Taylor says that after his concussion diagnosis, he'd considered quitting the team. "This stuff is serious," he says. "I've read up on it. You have to be on watch all the time after just one concussion. To tell you the truth, I wanted to quit, but I couldn't do that to myself or to you guys."

"Taylor," Bailey says, "you gotta take care of yourself."

The two boys make eye contact. It's not a stare but a frank acknowledgment that their fractured friendship might now begin to heal.

Suddenly this gathering of boys usually marked by groans and imagined injuries turns into a group therapy session, high school kids egging each other on.

"It's not that hard to come out here every day," Bailey says. "It's only four weeks, more if we make the playoffs. That's sixteen weeks of practice and games. One-quarter of a year. Then you're done."

"And if you want to win," Lane says hopefully, "you can will yourself to win."

"Even though we didn't win one single game last year, we got a letter from one of the referees praising our spirit," Bailey says. "A lot of teams in our place would have held their heads down. But we played through it."

Lane adds, "Man, if we get to play next week, I want one of us to get a penalty, to hit somebody really hard, to show them that McDermitt has

Fig. 28. Niyla Crutcher dancing. Photograph by Randi Lynn Beach.

arrived. Basketball season is still an entire month away. If we don't play football, we'll just go to school and then go home. That will drive me crazy. I want to play football."

He pauses. "If any of us are afraid of getting hit, there's an ambulance at the game."

Maverick scoffs at that suggestion. "We're out in the middle of nowhere. The ambulance takes an hour and a half."

Taylor stands up. "Anybody got anything else to say?"

"I'm tired," Maverick says.

Done with their huddle, the two coaches walk back to the team. Egan has left a phone message with Jaxon's father. "I don't know anything more than you, right now," Egan says. "Do you guys want to stay here or go home? I've never had to do this."

The boys decide not to practice; they'll return the next day and start fresh.

Bailey leads the final huddle. "Let's get out here tomorrow. We've got to get through this. All we can do is hope for the best. Dogs on three!"

The following afternoon after classes, students clamor onto two yellow school buses that will deliver them to scattered farms, ranches, and the reservation.

Lorraine is there behind the wheel of one bus. Lane's father, Kerry, is dressed in his cowboy hat and kerchief as always, patting kids on the back, laughing.

Life goes on at McDermitt Combined School.

The Bulldogs are in the locker room. They should be changing into their uniforms, fetching helmets, mouth guards, and shoulder pads from the equipment room. They should be ready to take the field, throwing the ball, doing stretches.

But they're not. They're slouched on wooden benches, slung so improbably low that an older man would struggle to rise from them. Many have their heads down. They're only seven strong, and that's the problem. They play eight-man football. They're one short.

At 3:00 p.m., Egan strides into the locker room, this big man with a linebacker's body, the great-great-great-grandson of Chief Egan, who moved from his birthplace in Owyhee to call McDermitt home and has won a state trophy as a Bulldog.

He's just been on a conference call from the principal's office, he begins, sighing like a coach who faces the press following a tough loss. Jaxon was on the line from home. Egan could hear the boy's voice. If he was going to play, the time to say so was now.

"I'm not playing," Jaxon had said.

The other boys knew this was coming, but it gut-punches them just the same.

The coach holds out a last possibility. "We'll give him until 3:30," he says. Maybe he'll change his mind and come walking through that door.

"If not," he continues, "we'll call it a season." His face is red. Rarely do you see big men so emotional, even the quiet ones. "You guys know this. It's not the way we want to go."

In small towns like McDermitt, the population scatters like a broken puzzle. And men like Egan are left to pick up the pieces.

As the team's leader he takes the blame. "The buck stops here. Maybe Jaxon has some personal problems. When the time comes, he'll straighten everything out."

The locker room fills with a strange sense of sadness mixed with elation as though a grueling physical test like a marathon or a football season is about to be avoided. "This might be the last time we get to hit," little Enzo says to big Elijah. "I want to hit you one last time. I want one last hurrah."

It's like a weight has been lifted. But not for Lane, who sits with his head in his hands.

Egan huddles inside Smith's office. The assistant knows what his late father, Moe, would say: get your ass into the gym and hit that bag. "Should we take one last walk out onto the field?" Smith asks. "You know, have one more practice?"

Egan shakes his head. "Without a real game to play for, there's going to be a lot of horseplay out there. Somebody's gonna twist an ankle. You know how kids can be."

At 3:15 p.m., Lane asks to call Jaxon at home with a last-minute plea, a move tantamount to phoning the governor for an eleventh-hour stay of execution.

The coaches reluctantly agree, and the boy walks into Smith's tiny office and closes the door. As the line rings he sits in the coach's chair and hunches forward like his stomach hurts. He wears a black ball cap on backward, sweats, and workout shoes.

Finally he puts the phone down.

"He's not answering," Lane says.

It's 3:23 p.m.

Minutes later the two coaches stand with their backs to the showers. Over all the practices, I've never seen any Bulldog use them. Most quickly change out of their uniforms, throw on their street clothes, and flee this place and its strong smell of sweat and, perhaps, its whiff of defeat.

The locker room door is open, bringing a much needed flow of fresh air to this cramped space. The hallways outside are quiet; everyone else has gone home. It's just them, these Bulldogs who are left. The boys sit in a single row, heads down. Their bodies seem heavier, weighed by something beyond their control.

"It's a shame it has to end this way," Egan begins. "I'd rather have a season and see you guys perform, especially you seniors. We would have only had four games, but I know it would have meant a lot to you."

"Better than nothing," Elijah says.

"Exactly right," Egan continues. "We've got to hold our heads high. We've got other sports to play. And we'll be there. Jack and I will be there for you guys."

Then Smith speaks up. Rarely without his clipboard, his hands are now empty, held by his side as though he doesn't know what to do with them. "It's just a weird feeling, kind of like when basketball season ends," he says. "I always feel lost that first day. So many days of practices and games, seeing you guys."

He pauses.

"I want to play football. I want to be up on the grass right now. It's tough. We're like this far from having a team. I know you guys want to go play."

Then Smith talks about Jaxon. "I was just dreaming that he'd come jogging in here or we would have gotten a hold of him and he'd said, 'I'll be there in ten.'"

He adds, "I'm a dreamer too."

Smith says he'll soon start holding open gym for basketball. While they usually lose more games than they win, the basketball team is at least competitive, without the disgrace of 100-point blowouts and canceled seasons from lack of players. All basketball takes is five players, and right now in this locker room, that's a relief.

Even hapless McDermitt can come up with that.

"But I don't even want to talk about that right now," Smith says. "I'd rather be up on the grass." He doesn't know what else to say. As a boxer he never made many concession speeches.

Egan steps in.

"It's a tough one to swallow, guys. I thought we'd have stories, something you guys could talk about as you and your teammates grow older together. We can't have that now. Like coach says, we've got to keep our head high."

Then the boys speak up.

"I don't know about anybody else here, but these four weeks of practice was a lot of fun," Bailey says. "I wish I could look forward to playing some games with you guys."

The men and the boys huddling in the locker room let the silence hang. What more is there to say? Once again, a town and its effort to sustain the legacy of its football program have stumbled and failed.

"Let's start packing up," Egan finally huffs, "so you guys can get outta here."

The players take few photographs. They shake hands. Not like boys, but young men.

Then they have one last team huddle, joining hands in a pyramid. "I had a helluva time with you guys," Bailey says. "Dogs on three!"

Taylor stands beside him, yelling the loudest.

"Dogs on three! One-two-three, Dogs!"

Then, one by one, the players and the coaches pack up their belongings and filter out of the locker room, this final ending to the season that wasn't.

The following morning, Egan is back on the field, looking lost. His shoulders are hunched, his face drawn with regret. A few students run on the surrounding track, but he seems utterly alone.

It's difficult to witness, this sudden one-man transition.

Just like that, Egan's gone from a proud veteran coach of a rural Nevada high school football team to the invisible role of school groundskeeper. Egan knows this is the price of living in such a small town with too few players. Football seasons, like waterless crops, can die on the vine.

Sure, high school sports can break a boy's heart, but they can also shatter that of a good man like Egan. They can rupture the spirit of a town that has already lost so much—the vibrancy of its mines, the shouts and laughter of the regulars at bars that once lined Main Street, and, in the end, most of its people, its very pulse.

On this cool morning, as gusts of wind bring the distinct scent of fall, Egan has a job to do. He heads a small crew, painting lines on the school football field.

Not for his varsity team, but for the Little Leaguers.

All year round, Egan collects his check as groundskeeper. Yet fall football season brings something sweet to anticipate as he lies in bed dreaming up new plays, sizing up new players, weighing the value each individual brings to the team as a whole—the way a boy might study his playing cards or fantasy league lineup.

For now that dream is gone, no matter how much Egan wants it back.

Now he's that finicky suburban homeowner, taking pride in the lushness of his field and mourning the dead spots that bedevil him each fall.

That cruel, rural sorcerer is at work again.

Egan pushes a gas-powered machine to spray white paint on the grass, following a rope stretched across the belly of the field so the lines are straight and true, lines ready to mark a player's progress with the ball, players that would not be his to coach.

The machine does not belong to McDermitt but to another school in Winnemucca. The one Egan bought the previous year had sputtered and failed like his dream of coaching football this season.

And so he had to borrow one, the kind of handout on which the school has long relied.

But Egan is proud.

One year he used handheld spray cans—the kind that rattle when you shake them—to paint his coveted field. He got on his hands and knees and produced those lines the only way he could.

The groundskeeper of Lowry High School, who drove the 75 miles from Winnemucca to deliver the device, now watches Egan walk behind the machine like a man mowing his lawn.

"My boy plays high school sports, and he's seen what's happening here," the groundskeeper says. "One day he asked me, 'How much longer is McDermitt even going to have a high school?'"

The boy's father imparted some unvarnished rural wisdom. "Unless you have enough young couples who want to raise a family, you won't have any kids in a town like that," he told his son. "You'll just have a place full of old-timers."

The men finish their work. The isolated patch of grass, which straddles two states and gazes out upon grazing wild horses, now looks like a real football field. Games can be played here. Players can hit hard, catch passes, score touchdowns.

They just will not be Richard Egan's kids.

Egan removes his hat and wipes his brow. His work is done, for now. Then the coach who has become the last man standing, the still-beating heart of a dying rural football program, walks off slowly toward his groundskeeper's shed.

23

Months pass before I return to McDermitt in the late spring of 2022. This time I make the long drive with Randi Lynn Beach, a veteran photojournalist who set out to capture this remote place with photographs, to add to my words.

Lorraine and Junior let us stay in her late mother's house on the eastern side of U.S. 95. In a way I feel like Dorothy waking up from her fever dream and seeing all the familiar faces peering through the bedroom window of that Kansas farmhouse.

I watch Lorraine and Junior tool around on their four-wheelers, two outliers happy with this place they call home. Jack Smith shows off the boxing gloves that contain the ashes of his father, Moe, and I peek inside the shed where Richard Egan plots his double life as football coach and groundskeeper. I visit Ardel Crutcher on the reservation and meet with Alice, Alana, and Martica, three generations of strong Paiute women, as Randi Lynn takes their portraits with sacred Red Mountain looming over their shoulders.

Cowboy Bob takes us to the town graveyard to look in on the burial plot where he will one join his mother and father. For now, though, he still plays the unofficial town greeter with tourists who stop along U.S. 95 for selfies at the "Welcome to Oregon" sign.

Some things never change.

I revel in the latest gossip. Junior tells me that Tickie, the determined reservation stray, was finally killed by one of those cars that he was still fast enough to catch on three legs. Egan later texts photos of the newest plague of Mormon crickets that beset the place, climbing over anything that doesn't move and some things that do.

The White Horse tavern is once again up for sale. A new investor moved around some dirt in the adjacent lot but nothing more. Such is life in McDermitt, where the glory days remained consigned to the past, near forgotten, at least for now.

Egan still copes with the strain of preserving a once proud rural football program. After an earlier newspaper story I wrote about the team, a Las

Vegas-area philanthropist dedicated an annual $10,000 allowance to help buy new uniforms and equipment.

The team purchased a tackling sled to replace the rusted contraption now abandoned near where the wild mustangs graze. Then school administrators decided to spend the money on other sports with a better turnout.

The lesson: you just can't throw money at McDermitt football. The problem goes beyond that. The donation would have been better used attracting more young families to relocate to this town so that football can continue.

Frustration over the football program's decline still lingers over the town. "They've embarrassed us," Junior says. "It's just hard to support them when they haven't won in years." Missing, he says, is that sense of hometown pride. "When they're winning, people can say 'This is *my* team. They represent *my* town.' You just don't feel that way when they lose and lose and lose."

Or when they don't take the field at all.

The school still has a hard time attracting teachers who will stay, and, despite a stipend to move here, most don't stay very long.

But there is good news. Thierry Veyrié has helped secure a $1 million federal grant for a three-year program to teach the Paiute language at the school. A half century after Paiute children were punished for speaking their native tongue, students receive class credit to learn the vanishing language of their forefathers. Perhaps this step will help encourage tribal elders to drop their suspicions of a white outsider who's trying to bring change and help preserve their language and culture.

Still, violence is fast becoming what McDermitt is known for, not football. In 2021 a forty-year-old man used a shotgun to murder two Paiute women here in a drug-related attack. The next year a sixteen-year-old boy from the reservation was shot to death outside a party in Winnemucca.

Egan had once tried to recruit that teen to play Bulldogs football. Maybe if he had played, maybe the team would've had another season, and maybe he wouldn't have been at that party. Maybe.

Tribal Chairman Maxine Redstar attributes the rising crime rate to the isolation and unemployment that turns many to meth, heroin, and fentanyl, bringing a rash of drug-related crimes. "This is a dangerous place to grow up," she says. "It makes kids callous to witness a pattern of crime all around them. When criminals aren't held accountable, kids say to themselves 'Nothing happened to that guy. Maybe I should try it.'"

On the reservation, grandparents—not parents—raise many children. "The older generation knows nothing about drugs or computers or smartphones," Redstar says. "The kids manipulate their elders."

Redstar is trying to buck that trend by helping raise her husband's two grandsons—ages fifteen and three. "If there's something going on with my grandson, I get involved," she says. "Kids here are marked as troublemakers, throwaways. But not mine."

When her eldest grandson showed an interest in ice hockey, the couple built a backyard rink that attracted bored reservation kids to gather and gawk. While there won't be a hockey team in McDermitt anytime soon, Redstar believes a youth center might help make it safer to walk the streets at night. It seems an elusive dream, as unreachable as trying to bring an NFL franchise to McDermitt.

Hope seems to be all McDermitt has left. Investors who bought a gas station and mini-mart opened a Subway sandwich shop. Gurpreet Mall says his family plans to develop the 5.5-acre property, adding a truck stop and a bar to the existing twenty-one-room motel.

Like the late historian Herman Hereford, Mall believes McDermitt is set to boom, that a new road, Interstate 11, to run between Mexico and Canada and pass close to McDermitt, will bring more visitors. Or maybe just make it easier to drive on.

Even Mall won't live here. He drives to town every day from Winnemucca. "Our interest here," he says, "is purely business."

Meanwhile some still look to mining as a savior.

Before my arrival, a Canadian-owned company received the rights to build a mammoth open-pit mine on federal land 50 miles from the reservation. This time, investors will dig not for mercury, but lithium, a vital component of the batteries that power electric cars.

Yet the site of the new Thacker Pass Lithium Mine is a place many here consider sacred, located near ancient Paiute burial sites that resulted from another historical injustice at the hands of the U.S. military.

I attended a protest where Myron Smart, head of a group called "People of Red Mountain," told the story. Dressed in Wrangler jeans, a cowboy hat, a turquoise shirt, and a bolo tie with an indigenous design, Smart pointed east into a vast valley. At 1:00 a.m. on September 12, 1865, the First Nevada Cavalry raided a campsite of a Paiute band that had refused to relocate to nearby U.S. Army forts. "The soldiers camped out there on the flat," Smart said. While the Paiute men were away hunting buffalo, the cavalry moved in. "They cut open their bodies and spread their intestines in the brush," he continued, slaughtering all the women and children left behind. "They massacred an entire village. That's what the cavalry did to our people, to all Indians. We are here to memorialize those who were not buried in the proper way."

A protestor read a horrific account of the massacre as recalled by one cavalry soldier. "Daylight was just breaking as we came in sight of the Indian camp. All were asleep," the account began. "We unslung our carbines, loosened our six-shooters, and started into that camp of savages at a gallop, shooting through their wickiups as we came. In a second, sleepy-eyed squaws and bucks and little children were darting about, dazed with the sudden onslaught, but they were shot down before they came to their waking senses. From one wikiup to another we went, pouring in our bullets. Those Indians who were only wounded we put out of their misery, and then mounted and rode away."

The Paiute hunters returned to find the carnage under a full moon and named the site of the desecration *Peehee mu'huh*, or "Rotten Moon."

As the woman read, the gathering was quiet. People sat in lawn chairs and the beds of pickup trucks, their children perched on their laps or standing beside them holding hands. In the center, a small fire fed with sticks, cedar, and tobacco, crackled softly.

The more things change, the more they stay the same here.

A federal judge struck down several lawsuits to halt construction, which is set for 2023. The mine pledges to bring three hundred jobs, hire workers from the reservation, and provide bus service to and from the mine site. In the end the McDermitt tribal council supported the mine.

But Smartt warned that Thacker Pass might match the notorious legacy of the now closed mercury mines. "These businessmen have got their minds made up to come here. But we don't know what this mine will do to our water. The snow and the rain could seep the poison into our well water."

He paused to face those gathered around him. Suddenly the children quieted.

"Then who are we going to turn to? Who is going to say 'Enough is enough'?"

They've had enough of broken promises.

Fig. 29. Niyla Crutcher on reservation. Photograph by Randi Lynn Beach.

One day in the early summer of 2021, Coach Egan received an email from Danny Lee Armstrong, who had coached the Bulldogs in the early 1970s when McDermitt was flush with football players.

"Coach Egan," the email began. "First, I want to recognize your work to keep the McDermitt football program alive with only 35 high school students."

Armstrong named players he still remembers a half century later for the way they played and the men they became—ranch kids and Paiutes alike, like Sid Kochamp, Ray Sam, Lyman Smart, Erman Smartt, Levi Abel, Loren Crutcher, Speedy Kavanaugh, Junior Horse, and Nathan Owyhee.

He included a donation "so the team can have a postseason awards dinner or wherever you feel the money is needed."

If there's ever a team again.

Armstrong also wrote the *Reno Gazette-Journal* and called for a return to the smaller, six-man football. "The boom and bust of the mining industry in Nevada results in tragedy for small-school athletic programs," he wrote. "Many Nevada small towns are connected to a local Native American community and these events bring everyone together to support the team. In many cases, there's little or no industry in these small communities and that makes after-school activities a vital part of the community life."

In the late summer of 2022, another crop of graduating seniors left McDermitt, including Taylor, the stalwart Bulldog, who dropped by Jack Smith's house before departing for the University of Nevada, Las Vegas.

After thirty-five years of coaching high school sports, a weary Smith is considering early retirement. The season forfeits and lack of player initiative have taken their toll. "This year could be it," he says.

Still, Taylor's visit reminded him why he coaches in the first place. "If it wasn't for you, my high school sports career would not have happened," the boy told his coach. "You made me work hard. You've given me memories."

When Taylor drove off, Smith felt rejuvenated. "I felt like I'd really mentored that kid," he says. "It felt good."

In 2022, for the second time in two years, the Bulldogs were forced to forfeit their football season because there weren't enough players.

Even Little League canceled its season. Not enough kids showed up to play.

But Egan hasn't given up. He'll be back to try again in 2023 and the year after that, he insists, mentoring new players while harboring the same old dream.

Egan wants to win, but he also wants something that's just as enduring: to stand on the sidelines of his humble home field and see lights. Friday night lights, the beacons that will allow his teams to compete after dark, feel the cool evening air through their sweat-soaked jerseys, and hear the cheers of their neighbors, friends, and families.

He wants his players to feel like any other kid, on any other team, in any other American town. To play at home on a frenetic Friday night.

"Just to see the looks on their faces," Egan says. "Imagine that."

Every evening during my days in McDermitt I took a walk down Cordero Road, the two-lane strip of asphalt named for the abandoned mine outside town.

The road runs west past the White Horse and Junior and Lorraine's house across the street before busting out of town like a runaway horse onto rangeland inundated by luscious orange light from the setting sun.

The long walks alone helped me cope with life in a small town where healthy food was scarce and prices high, where I battled to make a connection with moody high school boys and a reservation that often seemed like a foreign nation, which it is.

At dusk when the day's heat had dissipated and the road was quiet, the few passing drivers raised a hand in greeting, often pulling horse trailers or heavy equipment. They didn't know me, of course, but the fact that I was out there on a dead-end track used by a few ranching families qualified me as a neighbor, part of a rural family.

A few miles outside town, Cordero Road passes the canyon where in 1865 Cavalry Lieutenant Colonel Charles McDermit was ambushed by Paiute warriors, heightening the bloody conflict between Indigenous peoples and their white invaders.

Nearby, just off the tarmac, sits a white wooden marker where miner Todd Gibson rolled his pickup truck a few decades ago. His sister, McDermitt's postmaster, still comes out to pull weeds and chase away cattle that use the cross to scratch their backs.

Eight miles from its start, the road ends on a hillside graveyard of sorts, the vestiges of the two mercury mines that once provided McDermitt with money and jobs. Today abandoned elevators sit forlornly, and the worker housing that once sprung from the land has returned to rubble and dust.

As much as the football field, the reservation, and the Say When, the road became my anchor, helping my transition to a slower pace of life. One evening Coach Smith and his dog Hazel joined me on my evening routine. Our political beliefs could not be more different, but we had looked past that to become real friends.

We walked without a word as the last rays of sunlight resembled the fiery aura of a Renaissance painting, with muted colors of brown and gold and orange. I thought of Smith's father, the indomitable Moe Smith, and said that he was a great man. I could see pride flush the face of this football coach, Moe's boy.

And I realized that I loved this town and its people.

For months I'd left behind my life in Las Vegas to become a fledging resident of this state-line town, the sticks. Like everybody else, I made my weekly run south for supplies, trips that provided a release from McDermitt's numbing isolation.

Over Labor Day I attended the county fair in Winnemucca, sitting on hay bales under a tent for a youth dance performance. I watched old men in Wrangler jeans line up shiny vehicles they had doted on for years like girl-friends. Not vintage cars, but *tractors*.

In time I realized I had underestimated the pulse of life here. On road trips I used to refuse to stop the car in any town without rustic bars or a greasy hamburger joint. McDermitt isn't prettified like that. There's no tourist drag. Outside of the low-slung Say When casino, there's nothing that beckons out-siders here. Not at first blush.

Passing through McDermitt, I discovered, is like barreling through a country growing field, where you assume there are only stalks of inanimate corn swaying in the breeze. But if you stop the car, turn off the engine, and listen, you'll hear things—like the rustle a fox's tail makes as it scur-ries through the brush. You might spy a coyote or elk, make eye contact, acknowledge the presence of creatures you don't find when you're just hurrying through.

I had come to McDermitt in search of stories of youth and football. Even-tually in the shadow of Red Mountain, I found the people that give all this emptiness a purpose. Characters like Cowboy Bob, Todd Murrah, cranky Joe White Buffalo, and, of course, Junior and Lorraine. For them, McDermitt is a trade-off between isolation and being comfortable where your feet are planted. "I just want to be up in the hills," Lorraine says. "In the wide open spaces."

I looked past the small-town clichés of suspicious hearts, loaded guns, and wounding gossip to see something precious: a town with a foot in two

Western states, home to people whose lives approach both *Saturday Night Live* hilarity and Shakespearean tragedy, often in the same moment. Each day they negotiate alcoholism, spousal abuse, boredom, overwork, and the daily joy of living life to its fullest.

Some are connected to the high school football team, others not. Together they remain perhaps the last generation to call this town home—a place with captivating, complex people I would have never met anywhere else.

Slowly I accomplished what I had set out to do: pause my busy life just long enough to embrace lives far different than my own. Along that two-lane road, where the setting sun cast a twenty-foot shadow before me, I could hear the buzz of cicadas, smell the fragrant sagebrush, and detect the defensive warning of a mother skunk. Fat crows landed on fence posts to watch me pass, and I singled each one out in greeting.

One hot Saturday afternoon as I made my normal walkabout, a bearded local slowed his pickup beside me, leaned over the shotgun in his front seat, and, without saying a word, extended a cold can of beer. He seemed mystified as to why the heck anyone would be walking that road when a truck worked just fine.

Now I know the answer.

ACKNOWLEDGMENTS

For a book about such a small place, the list of those who helped make this project happen is comparatively large. Some are part of McDermitt's football community, others not.

Where to begin?

I'd first like to thank my landlords, good friends, and advisors, Junior and Lorraine Huttman, for their unfailing support and listening ears. I would not have lasted in town without you.

I'd like to thank French-born scholar Thierry Veyrié for his friendship and guidance on how to dig myself out of the many holes I'd dug for myself among reservation residents. I'd like to thank Cowboy Bob for, well, just being you. McDermitt would not be the same place without you. And hats off to your sister, Charlotte, and niece, Michelle, for the love they continue to show a hard-headed old cowboy. Thanks also to residents Joe White Buffalo and Vickie Easterday for insights on how to survive life in McDermitt, and to all of you for being friends with Cowboy Bob.

Also on the list of townsfolk are Pastor Dave Lewis, his wife Ashley, and their growing family, for bringing grace and the word of God to a place that still feels like the American frontier. And business owner Gurpreet Mall on the patience and acumen it takes to bring economic lifeblood to a small, out-of-the-way town. And I cannot forget the late author Herman Hereford, whose self-published book *McDermitt Days* painted a picture of this place when its people and bars and so many stories thrived.

McDermitt's football history is filled with the exploits of dedicated coaches, many of whom took the time to tell me their stories, so thanks to John Moddrell, Danny Lee Armstrong, and Burt Polkinghorn. And thanks to such former players as Todd Murrah and his son, Ryan, Cash Miner, and Frank Hill, and to others who have supported eight-man football across Nevada, including journalists Ray Hager and Guy Clifton, as well as Donnie Nelson, executive director of the Nevada Interscholastic Activities Association, referee Alden Donston, and Humboldt County School superintendent Dave Jensen, who offered bottomless support.

And, of course, Ron Kantowski of the *Las Vegas Review-Journal*, who gave his time to help shape this book and write an introduction.

From the Fort McDermitt Paiute and Shoshone Tribe, I'd like to thank former chairwoman Maxine Redstar as well as three women from the same strong Paiute family, Alice, Alana, and Martica Crutcher, along with Art Subori, Tilden Smart, Ardel Crutcher, Harley Jackson, and the late Erman Smartt. Thank you also to Wilson Wewa Jr. for your grace and time.

From the communities of Eureka and Jackpot, I'd like to thank Rich McKay, Tate Else, Jeff Evans, football coach Fred Minoletti and his assistant, Josh Auch, architect Jack Hawkins, former voice of the Vandals Jim Ithuralde, and from Jackpot, former coach Brian Messmer and his son, Isaac.

I'd like to give a special shout-out to all the players on the 2021 Bulldogs team, but especially Taylor and Lane, and their fathers, Scoobie and Kerry. Thanks also to Lowell and Lindsey Egan, the sons of longtime Bulldogs coach Richard Egan, as well as Richard's wife, Lori.

And, of course, a special tribute to Nancy Egan, Richard's oldest sister, who instilled in him much of his toughness and worked tirelessly to preserve the memory of family ancestor Chief Egan.

I'd like to thank Glenn Stout, a top-rate editor whose wisdom helped direct the narrative of this book, as well as Clark Whitehorn, acquisitions editor at Bison Books at the University of Nebraska Press, who has championed this project from its inception. And thanks to Oregon historian Dave Wilson, whose research helped guide this tabula rasa writer on the history and cultural significance of the great Chief Egan.

Special thanks go out to Randi Lynn Beach, my partner in crime and a photographer with a vision to bring my words into focus with stunning images.

And lastly this book could not have been written without the friendship and guidance of McDermitt head football coach Richard Egan and his friend, partner, and assistant coach (and head basketball coach) Jack Smith. I will never forget your humor and dedication as we stood there for so many practices on McDermitt's field of broken dreams. You guys are heroes to me.

And to my wife, Lily, who always encourages me to go where I need to go. To all of you, my heartfelt thanks.

FURTHER READING

Bolen, Robert D. *The Paiute Indian Nation*. Fort Boise Publishing, 2014.

Colton, Larry. *Counting Coup: A True Story of Basketball and Honor on the Little Big Horn*. Grand Central Publishing, 2000.

Deloria, Vine, Jr. *Custer Died for Your Sins: An Indian Manifesto*. University of Oklahoma Press, 1969.

Hittman, Michael. *Corbett Mack: The Life of a Northern Paiute*. University of Nebraska Press, 1996.

Hittman, Michael and Don Lynch. *Wovoka and the Ghost Dance*. University of Nebraska Press, 1997.

Howard, O. O. *Famous Indian Chiefs I Have Known*. The Century Company, 1916.

Parry, Darren. *The Bear River Massacre: A Shoshone History*. By Common Consent Press, 2019.

Peavy, Linda and Ursula Smith. *Full-Court Quest: The Girls from Fort Shaw Indian School, Basketball Champions of the World*. University of Oklahoma Press, 2008.

Powell, Michael. *Canyon Dreams: A Basketball Season on the Navajo Nation*. Penguin Publishing, 2019.

Riley, Jeff. *Big Time: The People, the Places and the Game of Oregon 8-Man Football*. Box Twelve Press, 2018.

Stowers, Carlton. *Where Dreams Die Hard: A Small American Town and Its Six-Man Football Team*. Da Capo Press, 2005.

Veyrié, Thierry. "A Historical Ethnography of the Fort McDermitt Paiute-Shoshone." Unpublished doctoral dissertation, Indiana University, 2021.

West, Stanley Gordon. *Blind Your Ponies*. Algonquin Books, 2011.

Wilson, Dave H., Jr. *Northern Paiutes of the Malheur: High Desert Reckoning in Oregon Country*. University of Nebraska Press, 2022.

Wilson, Laura. *Grit and Glory: Six-Man Football*. Bright Sky Press, 2003.

Winnemucca Hopkins, Sarah. *Life Among the Piutes: Their Wrongs and Claims*. Arcadia Press, 2017.

Zanjani, Sally. *Sarah Winnemucca*. University of Nebraska Press, 2001.

Milton Keynes UK
Ingram Content Group UK Ltd.
UKHW031014101024
449496UK00004B/126